The Beginnings of the Cinema in England
1894–1901

———

Volume Two: 1897

The University of Exeter Press edition of Volume 2 of *The Beginnings of the Cinema in England, 1894–1901* is a re-issue of the first edition published in 1983. Volume 1 (revised and enlarged edition 1998), Volume 3 (1988), Volume 4 (1992) and Volume 5 (1997) are also published by University of Exeter Press.

Frontispiece: Diamond Jubilee portrait of Queen Victoria, taken specially for the occasion by W & D Downey (*Barnes Museum of Cinematography*)

The Beginnings of the Cinema in England 1894–1901

———

Volume Two: 1897

John Barnes

UNIVERSITY
of
EXETER
PRESS

To my brother Bill

First published as
The Rise of the Cinema in Great Britain: Jubilee Year 1897
by Bishopsgate Press Ltd in 1983

Re-issued in 1996 by
University of Exeter Press
Reed Hall, Streatham Drive
Exeter, Devon EX4 4QR
UK
www.ex.ac.uk/uep/

Reprinted 2001

ISBN 0 85989 519 X

British Library Cataloguing in Publication Data
A catalogue record of this book is available
from the British Library.

Printed in Great Britain by Short Run Press Ltd, Exeter

Contents

Foreword

In the previous volume of this history I showed how the introduction of the Edison Kinetoscope in October 1894, led directly to the invention, by R. W. Paul and Birt Acres, of England's first cinematograph camera and subsequently to the adoption of screen projection as the ideal method of exhibiting films, so that by the end of 1896, the film had found a place in the programmes of almost every major music hall in the country. The present volume continues the story to the end of 1897.

The year 1897 marked the Diamond Jubilee of Queen Victoria's reign and practically the whole of the British film industry concentrated its attention on recording the celebrations connected with the occasion. The Queen's procession through the streets of London on the 22nd of June provided a marvellous spectacle for the cinematograph cameras which were situated at various vantage points along the route. So keen was the interest shown in the event, that by the end of the year there could hardly have been a person in England who had not seen this historic scene on the screen.

In other respects too, the year can be regarded as a spectacular one in so far as the cinema was concerned. The size of the cinema screen was spectacularly increased, especially by the American Biograph whose 70mm film when projected at the Palace Theatre in London, completely filled the proscenium area of that large house. Spectacular too in another way, was the 1½ hour coverage of the Corbett-Fitzsimmons fight screened at the Royal Aquarium Theatre. Such highlights of the cinema year are certainly an indication that the new medium was beginning to widen its scope in the field of entertainment and perhaps even to expand its creative possibilities as a medium of expression. But on the whole, the year 1897 was a period of consolidation and expansion. This is borne out by the number of new manufacturers of cinematographic equipment which began to appear and by the increasing number of films being offered for sale. In the pages that follow, I have endeavoured to examine the year's film production and methods of presentation, as well as to describe much of the cinematographic equipment that was produced; taking note also of any new development in film technique.

As in the former volume, particular attention is also paid to the cinema of other countries in so far as it effected the industry in England; thus by tackling the subject on an international plane rather than on a strictly nationalistic one, we are able to see the achievements of the English cinema in a truer perspective.

Further volumes of this history are planned to cover the period to the end of Queen Victoria's reign, thus documenting an era in the cinema's history which hitherto has been left almost untouched by the film historian.

John Barnes
Museum of Cinematography
St Ives, Cornwall
1979

1 Robert W. Paul and Birt Acres

The founder of the British film industry, Robert W. Paul (1), holds a unique position in the history of the cinema. His genius and talents were such that he combined not only the roles of inventor and manufacturer, but also those of exhibitor, producer and cinematographer. This in itself is a considerable achievement, but when one takes into account that he was also actively engaged at the same time, in the electrical trade as a scientific instrument maker, his versatility and industry appear formidable indeed.

Setting aside those activities concerned with the Kinetoscope and Kinetoscope films, which have been fully dealt with in the first volume of this history, Paul's involvement with the cinema in its more modern form can be said to have begun in March 1896. From then on, for several years, he was to hold the dominant position in the industry in this country. So successful in fact were his first year's operations that for the period 2 March 1896 to 17 March 1897, he was able to declare a net profit of £12,838. 15s. 4d., of which £6,585. 8s. 6d. accrued from the manufacture and sale of cinematographic equipment alone.[1]

For Paul, the cinema had become big business and in April 1897, he decided to form a limited liability company under the name of 'Paul's Animatographe, Ltd.' For this purpose a prospectus was circulated in which the aims of the new company were set forth. The capital was to be £60,000 in 15,000 ordinary shares of £1 each and 45,000 7 per cent cumulative preference shares of £1 each, the latter being offered for public subscription. The subscription list closed on 28 April, but the result was not disclosed.[2]

The prospectus stated that the Company was to acquire the inventions and patent rights, together with Paul's Animatographe or Theatrograph ('which is causing such wide-spread sensation by the display of animated photographs in the principal places of amusement') and to develop the resources of the invention and extend its present lucrative field of operations in various ways; these were to include: 1) The Manufacture and Sale of Animatographes and Accessories; 2) The Manufacture and Sale of Animated Portraits of Individuals; and 3) Animated Advertisements.[3]

Animated Portraits, the subject of clause two, may sound somewhat fanciful, for it was intended to open studios in London and the principal provincial towns for the express purpose of taking these portraits of the general public and to license country photographers to take negatives to be printed in the Company's factory.[4] A correspondent of *The British Journal of Photography* had reservations about the idea:

> I find it difficult to understand how this idea is to be profitably carried out. The taking of these animated portraits is easy enough, but how are they to be utilised by the sitters? Are the latter expected to possess a projection system, limelight, screen, and all, for the purpose of showing their friends how they look when animated? If so, the idea is surely calculated to be a somewhat costly luxury.[5]

Perhaps it was Paul's intention to issue these portraits in book form, so that the leaves could be flicked over to give the illusion of movement, like the pictures in the common 'flick book'. These pocket kinetoscopes were then coming into vogue and Paul's friend Harry Short was already in the process of forming a company to market his Filoscope.*

*The Filoscope is described and illustrated in the previous volume of this history, pp 107–8.

8

1   Robert William Paul, MIEE (1869–1943) (*British Film Institute*)

His plans may thus have included arrangements for issuing these portraits, as well as selected extracts from Paul's regular films. In any case, the basic idea behind Paul's scheme finally found realisation in the field of 'home movies', made practicable by the introduction of sub-standard film gauges, more especially in the 9.5mm and 16mm formats, which first became popular in the early 1920s.

The clause referring to Animated Advertisements, does not of course, imply the use of animation techniques such as cartoons, etc, but simply refers to regular films showing industrial processes or the use of basic commodities in 'lifelike operation' as the prospectus has it. There is no evidence to show that Paul made any such films for advertising purposes.

With the benefit of hindsight, one can say that Paul's Animatographe Limited offered a very sound investment, but at the time this was not so apparent and *The Optician* for instance urged extreme caution on the part of those proposing to acquire shares. Whilst upholding the good intention of all those responsible for the formation of the company, the journal seems to have had reservations about the future prospects of the film industry itself.[6]

However, Paul's film-making activities during 1897, continued the pattern he had previously followed the year before. A few films featuring music hall turns were made and also two comedies and a drama. But his main output comprised non-fiction films. In the latter class were a series taken in Sweden and Egypt. The Swedish series were photographed by Paul himself. The King of Sweden and Norway* had despatched a courier to London to purchase one of Paul's projectors, with a request that the maker accompany it and see it properly installed in the Palace at Stockholm. This Paul did to the apparent satisfaction of the King, who granted him special facilities during his stay, for taking Swedish pictures.[7] Paul was able to secure several subjects, of which one was of sufficient merit to be retained in circulation as late as 1903. His catalogue entry for that year, reads:

SWEDISH ELECTRIC RAILWAY. An electric trolley car coming through a Swedish pine forest. A very beautiful and clear picture.
    Code word — TROLLEY. Length 60 feet. Price 45s[8]

As an electrical engineer, this was a subject which would have had special appeal to Paul and he probably made doubly sure of obtaining the best possible results. Apparently the other Swedish subjects he took were not of a comparable standard and after 1898 were dropped from his lists.

The Egyptian tour (2) was undertaken by Paul's cameraman, Henry William Short, who had been responsible for a series of films taken in Spain and Portugal the previous year, and which had included one of the outstanding successes of the period — *A Sea Cave Near Lisbon*. This time he does not appear to have been so successful and none of the thirteen subjects he managed to bring back were accorded any special acclaim. Instead, they called forth a rather wry comment from Cecil M. Hepworth in the pages of *The Amateur Photographer*:

According to a contemporary, Mr. R. W. Paul's photographer has secured a series of kinetographs of the Egyptian Pyramids, among other things. Rather funny subjects for living photographs! One is tempted to ask: Cui bono? Yet animated Pyramids might be worth seeing.

*King Oscar II relinquished the crown of Norway on 27 October 1905.

2 Tour in Egypt (R. W. Paul, 1897) (a) Pyramids (b) Camels. Two of a series of 13 films photographed by
H. W. Short (*Barnes Museum of Cinematography* (a); *National Film Archive* (b)

The Psalmist says something about mountains skipping like young rams. Perhaps this is a fulfilment of a prophecy.[9]

Perhaps the truth of the matter was that foreign views were no longer a novelty in England, as the field had been extensively covered by foreign producers, in particular by Lumière. To succeed, the films had to be exceptionally well taken and have an intrinsic interest beyond that of the purely exotic.

Paul's other offerings during the year were mostly simple actualities, and included a series taken in Douglas, Isle of Man. *The Liverpool Landing Stage*, which was probably taken during the same excursion as the Douglas scenes, was sufficiently successful to be included in Paul's catalogues for several years; the 1903 entry reads:

> LIVERPOOL LANDING STAGE. A busy, animated scene, showing the departure of the Birkenhead ferries, the bustle of loading steamers, and the hurrying passengers.
> Code word — LIVERPOOL. Length 50 feet. Price 38s.

Another film which withstood the test of time, showed the Rottingdean Electric Railway, a subject which must have been of equal interest to Paul as the electric trolley car he filmed in Sweden. This too was included in Paul's catalogue for 1903:

> THE SEA-GOING CAR. The Brighton-Rottingdean Electric Marine Car coming through the sea to the pier, and passengers disembarking.
> Code word — ELECTRIC. Length 40 feet. Price 30s.

This unique sea-front railway plied the 3-mile distance between Rottingdean and Brighton and ran on rails washed by the sea. The passenger-car was kept clear of the waves by being raised upon stilts, and its rather odd appearance earned for it the nickname of 'Daddy-Long-Legs' (3). It was designed by Magnus Volk and opened on 28 November 1896, but in December, was partially destroyed in a storm. It was subsequently repaired and re-opened in May 1897. Paul's film was probably made shortly afterwards.

Among the topical events or news items which Paul and his cameramen covered were the victory of Galtee More in the Derby of 1897; the Prince of Wales reviewing Yeomanry at Cheltenham; the Fire Brigade Review at Windsor; and of course, Queen Victoria's Diamond Jubilee procession. This latter event was the one upon which his whole resources and attention were concentrated, as were most of the other film producers then active in England. The story of this historic filmic event is fully recounted in chapter 8.

None of Paul's fiction films made during the year, are of particular merit and are unlikely to have matched the standard of the best from France at this time. The vaudeville turns have an intrinsic interest, more especially that of the specialty dancers May and Flora Hengler, since a portion of this has been preserved in the leaves of Short's Filoscope, of which examples are to be found in the Barnes collection and the Kodak Museum (4). Two scenes of the Geisha, the Alhambra success, were specially staged for the Animatographe, but unfortunately no copies of either are known to have survived.

Paul produced one dramatic film called *Jealousy*, set in a garden, in which a jealous husband is shot; and two comedies — *You 'Dirty Boy' Statue Comes to Life*, which probably drew its inspiration from the Manneken-Pis at Brussels; and *Robbery*, in which a

3   Poster advertising Magnus Volk's Brighton & Rottingdean Seashore Electric Railway, the subject of R. W. Paul's film The Sea-going Car, taken in 1897 (*East Sussex County Libraries, Brighton Reference Library*)

4   The Sisters Hengler. The specialite dancers May & Flora Hengler, as they appear in R. W. Paul's film and reproduced in the Filoscope (*Kodak Museum*)

wayfarer is compelled partially to disrobe by a ruffian with a pistol. A copy of the latter is preserved in the National Film Archive[10] (5).

Concerning the exhibition side of the business, many of the London music halls continued to engage Paul's Theatrograph as one of the principal items in the programme. Paul's one set-back was the termination of his performances at the Alhambra Theatre, Leicester Square on 27 June, brought about by a dispute with the management over exclusive rights to the Jubilee films, a matter which is more fully discussed in chapter 8. Among the London theatres where Paul's Theatrograph was shown during the year were Sadler's Wells,[11] the Canterbury,[12] Oxford,[13] Paragon,[14] Royal,[15] and Tivoli.[16] The Theatrograph also continued to be exhibited throughout the provinces, receiving favorable notices in the local press. Paul advertisements mention engagements at the Royal Opera House, Leicester, Empire Palace, Sheffield, Theatre Royal, Brighton, Avenue Opera House, Sunderland, Grand Theatre, Newcastle-on-Tyne, Theatre Royal, Birmingham, and in Northern Ireland at the Grand Opera House, Belfast. Regional bookings remained in the hands of Paul's agent Tom Shaw & Co, 86 Strand, London.[17]

By 1897, the general public had grown accustomed to seeing films and there was not the same amount of attention paid to them in the press as had been the case during the previous year when they were still very much of a novelty. We find reviews, such as those published in *The Era*, no longer make a point of mentioning specific films, but are inclined instead, to review the programme in more general terms, like this one of 10 April:

> Mr. Robert W. Paul's Animatographe is a great attraction at the Oxford, some of the views exhibited being new to us, and being very ingeniously and effectively "taken".[18]

This did not apply however, to the Jubilee films, which continued to arouse interest for several months after the event itself had taken place. Many of *The Era's* reviews for 1897 are taken up with the Jubilee films, with only an occasional mention of the supporting subjects. It is interesting to note therefore, a review published early in the year of a

5 Robbery: A Wayfarer Compelled Partially to Disrobe (R. W. Paul, 1897) Frame illustrations from a
contemporary print (*National Film Archive*)

programme at Sadler's Wells, which mentions no less than nine films by Paul, although most, if not all, were subjects he made during the previous year. It might be as well to quote this review at length, since much of Paul's 1896 output was still being shown throughout Great Britain during 1897:

> One of the most attractive features of the current programme at this ancient home of the drama is undoubtedly Mr. R. W. Paul's Theatrograph, and this is all the more satisfactory because this particular item in the bill is one which would surely receive the approval of those who hold the strictest views with regard to the amusement of the people. In fact, these exhibitions of living pictures which are now the vogue may be claimed as the legitimate and greatly improved development of the magic lantern views in which a former generation found such huge delight. Since we last noticed Mr. Paul's Theatrograph some new and interesting pictures have been added, including "The Soldier's Courtship", which shows how a red-coated Romeo meets his Juliet — otherwise known as Mary Ann — how they take possession of one of the public seats, and how their love-making is interrupted by the intrusion of a severe-looking female, who is unceremoniously ejected, and the lovers resume their former affectionate attitude. Amongst the most familiar scenes is Blackfriars-bridge, the people and various vehicles crossing being reproduced with a startling fidelity which evokes loud applause. Those who did not witness the last Lord Mayor's show can obtain a very good idea of its principal features from Mr. Paul's reproduction. "The Twins' Tea Party" depicts two children taking tea together and having a slight tiff. An effective comedy scene is "The Husband's Return at 2.0am." The manner in which the indignant wife treats her festive spouse and his undignified retreat beneath the bed clothes cause much laughter. "Calling out the Fire Brigade" is a realistic picture of London life, and among other animated photographs which win favour are a dance by the Sisters Hengler, a serpentine dance, in which the colours of the dancer's dress are reproduced, the Music Hall Sports, and the Prince of Wales's Derby.[19]

This review, published in *The Era* on 16 January, is the first reference I have found to Paul's film of the Sisters Hengler. A list of films published by Paul in November of the previous year fails to mention it. Although its precise date is uncertain, I have decided to include it among Paul's films for 1897 (see Appendix 3).

In May occurred the disastrous cinematograph fire at a charity bazaar in Paris which resulted in such tragic loss of life. This disaster was widely reported in the English press and had repercussions on this side of the Channel. There was a sudden awareness of the dangers inherent in cinematograph performances and tighter controls were called for. During a trades exhibition in July at the Agricultural Hall, Islington, 'at which cinematographic pictures were to be shown, the management insisted that the apparatus be enclosed in a fireproof chamber, so a partitioning had to be erected and lined with sheet iron.' *The Optical Magic Lantern Journal*, reporting the matter, asked the question: 'Is this not carrying matters to extremes?'[20] But with time, the practice was generally adopted and portable iron projection booths were being advertised by dealers specialising in cinematographic equipment.[21]

The press was not slow in reporting any fire that involved a cinematograph performance and several such cases are also recorded in the photographic journals.[22] Furthermore, Cecil M. Hepworth and George Dickman, manager of the Eastman Photographic Materials Co, argued the pros and cons regarding the safety of cinematograph film, in the pages of *The Amateur Photographer*.[23] It was a situation which could not be ignored by the trade and practical steps were taken to reduce the risks by the applica-

6 Paul's Fireproof Animatographe, 1897 (Two views) Note the hollowed-out sprocket wheels (*Barnes Museum of Cinematography*)

tion of various safety devices to projection apparatus. For instance, the Cinématographe-Lumière, which was about to be placed on the open market at the time of the Paris fire, was now re-equiped with a special safety condenser in the form of a glass globe filled with water,* and R. W. Paul, in characteristic fashion, tackled the problem by designing a completely new apparatus which was placed on the market in September as Paul's Fireproof Animatographe (6). The film spools in this machine were entirely enclosed in metal casings, and the film passed through narrow slots to and from the mechanism, thus reducing to a minimum the amount of film which was actually exposed and likely to catch fire. The machine had a four-picture sprocket actuated by a four-star Maltese cross; it was far more portable than his previous projector and was used on a stiff tripod.[24] The price of the complete outfit, with iron lantern, condenser, arc lamp (or mixed jet), on portable oak tripod stand was £15.[25] The various features of the apparatus are set forth in an advertisement published in October[26] (7). Reviewing the machine in its issue of 29 October, *The Amateur Photographer* had this to say:

> ... the picture-strip is only in motion for about a fifth as long as it is stationary, the shutter is quite small, and the flicker is, consequently, much reduced. In short the whole effect upon the screen is as good as in many an instrument of far more elaborate and expensive design.[27]

Perhaps its most striking and important feature, apart from its 'fireproof' qualities, was in the design of the hollowed-out sprocket wheels, which adopted a form which is followed to this day. This feature of the machine was also commented upon by *The Amateur Photographer*:

*The Lumière condenser is described in chapter 6.

17

PAUL'S
FIREPROOF ✦ ANIMATOGRAPHE.

With driving gear, fireproof spools, and 2 inch objective, giving an 8 feet picture at 15 feet distance, in travelling case, ready for attachment to lantern **£10 0 0**

Do do complete with iron lantern, condenser, arc-lamp (or mixed jet), on portable oak tripod stand ready for work **£15 0 0**

Interchangeable objectives of any focus can be supplied.

The tripod is suitable for use with the apparatus when adapted as a camera.

The mechanism is supplied to order fitted for use as a camera or projecting apparatus at will. Price quoted according to quality of photographic lens.

PAUL'S ANIMATOGRAPHE has the following proved advantages :—

A whole series of Films may be joined up and put on the Machine at once, and run through without resetting the Machine. This saves time and handling of Films. The Films are kept clean, there are no loose Films lying about, and a smart show results.

The patent continuous feed obviates all jerking actions and relieves the Film of intermittent strain, so that Films have been used a year without serious depreciation. The picture surface is not rubbed in the Machine and the Film therefore does not show scratches, so objectionable to the spectator.

It is important to exhibitors that the Machine should be open to view when working, and the few adjustments easily accessible. In Paul's Animatographe the side of the sprockets are open, the first Film can be put into position in two seconds, and the whole series is then ready for running. The arrangement for centering or masking the picture is simple and exact.

Paul's Animatographe is most solidly constructed, the spindles and important gears being of steel. The bearings are of great length in solid gun-metal, and the parts are fixed together by split taper pins which cannot shake loose. Every detail has been strengthened in accordance with experience and observation of working.

Steadiness has been attained by accuracy in construction and the employment of a definite locking movement. Paul's Animatographe is well known as being unrivalled in this respect.

Absence of flickering results from the rapidity of the intermittent motion, requiring the light to be cut off during a very small interval of time only. In fact, the small shutter is not essential to the working of the Machine.

The mechanism is probably the most compact ever constructed, and measures, without the film-spools, 6 inches by 4 inches by 4 inches only. The complete outfit is easily carried in one hand.

Objectives of any focus may be attached to the fitting supplied, and are interchangeable, making the apparatus suitable for working at any distance from the screen. It is easily set up.

The Film cannot be ignited at all except by wilful carelessness, and if ignited only a few inches can burn, the bulk being enclosed in metal casings.

A heap of shavings, piled over a Machine fully charged with Films and ignited, failed to cause ignition of the Films.

This Machine is nearly silent in working, making no more noise than a sewing machine, and is easier to work, the motion being very smooth.

ROBT. W. PAUL. 44, Hatton Garden, London, E.C.

Telegraphic and Cable Address—" CALIBRATE, LONDON."

[For List of Films, see next page.]

X

7   Advertisement for Paul's Fireproof Animatographe. From The Magic Lantern Journal Annual 1897–8 (October, 1897) p xciv (*Barnes Museum of Cinematography*)

A noteworthy feature of the instrument was the hollowing out of the sprocket wheels and all the other surfaces that come in contact with the travelling film, so that at no point of its journey does it touch or rub against anything except at the edges where the perforations are, and where slight abrasions and numberless scratches are of no consequence.[28]

Once again Paul was in the forefront of film projection design and the lessons he set were not to go unheeded by other manufacturers.

The mechanism of Paul's Fireproof Animatographe was so designed that, with only slight modification, it could be enclosed in a wood case and supplied as a cinematograph camera, the price varying according to the photographic lens fitted. I have not seen an illustration of the apparatus in this form, but contemporary accounts clearly establish that such a camera was readily available on the market.[29]

Another field in which Paul pioneered the way, was in mobile generators for supplying electric current for travelling showmen:

The report has gained currency that Mr. R. W. Paul, famous for the invention and even more so for the energetic exploitation of the animatogrephe, (sic) is contemplating an eruption in another place. His idea is to start a more than usually animated autocar, for it will be destined to carry from place to place a first-class cinematograph. Having arrived at a small town, say, where a living photographic performance is to be given, the operator will be quite independent of the lighting arrangements of the town or the obstinacy of the railway companies on the matter of compressed gas [for limelight]. He will merely gear the motor of the carriage on to a dynamo which he has brought along with him, and there you are.[30]

The idea of a mobile generator may have occurred to Paul after witnessing the electric trolley car which he had filmed in Sweden, or maybe, as *The Amateur Photographer* suggested, it was born from an idea first mooted in its pages about a year previously.[31] Whatever the source of Paul's inspiration, its realisation subsequently became a boon to fairground showmen and instigated the era of the travelling Bioscope. Paul himself had foreseen such a development, as is evident from a statement he made as early as April 1897:

A new and extensive field will be opened up by the Travelling Shows now in preparation, which it is proposed shall contain their own means of locomotion, and have the whole apparatus set up ready for work with electric plant. This will enable side-shows to be worked in country towns and fairs . . .[32]

Whereas Paul was successfully launched on a fruitful and prosperous career in the film business, Birt Acres (8) who had been associated with the industry for almost as long, was failing to achieve the success he perhaps deserved. His activities during 1897 are frequently reported, more especially in the pages of *The Amateur Photographer*, but his work during this period did not amount to anything of real significance. He certainly endeared himself to photographic and other societies by attending their meetings, giving demonstrations with his Kineopticon.[33]

Among the functions which Acres attended in person, was the Birmingham & Midlands Institute's annual conversazione, held on 12–15 January. Here he gave performances each evening of such old favourites as the Marlborough House events connected with Princess Maud's wedding which he had filmed on 22 July 1896; *Henley Regatta; Rough Sea at Dover*; and the *Derby* of 1895.[34] The programme was repeated on

8   Birt Acres, FRMetS, FRPS (1854–1918) (*Mrs Sidney Birt Acres*)

the 16th at the Burlington Hall, Aston, this time being shown by a representative of Birt Acres, whose name is not recorded.[35] Other engagements during January included demonstrations at the Beverley Photographic & Sketching Club,[36] and the Colne Camera Club.[37] During the same month the Nottingham Camera Club, in conjunction with the Mechanics' Institute, announced that they too had decided to enlist his services.[38] On Thursday, 11 February, he delivered a lecture at the Camera Club (London) on 'the making and exhibiting of living pictures'.[39] The lecture was accompanied by a demonstration and explanation of Birt Acres's camera and projector, for which, he said, he took out a patent two years ago. This must refer to British Patent No 10474 of 1895 (already discussed in the first volume of this history). It is interesting to note the description of the apparatus as it appeared in the Club's journal:

The machine was constructed to carry a spool containing 250 feet of film, upon which photographs were taken at the rate of twelve per foot, the exposed portion being wound on to a second spool; in projecting, also, the film which had passed through the lantern was received upon an empty spool, instead of being run out loose into a box or basket, as was the case with some apparatus. The camera was fitted with a simple form of revolving shutter, and a finder was placed on the top, the whole being enclosed in a box which could be readily carried, and all that was necessary for taking the pictures was to turn the handle on the outside. The entire process had been reduced to the utmost simplicity, for in taking the negatives, printing the positives, and showing them in the lantern, nothing had to be done but to turn the handle.[40]

The lecture also included some remarks about his method of processing the film:

For the development of the film Mr. Acres used a wooden frame in which were fixed a number of pegs, about 1½ inches apart, round which the film was wound, a hundred feet of film requiring a frame about 30 in. × 24 in. This frame fitted into an upright dish containing the developer, and he was able in that manner to develop a film up to 200 feet in length absolutely evenly from beginning to end. To print the positive the two films were placed together and exposed by turning the handle in the same manner as when taking the negative, the speed depending upon the rapidity of the sensitive coating, the quality of the light, and the density of the negative. The films could be dried upon similar frames to those used for developing, but a better plan was to wind them upon drums, and the drying could be accelerated by rapidly revolving the drums.[41]

In the course of his lecture, Birt Acres said that he was now pursuing a series of experiments with the object of adapting the three-colour process to his apparatus, and had nearly completed an instrument of which it would be possible to take photographs and project them in natural colours. Other matters mentioned by him, included daylight loading spools and an alternate method of cinematography using two films side by side for the purpose of reducing the flicker apparent in normal methods of projection, but in practice he had found the results unsatisfactory as it was very difficult to make the two pictures coalesce on the screen, and a side movement resulted, which was more unpleasant than the flickering. Of particular interest is the reference Birt Acres makes to time-lapse cinematography, utilised by him to show the movement of clouds. For this purpose, he took about one frame per second and projected the resultant film at a speed of from sixteen to twenty frames per second, 'thus exaggerating the movement but retaining the form.'[42]

On 22 April he appeared before the London & Provincial Photographic Association. Here the performance was prefaced by a short talk, in which Birt Acres outlined his own part in the development of the invention and spoke of his future plans for its perfection.[43] He also informed his audience that he proposed to film the Jubilee in colour and with enough film in his camera to last between two and three hours, all of which of course turned out to be pure fantasy, although taken seriously enough to be repeated by at least one leading photographic journal, viz: *The Amateur Photographer* (vol 25, pp 202 and 310).

The fact that his programmes still included films originally intended for the Kineto-scope and taken as long ago as 1895 with the Paul–Acres camera, leads one to suspect that his progress as regards film production had been minimal, despite frequent rumours that great things were to be expected of him at any moment. A case in point arose out of the preparations for the forthcoming Jubilee celebrations, when it was announced in March that Birt Acres 'has in preparation apparatus that will take an animated picture three hours long at the rate of twenty impressions per second.'[44] As if this were not enough, the following month the same paper (*The Amateur Photographer*) printed an even wilder statement:

> The latest news is that our only Birt has adopted a method of taking these animated pictures in the colours of nature. If this be so, his set illustrative of the great Diamond Jubilee pageant on June 22nd, taken from a privileged place in the precincts of Buckingham Palace, will be absolutely unique.[45]

These rash statements evidently emanated from the lecture Birt Acres gave at the meeting of the London & Provincial Photographic Association mentioned above. How successful he was in obtaining Jubilee films of any kind, is not known, since no evidence apparently exists of him having achieved any results whatsoever. This also applies to the Oxford and Cambridge University Boat Race which he is also reported to have taken:

> "ON DIT" that Mr. Birt Acres was to be seen taking animated photographs of the Boat Race from a parlous place on the umpire's launch. An adventurous spirit is Mr. Acres, and a daring one. We hope his efforts to catch the fleeting flotilla on the photographic film were attended with the success they deserve.[46]

In fairness to Birt Acres, it must be owned that the weather on the day (3 April) was not propitious for cinematography, a matter upon which the *British Journal of Photography* commented:

> This year the light, at the time, was as exceptionally disappointing to photographers as the temperature and wind were unpleasant to visitors generally. We know that preparations were made by "animatographers" to secure pictures of the event, but we have not yet heard the results obtained. Although fully exposed pictures may have been secured, they must, necessar-ily, lack the brightness and sparkle they would have possessed had they been taken in bright sunshine.[47]

More successful was a film he took of a visit to his works during the same month, of the editors of the principal photographic journals. The film was taken in a yard adjoining his premises,[48] which were then situated in Salisbury Road, Barnet. *The Optical Magic Lantern Journal* gives a brief summary of the film's contents:

... Mr. Acres [is] discovered sitting by the side of one of his projection machines. He then receives the editors one by one, Mr. Bedding, of the *British Journal of Photography*, being the first to appear on the scene; then Mr. Wall, of the *Photographic News*, next appears, closely followed by Mr. Rowe, of *Photography;* then ourselves [Mr. J. Hay Taylor], of the *Optical Magic Lantern Journal*; Mr. Snowden Ward, of *Photogram* fame; and finally, Mr. Welford, as representing the latest addition to photograph literature in the shape of *Photographic Life*.

After the usual salutations, Mr. Acres explained the working of the apparatus practically. One of Mr. Acres' assistants then removed the apparatus from the table on which it was standing, and in true English fashion another assistant brought on some liquid refreshment and cigars.[49]

The occasion also provided the visitors with an opportunity to inspect the plant. The editor of the *Optical Magic Lantern Journal* noted: 'We saw the film coated in length of 1,200 feet without break, cut up and perforated, also the printing machine and special apparatus for developing, washing, and drying the prints.'[50] The account in the *Photogram* gave more specific details of these processes:

He [Acres] purchases the celluloid substratum in long rolls of considerable width, and by means of machinery ... he cuts and perforates it to the well-known standard gauge.

... The coating machine is on much the same lines as any ordinary plate-coating apparatus, save that the details have been immensely simplified by Mr. Acres ... The film passes through a long ice chamber, at the end of which it is received and wound upon an immense drum of some six feet diameter in a drying room ... For development the exposed strip is wound round a light, square frame of wood on which it is immersed, after carefully wetting and brushing to remove air bells, in an upright dipping trough of very dilute developer. Pyro is used, and the strength is about one grain to the ounce. When development is complete, washing and fixing are carried through without removing the film from the frame. The printing apparatus is very simple and works very satisfactorily.[51]

Further details of Birt Acres' method of developing the film were given by Thomas Bedding, editor of the *British Journal of Photography*, in the Almanac published 1 December:

He uses a rectangular frame, the top and bottom bars of which each have a row of small wooden beads. The film is wound taut round this frame, the wooden beads engaging the perforations. The ends of the film being secured to the frame, the whole thing is placed in a vertical bath containing the developer, and is fixed and washed in similar vessels. This appears to be a simple and economical way of working, especially on a small scale.[52]

The film of the visiting editors was shown for the first time on Thursday 22 April at the London & Provincial Photographic Association, and,

as each one of the editors put in an appearance he was loudly applauded, and when it came to the refreshment part of the programme the applause was loud and long. It was admitted by all present that this series of pictures, representing as it did Mr. Acres' latest work, was second to none of the pictures that have ever been shown by anybody — the absence of flicker and jump being specially remarked upon — and we heartily congratulate Mr. Acres upon his unqualified success.[53]

This favourable verdict of the performance was perhaps a trifle flattering, for according to a letter received by *The Amateur Photographer* and mentioned in its issue for 21 May, it was therein intimated that at an early date Birt Acres will exhibit still further advances in animated photography 'in which every trace of the objectionable flickering will be entirely eliminated.'[54] We know from a patent of 18 April 1897 (Brit. Pat. no 114) that Birt Acres was experimenting with a form of cinematography which aimed at eliminating the interval between successive frames by employing a two-lens system in the camera and projector. A similar principle had been attempted the year before by Friese-Greene, in association with J. A. Prestwich, but without any apparent success.[55] As far as the two-lens camera of Birt Acres was concerned, the prospects for success were doomed from the start, for, as Hopwood has pointed out,

> . . . cameras having a double point of view must induce an apparent vibration of foreground objects on the screen by reason of the varying perspective of alternate views and, indeed, there appears to be little advantage in employing a duplicate system *for obtaining negatives* unless it be so arranged that both systems work through one objective, or at least from one point of view. The great need is not that the views should be photographed without interval, but rather that they should be *projected* without intervening darkness; and this is perfectly feasible, for the separation of projection lenses does not alter perspective.[56]

Birt Acres's two-lens projector, although perhaps feasible in theory, obviously proved impractical in use. It employed two mirrors, one stationary and the other revolving, so that the light from the illuminant was deflected through alternate frames of the film. One obvious drawback was the loss of light which such a system entails. A difficulty might also arise in maintaining a proper constancy in the brightness and definition of the alternate images as these were dependent on separate mirrors, separate lenses and an inequality in their distances from the source of light. The invention, not surprisingly, was never brought to a successful conclusion, and Birt Acres instead, turned his attention to other matters.

Well aware of the hazards presented by cinematograph fires, he too decided to tackle the problem and on 13 May 1897, applied for a patent on 'a safety appliance for kinematoscopes and the like' (No 11918). We do not know the nature of the appliance since the full patent never issued. In the same month, Acres also made application for a patent covering 'improvements in apparatus for taking, viewing or projecting photographs of moving objects' (No 13421, 21 May); but this too was either rejected, or for some reason never completed, so consequently we do not know the nature of these improvements either. Much of his time at this period must have been taken up with these experiments and was probably the reason why so little was heard of him for the next few months, a silence which prompted *The Amateur Photographer* to remark in its issue of 24 September: 'We have not heard much of Mr Birt Acres lately.'[57] This brought an immediate response from Acres in a letter which was published the following week:

> . . . you say you have not heard much about me lately. The fact is I feel that there is a great future for animated photography, but there is also great room for improvement, and as I have

set my heart and soul in the subject, it is not to be wondered at that instead of seeking a bubble reputation as a music hall showman, I have been endeavouring to perfect my system for working, etc.[58]

It would seem that Birt Acres' incessant experimenting was, for the most part, devoid of practical results, yet he must have had a camera and projector capable of giving reasonable results, for otherwise he would not have been able to fulfill the numerous engagements of which we have spoken, nor indeed been able to take the successful film of the visit to his works of the editors of the photographic press. But what exactly this apparatus was, we have no means of telling. Neither had Cecil M. Hepworth, who had asked Birt Acres for details of his apparatus for inclusion in a review of 'some present day machines', to be published in *The Amateur Photographer* on 24 September.[59] The editor of the same journal had also requested particulars, but he too received no response.[60] We can but conclude, that the apparatus which Birt Acres was using for all practical purposes was not entirely of his own devising. This conclusion seems to be borne out by an experimental camera, now in the Science Museum, London, which probably dates from this period, and employs the common 'dog' or beater movement, already extensively used by other manufacturers at this time. I have already suggested that this camera was the prototype for his sub-standard cinematograph, patented the following year and successfully marketed as the Birtac.[61]

According to a report published in June, Birt Acres was already devoting his attention mainly to the manufacture of cinematograph film and to its development and printing, etc.[62] This was carried out at his Northern Photographic Works, which were then situated at 45 Salisbury Road, Barnet. It seems unlikely however that the volume of work carried out was very large. By that time, nine tenths of the trade was said to be in the hands of the Eastman Company.[63] and there were besides several other firms engaged in the same line of business, namely, T. H. Blair,[64] E. H. Fitch & Co,[65] Marion & Co,[66] The Reliance Roller Film & Dry Plate Co,[67] and Dr. J. H. Smith & Co.[68] It perhaps says something for Acres' expertise that he was able to expand his business inspite of this formidable competition. In September 1897, the business was registered as a limited liability company, with himself as managing director.[69] Henceforth it was known as The Northern Photographic Works Limited, with a capital of £2,000 in £1 shares.[70] The new company evidently got off to a good start, for in November it was deemed necessary to move from Salisbury Road to larger premises in Nesbitt's Alley, High Street, Barnet.[71] Thus it would seem that the film and processing side of the business was more successful than his other endeavours.

Averse as he was (or professed to be) to the purely commercial exploitation of cinematography as a music hall turn, nevertheless, Birt Acres had flirted with the idea of public performances. As long ago as March 1896, he had rented a hall off Piccadilly Circus in which to exhibit his Kineopticon. In that year too, his apparatus had been exhibited at several theatres under the management of Lewis Sealy. But the name of Birt Acres had been connected with these performances only unofficially so to speak. During January and February of 1897 however, we find his name openly linked with the Dramatic & Musical Syndicate of 19 Buckingham Street, Strand, which was advertising his apparatus for these months as 'The Birt Acres Royal Cinematographe'.[72] According to the advertisements this machine was the same as that shown at Marlborough House and was also described as 'the first machine which was shown in England.' However unlikely this may be, there is no means of knowing exactly what the Royal Cinematographe was actually like, since to my knowledge, no adequate descrip-

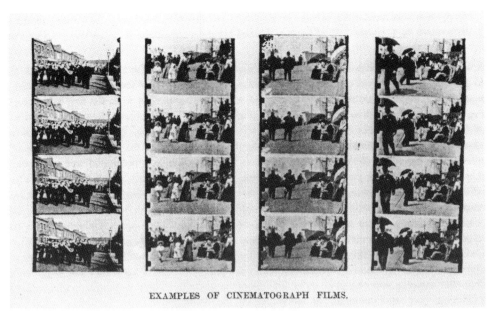

EXAMPLES OF CINEMATOGRAPH FILMS.

9 Suppressed plate showing frame illustrations from two films by Birt Acres. Note the slanting frame lines and unusual perforations. From R. Child Bayley, Modern Magic Lanterns, 2nd edition, 1st state, undated (*David Henry Collection*)

tion or illustration of it was ever published. In any case, Birt Acres' association with the agency just mentioned, seems to have been short lived and I am unable to find any further mention of it. At best, Acres' incursions into the field of commercial film exhibition were somewhat perfunctory.

Could his lack of success as a film exhibitor be due in part to the poor quality of his films? There is evidence to show that not all his films were of a very high technical standard. Some frame illustrations reproduced in the book *Modern Magic Lanterns*, by R. Child Bayley (9) show strips of two of his films in which the individual images are rather ill placed in the frame. The perforations too, do not conform to the usual Edison type then generally in use. The films are unidentified and difficult to date precisely. The indications are that the edition of the book in which they appear, was probably published early in 1897. This would suggest that the films themselves were made sometime during the previous year.

Modern Magic Lanterns was first published in 1896 (the preface is dated November, 1895). The edition of the book in which the frame illustrations appear is undated and contains an added chapter (XVI) on cinematography, titled, 'Animated Lantern Pictures'. The text on page 102 refers to the plate as follows: 'By the courtesy of Mr. Acres we are enabled to reproduce here a few of these little pictures.' It would seem, that no sooner had this edition appeared than Birt Acres persuaded the publishers to suppress the plate and delete all reference to it in the text, for in the next edition of the book (the official second edition) the matter has been omitted. It must be concluded therefore, that by the time the frame illustrations had appeared in print, Birt Acres realised that they did not compare favourably with those of other producers, and in order to safeguard his reputation, ordered their deletion.

26

The edition of *Modern Magic Lanterns* containing the suppressed plate, is now extremely rare, and I am indebted to Mr. David Henry for placing his copy of the book at my disposal. I am also grateful to him for bringing it to my notice in the first place. The two films illustrated show a band marching down a street, and a promenade scene. Could the location be Ilfracombe in Devon, where Birt Acres is known to have filmed?

2 Manufacturers and Dealers in London, 1896–7

Among the leading manufacturers of cinematographic apparatus in the years 1896–7, were several firms already engaged in the optical magic lantern trade. To begin with, cinematography was considered a logical extension of the ordinary lantern and many of the early film projectors were specifically designed to fit into, or in front of, most makes of professional lantern; whilst others were designed as dual purpose machines performing the function of combined slide and film projectors. Moreover several of the early film exhibitors were themselves formerly exhibitors of magic lantern slides. Indeed, so closely were the two functions related that we find cinematograph films referred to as 'cinematographic slides', or 'cinematograph film slides'.[1]

The close relationship between the ordinary lantern and the cinematograph, and the increasing popularity of the latter, caused one commentator to remark, 'If this boom continues, no lanternist's outfit will be complete without a kinetoscopic camera-projector, and no lantern show will be complete without a series of animated pictures.'[2] It is hardly surprising therefore, to find the principal manufacturers of lantern equipment turning their attention to cinematographs and films. Among the first to do so in London were J. Wrench & Son; W. Watson & Sons; and J. Ottway & Son.

J. Wrench & Son

The Cinematograph manufactured by J. Wrench & Son (10), which first appeared on the market in the middle of 1896, continued to be sold throughout most of the following year and, presumably, was still being made during that period. An advertisement of March 1897, states that over one hundred of these machines are now in use,[3] and a report published as late in the year as October, states that 'this apparatus is simple, effective and enjoys great popularity.'[4] This was the machine which eventually replaced Paul's Theatrograph (Animatographe) at the Alhambra on 8 July (see chapter 8) and where it was in use for sixteen weeks, soon afterwards to be re-engaged for a further term,[5] so that by December it had fulfilled engagements at that theatre amounting to twenty weeks.[6] The Wrench Cinematograph also had the distinction of being used at Balmoral Castle for a performance given by W. Walker & Co, of Aberdeen, before Queen Victoria, on 25 October.[7] Some other places where it was used during the year were the Grand Theatre, Islington; Forester's Hall, London; Theatre of Varieties, London; Palace Theatre of Varieties, Manchester; Empire, Southampton; Palace, Chatham; Royal, Woolwich; Queen's, Poplar; and the Alhambra, Sandgate.[8]

The firm of J. Wrench & Son, 50 Gray's Inn Road, was established in 1816 by John Wrench, and like so many businesses in the 19th century, was essentially a family concern. Towards the end of the century its principal member was Alfred Wrench, and it is his name which appears on the patent specification, where he is described as a wholesale optician.[9]

On 7 January 1897, we find Alfred Wrench demonstrating his Cinematograph at a meeting of the Camera Club, Charing Cross Road, where it was put through its paces in the presence of several experts and pronounced 'practically noiseless and steady.'[10] In fact we are told that the machine worked 'with much less noise than most of those now in public service.'[11] In the course of the demonstration the apparatus was first used

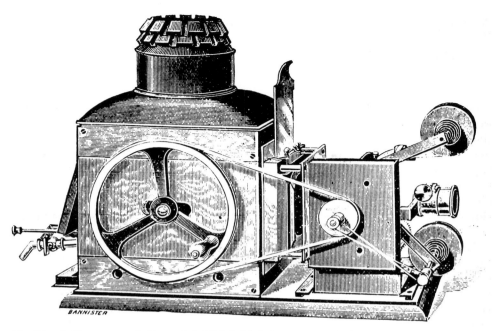

10   Wrench Cinematograph (1st model) 1896–7. Made by J. Wrench & Son, London. One of the most popular and reliable film projectors of the period (*Barnes Museum of Cinematography*)

with limelight as the illuminant, Locke's patent high-power mixed-gas jet being the one employed.[12] Then an electric arc lamp was tried, under the management of Cecil M. Hepworth.[13] It was found that a good powerful limelight jet was sufficient for all ordinary purposes and that the results were not far behind the electric arc lamp.[14] It was also established that the operative rate of the machine was twenty frames per second and that the period of rest and movement was about 1-40th of a second, but on this point Alfred Wrench explained that 'the present instrument was under revision, with a view to produce an instrument whereby the period of light would be double the period of darkness.'[15] This is our first intimation that in this respect the apparatus was not quite perfect and no doubt the projected images were not entirely devoid of flicker, but after all, this was a common defect of most projectors at that time.*

Cecil M. Hepworth's assessment of the merits of the projector were made known on 5 March:

. . . it is a pleasure to use an instrument that not only gives no trouble to the operator, but is at the same time as satisfactory to the onlookers as these things well can be. It is less noisy than any other instrument I have tried, or seen tried, while, if good films are used, the picture is as steady as may be, and accompanied with but little of that distressing flickering which is generally so noticeable. Moreover, it is so easy running that many a sewing machine might be ashamed to try conclusions with it in this respect, while the vibration of the instrument is practically *nil*, and any ordinary table is strong enough support for it.[16]

Unlike other projectors of the period which could be readily adapted for use as a camera, the design of the Wrench Cinematograph obviously precluded its conversion

*For a discussion of this problem see page 140.

in this way and so an entirely separate apparatus had to be designed if successful films were to be taken. To achieve this aim, Alfred Wrench enlisted the services of Alfred Darling, a clever mechanic and engineer of 47 Chester Terrace, Brighton, and together they designed a camera on entirely different lines to the Wrench projector. The movement chosen was of the claw variety, in which a single double-action cam raises, lowers, inserts, and withdraws the claw. The shutter was composed of segments sliding over one another, by which means the area of the shutter could be varied. Most likely, this was one of the earliest instances of a variable shutter being applied to a movie camera; I know of only one earlier, that of the Prestwich camera, to be described later.

The Wrench-Darling apparatus is not unlike the Cinématographe-Lumière both in appearance and mechanism (11). Even so, it would be wrong to suppose that it is a flagrant copy. Rather it is an attempt to improve on Lumière's already successful apparatus. Like the latter, it can be used as a camera, printer and projector. But whereas in the Lumière machine, the film is moved by one tooth, or pin on each side, here two sets of three pins are employed. The method by which these pins are inserted and withdrawn from the perforations in the film also differs. In the Wrench-Darling machine, the pins are attached to a frame bearing a small projection which enters a groove on the edge of a disc, the groove being designed in such a manner that when the pin-frame is being lowered by the cam, the pins are engaged with the film perforations, but when the pin-frame is being lifted, the pins are disengaged. The Wrench-Darling cinematograph has been placed on permanent loan to the Science Museum, London, by Messrs. A. Darling & Sons of Brighton (Inv. no. 1978–281). I am indebted to Dr. D. B. Thomas for a description of the apparatus, from which my own account has been adapated.

The Optician was given a preview of the new camera and published the following account in its issue for 3 June:

> We had pleasure, a few days ago in viewing the first perfected instrument. It is built on the same lines as the cinematograph except that it contains many improvements. As a camera it is encased in mahogany, the shell being absolutely light-proof, for the side which opens has first a movable shutter fitted into a rabbet, which is again enclosed by a sliding shutter. The operating crank is located upon the opposite side of the case. The shaft is so bushed as to also exclude the light. All the best principles of the old cinematograph are retained in the new, and to use it as such, all that is necessary to be done, is to remove the shutters and then release the machine from the case by unscrewing two thumb-screws, and it is then ready to reproduce upon the screen the pictures it has previously "taken" as a camera.
>
> The machine which we allude to is made to carry a roll of film 150ft. in length, but can be made to take a reel of very much longer dimensions.
>
> We saw one of the first films taken by this apparatus, and certainly have to pronounce it very excellent indeed. It shows the subject evenly and well-defined. We predict that this instrument will become exceedingly popular.[17]

The camera was patented by Darling and Wrench on 21 July 1897 (No 17248), but was apparently in service before the patent was officially lodged at the Patent Office. It was with this camera that Alfred Wrench obtained 'an excellent series of pictures' of Queen Victoria's Diamond Jubilee procession, and was also used by him to film the Naval Review at Spithead which took place on 26 June 1897.[18]

Wrench's Jubilee films were shown at the Alhambra Theatre, Leicester Square,

11   A combined camera, printer and projector, made by Alred Darling of Brighton. Patented by Wrench & Darling (No 17,248. 21 July, 1897) (*Science Museum, London*)

where they comprised a programme lasting about five minutes and which was said to be 'a very creditable production.'[19] However, the camera which Alfred Wrench managed to put to such good use, was probably not manufactured for the commercial market until the following year, despite the fact that an advertisement published in October, lists among the firm's products, 'Patent Cinematograph Camera.'[20] In fact Cecil M. Hepworth informs us in his 'review of some present day machines' (*The Amateur Photographer*, 24 September) that the camera used for taking the Jubilee films 'will be ready about next spring',[21] and I feel sure that if such a camera had indeed been marketed before then, it would have been noticed by one of the photographic journals. The conclusion to be drawn, I think, is that for the time being, Wrench's Patent Cinematograph Camera was reserved solely for the firm's own use. The camera was probably withheld from the market until the complete specification was lodged at the Patent Office. This did not take place until 18 May 1898, and it was another month before the patent was finally granted.[22]

Wrench did however, introduce a new cinematograph projector during the latter half of 1897. This was a low priced machine, which was just being put into full production at the time Hepworth was writing the article just mentioned, for he writes that one had been made ready just in time to be shown to him before his article went to press.[23] Known as Wrench's 'Cheap Form of Cinematograph' (12) it was probably not ready for the market until about November. The price of the apparatus was nine guineas [£9.45].[24] It employed the common 'dog' or eccentric cam movement, which struck the film at each revolution, drawing down a length of film equal to one frame. The machine was also fitted with a picture racking device which was actuated by a small lever at the side. Although relatively cheap, the projector seems to have given good results and the *Optical Magic Lantern Journal* wrote: 'We have lately had one of these instruments in use and found it to work excellently.'[25]

A modification was later made to the first Wrench Cinematograph. The original model had been on the market since August 1896, but the exact date when it was superceded by the new version has not been determined; it was probably not before 1898. It still retained some features of the original, but was re-geared and the old-type mangle wheel* which had been situated on the lantern body was now discarded and a crank-handle fitted directly on to the driving shaft. The baseboard was also widened and the projector mechanism swivel-mounted so that it could be drawn aside to allow the lantern to be used for slide projection. For this purpose a metal ring was fixed to the edge of the front plate to support a second objective lens for showing the slides.

A feature of both versions was the unique means employed for imparting the intermittent movement to the sprocket-wheel (situated immediately below the gate). This comprised a six-toothed rachet-wheel with a deep notch at the foot of each tooth into which fitted a small pawl for holding the ratchet-wheel rigidly in place. A second, larger pawl, which jogged backwards and forwards when the crank-handle was turned, pushed the smaller pawl out of its locking position and itself acted on the ratchet-wheel, moving it round the distance equivalent to one picture frame. It then retired and the smaller pawl took up its original position, once more locking the ratchet-wheel until the next time when the whole procedure was repeated. This occurred fifteen times per second provided the crank-handle was turned at the correct speed.[26]

The revised model[27] was also fitted with a racking plate adjustable by a vertical

---

*So called because of its resemblance to the crank-wheel employed on domestic mangles used at that time for wringing clothes.

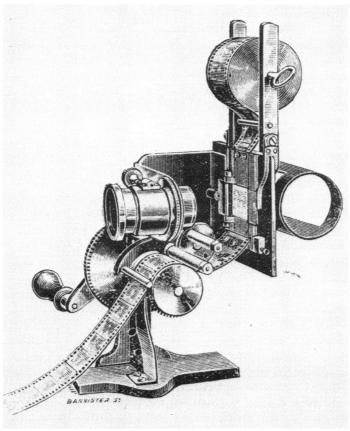

12   Wrench's cheap form of cinematograph, 1897 (Two views) (*Barnes Museum of Cinematography*)

13   Trade Mark of J. Wrench & Son, Manufacturing Opticians, 50 Gray's Inn Road, London. Registered no 188943, 26 July, 1895, Class 8. In use since 1870 (*Barnes Museum of Cinematography*)

pinion which extended beyond the top of the mechanism and terminated in a milled-head for holding. Like its predecessor, it had a segmented barrel shutter situated at the rear of the gate. Rather surprisingly, the sprocket-wheels were still turned from a solid piece of brass, or bronze, without any allowance being made for a recessed path between the edges. Consequently the whole surface of the film came into contact with the sprocket, much to the detriment of the former.*

Wrench also installed a film developing and printing department, which was in operation by early June. The plant was situated in the basement of their building at No 50 Gray's Inn Road, and catered for amateurs as well as the trade.[28] But J. Wrench & Son were essentially wholesale opticians and their products are seldom, if ever, marked with their name and address. Instead, a distinctive trade mark is used, which takes the form of a little emblem composed of a stop-cock or tap, bearing the letters J. W. (13). The business flourished well into the present century, but was finally absorbed in about 1925, by Cinema Traders Ltd, Scientific & Illuminating Engineers, of 26 Church Street, London, W.1., who specialised in a wide range of equipment and accessories concerned with the exhibition side of the film industry.

W. Watson & Sons

W. Watson & Sons, of 313 High Holborn, established in 1837, specialised in a wide range of optical goods, including still cameras and photographic accessories. Towards the end of 1896, this firm introduced its popular cinematograph called the Motorgraph (14), which remained on the market throughout the following year.[30] It was of the type that could be attached to most makes of optical lantern and could also be quickly adapted for use as a cinematograph camera. It was exceedingly compact, the mechanism being contained in a small walnut wood case measuring 6 × 4⅜ × 5½ inches.[31] The price of the instrument was twelve guineas [£12.60].[32]

When used as a projector, the front lens of the magic lantern was first removed and the Motorgraph placed close to the front tube. It was necessary of course to insure that the Motorgraph coincided with the exact optical centre of the lantern, which could easily be achieved by mounting it on appropriate wooden blocks fixed to a baseboard, as shown in the illustration. The roll of film was placed in position between the two uprights at the top of the instrument and held in place by inserting a spindle through holes in the uprights so that it passed through the centre of the coil of film, no spool being required.[33] The loose end of the film was then inserted in the slot at the top of the box and fed through the gate to the sprocket-wheel below, and then out through

*Projectors with unrebated sprocket-wheels can usually be ascribed to the years 1896–8. Most machines after this period had modern type sprocket-wheels.

34

W. WATSON & SONS,

Opticians to H.M. Government,

313, HIGH HOLBORN, LONDON.

THE MOTORGRAPH,

£12 12s.	For Projecting Animated Pictures and Exposing Films for Producing Same.	**£12 12s.**

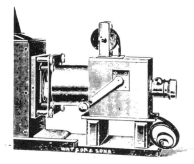

CONSTRUCTION:
Very Strong without Complications.

WORKING:
Simplicity itself.

ACTION:
Steadier than High Priced Machines.

Can be Used with any Magic Lantern

Takes Films of Standard Perforation.

Produces most brilliant picture, passing more light than any other machine.

Absolutely Reliable.   Cannot be Deranged in Working.
Very Compact (Outside size, 6 × 4⅜ × 5½).

Price of MOTORGRAPH, with Special Large Aperture Projection Lens,

···⟩ **£12 12s.** ⟨···

For full particulars of Motorgraphs for Projecting and Taking, see Catalogue No. 8.
Write for New List of Films, New Subjects Weekly.

DEVELOPING AND PRINTING CUSTOMERS' OWN FILMS UNDERTAKEN.
Demonstrations of the Motorgraph given by appointment.

The Latest and Best of everything used in connection with Animated Photography.

Troughs, High-Power Jets, Arc Lamps, Film Winders, &c., &c.,
KEPT IN STOCK.

14   Advertisement for Watson's Motorgraph published in The Magic Lantern Journal Annual 1897–8 (October, 1897) p civ (*Barnes Museum of Cinematography*)

another slot situated at the lower edge of the case. Since no adjustable racking plate was provided, it was necessary to insure that the picture frame was correctly registered in the gate aperture, where it was held in place by a spring flap.[34] The film was advanced by a single sprocket-wheel to which an intermittent movement was applied by the interaction of an eccentric cam and lever in combination with a ratchet-wheel and coiled spring. This form of intermittent mechanism was unique and has been described by Cecil M. Hepworth in the following terms:

> In this machine the sprocket wheel runs loosely upon its axis, which is connected directly to the driving handle of the instrument. But it is connected with this axle by a spiral spring, one end of which is attached to the sprocket and the other to the axle. Consequently, when the handle is turned the sprocket wheel would move regularly with it if there were nothing to interfere. But there is a pawl which engages with the teeth of a ratchet attached to the sprocket, and this prevents any movement of the latter, and turning the handle, therefore, puts tension upon the spring. To the axle, however, is connected directly a cam of peculiar shape which releases that pawl periodically, and so the sprocket shifts round quickly until another tooth of the rachet brings it to rest again. In that time, of course, it moves the film to the extent of one picture, and simultaneously the lens is covered with a translucent shutter of xylonite.[35]

A report published in October 1897, says that the Motorgraph 'has recently been provided with a supplemental condenser.'[36] As far as I know, this was the only modification made to the apparatus during the whole of its commercial life, a factor which speaks well for its efficiency, although it was probably more suitable for amateur use than the professional exhibitor, especially since the film capacity of the apparatus was restricted to lengths of up to about 75 feet.

15 The Motorgraph, 1896–7. Made by W. Watson & Sons, London. View of the interior mechanism (*Barnes Museum of Cinematography*)

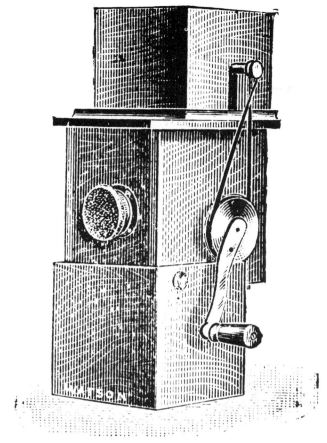

16 The Motorgraph Camera, 1896–7. From an illustration in The Optician (3 June, 1897) p 194 (*British Library*)

There is a Motorgraph in the Barnes Museum of Cinematography, unfortunately not in original state; the outer case has been altered and some of the brass adornments are obviously spurious. However, the interior mechanism is genuine although the spring-plate to the gate is wanting (15).

To adapt the Motorgraph for use as a ciné camera, all that was required was to fit two film boxes to the top and bottom of the instrument, and substitute a different lens and shutter. These attachments could be had from the makers for a few pounds extra, but it was advisable to return the instrument to the makers for conversion[37](16).

In addition to the Motorgraph, W. Watson & Sons were able to offer 'the latest and best of everything used in connection with animated photography,' which included troughs, high-power jets, arc lamps and film winders, &c. They also undertook the developing and printing of customers' own films, and could arrange demonstrations of the Motorgraph by appointment.[38] In its issue of 3 June, *The Optician* reported that 'this firm has a large line of English films, among the latest of which is "Football" and the "Charge of Guards," both of which we have seen, and have to pronounce very fine indeed. They make a special feature of private and public entertainments, having given nine shows only last week.'[39] The football film was made by G. A. Smith (see Appendix

1, p 203), and the one of the guards may have been a Lumière film. In October 1897, Watson issued a catalogue of cinematographic apparatus which also contained a list of some hundreds of films.[40] No copy of this catalogue seems to have survived, but no doubt some of the films listed were photographed with the Motorgraph Camera. For instance, we know that 1000ft of film was exposed in this camera during the Jubilee procession and sold by Watson in lengths of about 75ft.[41]

J. Ottway & Son

J. Ottway & Son, of 178 St. John's Street Road, established in 1859, were also well known manufacturers of still cameras and optical magic lantern equipment who had turned their attention to cinematography in 1896.[42] By November of that year, they had placed on the market a very substantial apparatus called the Animatoscope, specifically designed for use in large halls (17). It was mounted on a strong metal pillar which also carried a large crank-wheel (of the mangle-wheel type) and connected to the main driving shaft by a belt. The apparatus was a dual purpose machine, projecting both films and lantern slides. By means of adjusting screws, the desired tilt of the projector was easily attained, and the change over from film to slide projection was ingeniously effected by means of a lever which raised a reflecting mirror to the requisite angle in front of the condensing lens, and at the same time shifted the illuminant closer to the condenser to better illuminate the slide. The slide itself was placed on a small platform which also supported the vertical lens attachment which was similar to that used on science lanterns.[43]

The overall design of the Animatoscope was reminiscent of Paul's Theatrograph, as was also the form of the intermittent mechanism. Two sprocket-wheels, situated above and below the film gate, were moved intermittently by two star wheels based on the principle of the Maltese-cross. The shutter was of the double-fan type but with serrated edges (like the old-fashioned fans used in dissolving views) with the idea of reducing flicker.[44] The Animatoscope was an expensive machine, costing £60.[45] Additional information about this projector will be found in the previous volume.

A report published in October 1897, states that J. Ottway & Son 'are also making a smaller and lighter apparatus for private rooms. In this instance, the heavy stand is dispensed with, and the driving wheel attached in a convenient position.'[46] I have not found any further information about this apparatus and am unable to say whether or not it appeared on the market before the year ended.

Newman & Guardia Ltd

Newman & Guardia Ltd, of 90 Shaftesbury Avenue, makers of high quality cameras and accessories, also had intentions of including cinematographic equipment in its range of products, but the first attempts to design suitable apparatus all proved abortive. As we have already noted in the first volume of this history, A. S. Newman had constructed an experimental machine early in 1896, but the results did not come up to expectations and it was never commercially produced. An entirely different machine was then designed which was patented in October, but this too apparently failed to meet the exacting standards set by the firm, with the result that the year slipped by without the company achieving a marketable product.

Work went ahead throughout most of 1897 in an endeavour to find a satisfactory solution to the problem, only to be met with further setbacks, until finally a successful conclusion was reached towards the end of the year. The first indications that some sort

17 Ottway's Animatoscope, 1896–7. Made by J. Ottway & Son, London (*Barnes Museum of Cinematography*)

of apparatus had possibly been built by July, is contained in a description of the new premises which Newman & Guardia had then recently acquired:

> Newman & Guardia, Limited, have added to their town premises the adjoining building, No. 90 Shaftesbury-avenue, W. The complete premises thus obtained at the corner of Macclesfield-street and Shaftesbury-avenue form a very fine suite of rooms, and are partly rendered necessary by the determination of the firm to go much more fully into apparatus for optical projection. The optical projection room is specially arranged so that lanterns, including the firm's new Kinetographic lantern may be seen in actual work.[47]

We also have notice of a proposed series of cinematograph shows to be given by "N. & G." at the Royal Agricultural Hall, Islington, where the Printers and Allied Trades Exhibition was to be held:

> ... Messrs. Newman and Guardia, of 92, Shaftesbury Avenue, W., will give six exhibitions of animated photographs daily, their recently completed apparatus being used for the production of the pictures. These entertainments will all be free to visitors to the exhibition, which will be open from 23rd to 30th June inclusive.[48]

But it is not at all certain whether indeed these shows ever took place. According to Cecil M. Hepworth, there is some doubt about the matter, as the following extract from his 'review of some present day machines,' indicates:

> Messrs. Newman and Guardia are not quite ready with their long-talked-of instrument yet, and this is a firm that never bring out anything until it has quite satisfied their own high standard of excellence. Any one who is familiar with the mechanism of an "N. and G." camera will admit that great things must be expected from this firm when at last their cinematograph is ready for sampling, and we should all be disappointed if those expectations be not realised. By the way, I suppose that the recent launching at the Agricultural Hall must be regarded as abortive. I thought that the new cinematograph was ready to start its career on the troublous sea of public opinion.[49]

The above paragraph was published 24 September, so it would seem that as of that date, "N. & G." had not in fact completed the final stages of their apparatus, but obviously something was in the offing. Then finally two months later, on 24 November, it made its belated appearance at a meeting of the Photographic Club, where 'a very successful exhibition of Messrs. Newman & Guardia's kinematograph was given before a large audience.'[50] The editor of *The British Journal of Photography* was able to report in the issue for 3 December, that he had been informed by Mr. Newman 'that the machine will shortly be ready for the market,' and that 'considerable time and labour have been spent in bringing it to a high degree of perfection.'[51] It was too late in the year, one would suppose, for the machine to be put into commercial production and be ready for sale before the year closed, so one must conclude that yet another year passed without a "N & G" cinematograph reaching the market.

Chard & Co

Chard & Co of 8 Great Portland Street, had been exhibiting films since September 1896,[52] if not earlier, and during the year under review also established themselves as film producers. They dealt too in cinematographic apparatus, but whether this was actually made by them is open to question. Among the goods which they offered were projecting and perforating machines, photographic apparatus and 'all requisites for animated photography.'[53] They also operated a film developing and printing service and undertook the perforating of film.[54] The exhibition side of their business was advertised as Chard's Vitagraph, so it would seem that they were users of the French Vitagraphe, made by Clement & Gilmer of Paris. Such performances are recorded at Argyle, Birkenhead; the Winter Gardens, Morecambe;[55] and the Myddelton Hall, Islington, the latter engagement receiving an enthusiastic notice in *The Era*:

Chard's Vitagraph scored another success last Sunday night [7 November] at Myddelton Hall, Islington, in connection with the National Sunday League Concerts. Scenes from the Jubilee Procession, including the now historic ceremony at Temple Bar, a new and startling train film, a realistic bolster fight, a laughable film of marines at vaulting exercise, were all loudly applauded. Contrary to rules, an encore was insisted on by the audience, and by kind permission of the management "The Flying Dutchman at full speed" was repeated.[56]

Chard's theatrical bookings were augmented, whenever possible, by local scenes taken specially for each engagement.[57] The whole of their film making activities seem to have been confined to the non-fiction class, and in particular to news films. They were particularly proud of their Jubilee film depicting the Lord Mayor handing over the City Sword at Temple Bar, which they described as 'the finest film taken of the Jubilee Procession.'[58] They had exclusive coverage of the Roman Catholic St. Augustine Centenary at Ebbsfleet, which they claimed was 'the only animated photograph taken of this world-famous ceremony.'[59] Also covered was the launching of H.M.S. Canopus at Portsmouth, again said to be the only film taken of the event.[60] Other films included the Derby and the Oaks.[61] It was during the filming of horse races at Epsom that one of their cameramen became involved in a fracas with a titled lady and her daughter, which ended up in court. The case arose out of an incident which took place at the Epsom Downs Hotel on 27 April. Vernon Henry Tovey, a journalist and photographer, employed by Chard & Co to film the races, had erected his camera on the balcony of the Hotel. The Countess R. Sztaray was accustomed to using the balcony and objected to this intrusion. After Tovey had been there some time, she enquired whether he intended staying all day, to which he replied that he had the perfect right to do so, since he had paid for the use of the stand. A little later, as he was preparing to film the finish of a race, the Countess asked if he would move the camera to allow her to pass. This he refused to do until the race was over, whereupon the Countess's daughter, Flora, overthrew the apparatus and in so doing slightly injured the cameraman in the eye and caused considerable damage to the camera and negatives.[62] Tovey sued for assault and Chard & Co for damage to their equipment and films. The case came before Epsom Crown Court on 26 June and 16 July. Rather unreasonably perhaps, the verdict went in favour of the defendants.[63] Tovey, the cameraman involved, is also known to us from an advertisement in *The Era* where he offers for sale a number of films and a complete outfit. His address is given as 1 Valmar Road, Coldharbour Lane, Camberwell, S.E.[64]

J. H. Steward

I have yet to find a cinematograph which can be attributed to J. H. Steward, manufacturing optician of 406 & 408 Strand. In November of 1896, this firm was advertising a portable cinematograph at £36, which was described as 'simple, certain and noise-less.'[65] When one remembers that the price of the original Wrench Cinematograph was also £36, one immediately suspects that it was this apparatus that was being offered for sale by J. H. Steward. Almost one year later, another advertisement appeared, listing among the firm's products, 'Cinematographs, of best design, from £18.'[66] An advertisement in the *British Journal Photographic Almanac for 1898*, which was published in December 1897, lists three cinematographs priced at £20, £36, and £9.9s., the last two, we know, were the prices of Wrench's two machines. Also advertised are 'high-class films of new subjects.'[67] J. H. Steward was established in 1856 and built up a considerable reputation as a maker of optical lanterns, but the absence of more precise details concerning cinematographic equipment leads one to believe that this part of the business was entirely supplied from outside sources.

Philipp Wolff

Philipp Wolff (9 & 10 Southampton Street, High Holborn) entered the film business late in 1896. He dealt principally in films, of which he had one of the largest stocks in England. His speciality was foreign films, particularly French, but he also sold English subjects, some of which may have been his own productions. Advertisements published during 1897, state that he has 100 English subjects at 30s each (£1.50),[68] and according to another statement he was able to supply all Paul's films without restrictions.[69]

Apart from a series he produced on the Jubilee procession (see p 189) little is known about his own productions. A film called *The Death of Nelson*, was one of his most successful English subjects and was said to have been prepared to commemorate the anniversary of Trafalgar [21 October].[70] The film proved to be extremely popular, and the demand at first, exceeded supply.[71] Wolff also issued films 'illustrative of scenes in connection with the Indian Mutiny, and also an excellent scene depicting Charles I taking leave of his family.'[72] But whether these films were actually produced by Wolff, or indeed made in England, is open to question. They could very well have been made in France under his instructions, since he had special facilities in that country, which included his own offices. Whatever the true facts may be, the films were undoubtedly well produced and were described as 'wonderfully sharp, clear, and full of detail.'[73] The majority of the films issued by Wolff were foreign importations and this aspect of his business is more fully discussed in chapter 6.

By the beginning of 1897 Philipp Wolff was also dealing in cinematographic equipment,[74] but this may have been supplied from an outside source, as there is nothing to suggest that he himself was a manufacturer. By June he had placed on the market a rather expensive projector, under the name of Wolff's Vitaphotoscope (18)* The lantern and film mechanism were separate components but mounted at each end of a strong oak baseboard which, for exhibition purposes, was fastened on top of the travelling case by means of two sash screws. Bolted to the side of the case was a large pulley or mangle-wheel, connected by a belt to the main drive. A small drawer or box was also provided in which the films and tools were stored. When the projector was not in use, all the components could be dismantled and neatly stowed inside the oak chest, which was fitted with massive brass handles. The intermittent movement of the projector was of the Maltese-cross and cam variety. The machine was described by *The*

*I have not been able to find an illustration of this machine in its original form, so the model of 1898 is shown. This was similar in most respects, except for the addition of the reel standards and spools.

18 Wolff's Vitaphotoscope (1898 model). Similar to the original 1897 version except for the addition of the spool standards and reels (*Barnes Museum of Cinematography*)

Photogram as 'a fine specimen of engineer's work, beautifully designed and finished, substantial and rigid.' The price was £35, but as *The Photogram* observed, 'anyone who examines it in detail must admit that the price is not extravagant.'[75] As an added bonus, each purchaser of the apparatus was given a written guarantee for two years.[76]

The Photographic News described the Vitaphotoscope as 'not only extremely simple in design, but effective in action. The flicker too often seen with some of these instruments is absent, the pictures are immovable on the screen, and the whole apparatus packs away into a neat box, which may be used as a support while showing. This is, we think, one of the best machines we have seen yet.'[77]

Wolff's cinematograph camera was expensive too, costing from £20 to £80 according to the number of accessories supplied.[78] These included two Zeiss lenses, about 2in and 3½in focus respectively, and no less than eight film boxes, as well as a massive and rigid tripod which, it was stated, 'would withstand even the surgings of a race-course crowd.'[79]

Fred Harvard

Cecil M. Hepworth mentions an apparatus called the Cinematoscope, invented by Fred Harvard of 31 Reedworth Street, Kennington Road, but not having had the opportunity of inspecting its interior mechanism, he was unable to give any precise details concerning it, except to note that it was uncommonly like the Wrench Cinematograph.[80] According to the claims of its inventor, it had special facilities for changing the films, so that tiresome waits between the pictures were avoided. It could also be used with or without a shutter, and was steady in operation and did not tear the film.[81] Hopwood, in his book *Living Pictures* (London, 1899) mentions the apparatus by name without describing it.[82] I have been unable to find an illustration of this machine.

Harvard was active during the latter half of 1896, as an exhibitor, although he also advertised machines and films for sale. His performances were variously billed as Harvard's Animatoscope, Cinematoscope, or Cenematoscope.[83] In January 1897, he was advertising his apparatus as 'Harvard's Cinematoscope (Protected) Large Pictures. No Vibration. Can work with equal success with limelight or electric light.'[84] Although dealing in films and equipment, he seems to have attached more importance to the exhibiting side of the business. He claimed to have nine machines and operators working and was 'open for engagements for any part of the world',[85] this last more likely, hyperbole than hard fact. That his activities were on a rather minor scale is apparent from his advertisement in *The Era*. Here he gives the Grand Theatre, Blackpool, as his immediate address[86] obviously because he was then fulfilling an engagement at that theatre. Such practice is typical of the small-time exhibitor, who was likely to be away from his permanent address for long periods at a time.

The European Blair Camera Co, Ltd

Hepworth also refers to an apparatus brought out by the European Blair Camera Co, Ltd, (9 Southampton Street, Holborn) but without being able to supply any details. He merely states that 'this is another self-contained instrument, so much so that I could not find out anything about it, except that it works with a claw, and apparently works very well. It seems to be thoroughly well made, and is certainly pretty silent and quite simple in its working.'[87] Most likely, this was the subject of patent No 17505 of 7 August 1896,[88] of which Hopwood gives the following summary:

> The film is driven by two sprockets, one feed, one take-up, both continuous. Between these the film is sufficiently slack to allow an intermittent feed to be given by an arm rocked from an eccentric. Another eccentric forces pins into the perforations to steady the film during exposure. These pins have taper points which act to finally adjust the film.[89]

The Blair company was one of the very first in England to supply film stock for cinematographic work, a topic we have already discussed in the previous volume. But the company had also been experimenting with chrono-photographic apparatus from a very early date and its first patent in this respect is dated 27 June 1895 (Pat. No. 12458).[90] On 16 June of the following year, Blair took out a second patent (No. 13284)[91] on a cinematograph which however, never appears to have reached a practical stage, but seems to have been abandoned in favour of the patent of 7 August 1896, mentioned above. Even so, it seems unlikely that this latter apparatus reached the production stage before the middle of 1897. Hepworth's brief mention of the apparatus is the only record I have of its existence. The possibility exists of course, that this

44

apparatus may have been developed by the parent company in America, in which case it cannot qualify as an English invention.

The European Blair Camera Company Limited, continued to specialise in film for cinematography and during 1897 were advertising two brands, a 'matt' film for negatives and a 'transparent' one for positives. This they were able to supply in any width up to 20 inches and any length up to 120 feet, without joins.[92] The company's main business however, was concerned with plates and films for still photography and, of course, with photographic equipment of all kinds.

Bender & Co (The Velograph Syndicate Ltd)

During the latter part of 1896, probably in September or October, Messrs Bender & Co, specialists in photographic enlargements, of 242 London Road, Croydon, acquired the rights to a machine called the Grand Kinematograph.[93] This apparatus had been invented and patented by T. J. & G. H. Harrison,[94] and was designed to take a large gauge film, about 70mm wide. The apparatus had been exploited for a time by W. & D. Downey, the well known portrait photographers, but after passing from their control, it had been taken up by Bender & Co, who, with the assistance of the original patentees, proceeded to effect improvements in its construction. The new improved model was to have been demonstrated at a meeting of the Croydon Camera Club on 13 January, 1897, but owing to some impediment the machine was not available and the original model had to be exhibited in its place. During the meeting, ten films were shown, of which two were selected for special praise, *Demolition of Old Railway Station, Croydon*, and *Yacht Landing Pleasure Party, Hastings*. Both these films had been taken by Adolphe Langfier, a partner in the firm, who was to have given the original demonstration with the new apparatus, but was prevented from attending through illness, his place being taken at the last moment by the president of the club, Hector Maclean.[95]

Eventually, Adolphe Langfier was able to demonstrate the new model at the next meeting of the club, which was held on 27 January. A comparison was then made with the original design and the various improvements pointed out. According to the published reports of the meeting, 'the main improvements consisted in less power being needed to work the machine, much less noise, less flicker; finally, much steadier pictures were obtainable due to an improved film perforator, which ensures accurate registering.' Langfier was also able to show a film which he had taken at 11.30 that morning, of skaters on Morland Pond. The estimated exposure of the negative was said to have been between $1/200$th and $1/100$th of a second.[96]

No attempt was made to place the Grand Kinematograph on the market, since it would have been difficult to induce the public to buy a machine using a large gauge film. Its makers thus preferred to use it for their own exhibitions.[97] This restrictive use of the apparatus was only temporary, for it was soon realised that the machine could be easily modified to take film of the Edison standard and in this form would have decided commercial possibilities. By June, the apparatus had been converted to its new role and renamed the Velograph (19).

To exploit the new machine, the Velograph Syndicate Limited was formed in June, with a capital of £5,000 in £1 shares, to take over the cinematographic section of the business of Bender & Co,[98] and an extensive programme of film production was also embarked upon. Among the earliest successes were a 120ft film of the Derby[99] and a series of films of the Jubilee procession taken at two different points along the route[100] (see illustration 98).

19 The Velograph, 1897. Introduced by the Velograph Syndicate of Croydon. This was a 35mm version of the Grand Kinematograph which was patented in 1896 by G. H. & T. J. Harrison and originally designed to take 70mm film (*Barnes Museum of Cinematography*)

The mechanism of the Velograph was similar in most respects to the Grand Kinematograph which has been described in volume one. The new machine was fitted with a short focus Dallmeyer projection lens, a Gwyer jet, and a firm iron stand and packing case, which included a liberal supply of tools and accessories. The complete outfit cost £55.[101]

Interchangeable Ltd

The Interchangeable Automatic Machine Syndicate Ltd (known more simply as Interchangeable Limited) of 57 St. John's Road, Holloway, had entered the film business in 1896 and at one time were associated with the Edison projecting machine.[102] By March of 1897, they were advertising 'The Showman's Kinematograph' at £20, and 'The French Cinematograph' at £15,[103] but nothing is known about either of these two instruments, unless the former was the same as a machine they advertised in December under the name of Le-Biograph.[104] This last cost £12 for the mechanism only, but £20 complete with lantern, &c, the same price, it will be noted, as the machine advertised in March. No actual description of this apparatus can be found, but it probably employed a claw-type mechanism, since it was specifically stated not to have had a sprocket wheel.[105] Most likely the apparatus was of French origin, as its name would suggest.

Interchangeable Limited were dealers in apparatus and films, but there is no evidence to suppose that they themselves were manufacturers. The films which they offered included both French[106] and English subjects, and among the latter were films of the Jubilee and Henley Regatta. Also offered was *A Magnificent Glove Fight*, which was 150 feet long and cost £4.15s.[107] This was probably an American importation.

H. Heinze & Co, Ltd

In the first volume of this history, I described two patents relating to an apparatus invented by a mechanical engineer by the name of Horatio John Heinze.[108] Application for the first patent was made on 14 July 1896 (No. 15603), but evidently proved unsatisfactory, for Heinze applied for a second patent on 12 October (No. 22627). This latter materialised in January 1897 as the Pholimeograph and was advertised in *The Era*:

> At Last, at last. The dream of inventors an accomplished fact. The Pholimeograph (Heinze' Patent) just completed, is the only machine for showing animated photographs in which sprockets (so destructive in tearing films) are not used, and in which perforations in films are not required. The life of the film is practically insured. Damaged films rendered useless on sprocket machines, as good as new on Pholimeograph. Immense saving for exhibitors obvious. Is worked by hand. Absolutely steady. No flicker. Almost noiseless. Easy to operate. Very small and portable . . .[109]

The means by which all this was supposedly accomplished is revealed in the patent specification. In lieu of sprocket wheels, two blocks were driven forward to grip the edges of the film against a plate on the other side. The gripping-blocks and plate then sank together, carrying the film with them. It was an ingenious idea, but one rather suspects that if the film were to slip the exact registration of one frame with the next would be prevented and the effect on the screen would be a hobbling or jumping motion, as sometimes experienced in sprocket machines when the perforations of the film are torn or damaged.

The Pholimeograph was probably capable of giving a satisfactory performance when under the control of an experienced operator, but it is doubtful whether the machine would be quite so successful in the hands of the average showman. However, a satisfactory performance is said to have occurred at the Albert Hall before an audience of 20,000 [!] and pronounced 'a triumph of mechanical skill in both workmanship and results. The size of the picture shown on the screen was 40 × 30 feet.[110] The sole manufacturers and owners of this instrument, were H. Heinze & Co, Ltd, of 16 East Road, City Road, London, but the apparatus was also being advertised by another member of the inventor's family, A. J. Heinze, of 21 Hackney Road, who was a dealer in spare parts and accessories for phonographs and graphophones. His advertisements are to be found in the *English Mechanic* during October and November 1897 (pp 170 and 285).

Bonn's Kinematograph Ltd

In April 1896, Jacob Bonn, an electrician of 1 Holborn Place, High Holborn, WC, had applied for a patent on a projecting machine which was briefly described in my previous volume.[111] At the time, I was unaware that this patent had any practical results. Recently, on re-reading Cecil M. Hepworth's autobiography, *Came the Dawn*, I was surprised to find a reference to it:

> Early in 1897, [writes Hepworth] we took a shop in Cecil Court, Charing Cross Road, and set up there to work an agency we secured for the sale of cameras and dry-plates. We enjoyed the lark and waited for custom — which never came.
>   I was still being bitten by the thought of those film pictures of Robert Paul's, and it was at

some time during the first months at Cecil Court that I discovered the possibilities of buying an experimental film-projector from a man named Bonn in High Holborn. I bought it for a pound, modified it and coupled it to my existing lantern, and thus I had a means of projecting film's.[112]

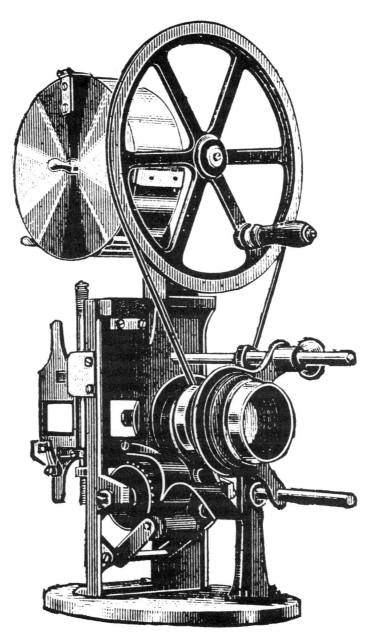

20 Rosenberg's Cinematograph, 1896–7. Introduced by A. Rosenberg & Co, Newcastle and London (*Barnes Museum of Cinematography*)

So, equipped with a modified Bonn projector, Hepworth set off to tour the country with a cinematograph show.[113] But perhaps the original Bonn machine was not quite so inadequate as Hepworth would have us believe, for the following advertisement in *The Era* for 20 March 1897 proves that it was practical enough to warrant commercial exploitation, without Hepworth's help:

Animated Photographs
Easter Holidays
Bonn's Kinematograph, Limited, are
prepared to Arrange for Exhibitions of
their Life-size Pictures, Plain and
Coloured. Apply for Prospectus to
George Offor
Managing Director,
78, Mansion House-chambers, London E.C.[114]

A. Rosenberg & Co

Sometime during the first half of 1897, A. Rosenberg & Co transferred their business from Featherstone Chambers, Newcastle-Upon-Tyne to 17 Southampton Row, London. The exact date of the move has not been determined, but as of 2 January the firm was still advertising from the old address.[115] However, by 29 May the new address was being used,[116] so the move had obviously taken place between these two dates. The projector associated with this firm was called the Kineoptograph, but was more often referred to as Rosenberg's Cinematograph (20). It was invented by William Routledge, of 46 Low Friar Street, Newcastle, and patented on 21 July 1896 (No 16080). A description of the apparatus appeared in the first volume of this history, so need not be repeated here.

The apparatus had remained on the market since July 1896, but I do not know whether it underwent any modification during that period. An advertisement of 2 January refers to it as Rosenberg's Improved Cinematograph,[117] which may suggest that some change in design had taken place. The price however, remained unaltered at £35. A patent jet for use with the projector was also available, which was said to be capable of 2,000 candle power.[118]

Since taking up its London address, the business of the firm seems to have greatly increased, and in addition to its own machines and films, those of other makers were now offered for sale, including those of Edison and Lumière.[119] The Lumière films were available with Edison perforations and comprised some 360 subjects. Méliès' Greco-Turkish War series were also available, as well as films of the Jubilee.[120] Rosenberg & Co were also engaged in the exhibition side of the industry and we have records of shows being given at the Royal Clarence Theatre, Pontypridd,[121] and the Tivoli, Middlesbrough.[122] The business also traded in graphophones and other scientific novelties, and during May, a large stock of pocket kinetoscopes had been received, comprising various subjects.[123]

So far, we have been considering those London firms whose connections with cinematography began in 1896 and continued throughout 1897. 1897 was a year of expansion as far as the manufacturing side of the British film industry was concerned, and we shall find no less than a dozen firms came new to the trade during that year. It is these firms that we shall be discussing in the next chapter.

3 London Manufacturers and Dealers 1897.

W. C. Hughes

One of the earliest of numerous cinematographs to appear on the market for the first time during 1897, was the Moto-Photoscope (21) introduced in January by W. C. Hughes, of 82 Mortimer Road, Kingsland.[1] The mechanism was contained in a very portable wooden case, measuring only 11in high, 7¾in wide and 4¾in deep.[2] The case had a door on each side which gave easy access to the working parts, since these were mounted on the inside of the doors themselves. One door, the larger of the two, carried the main projector mechanism and the other, smaller door, held a slide-carrier for small transparencies or diapositives. Thus, should the main door be open for the operator to lace up or change the film, the opposite door holding the slide, could be closed and a still picture, or the title of the next film,* could be projected on the screen during the change over period.[3]

The film was drawn forward through the machine by a cam or 'dog', which advanced the film one frame at a time and the resultant slack was taken up each time by a sprocket-wheel. The mechanism was so arranged that the film was in movement only one eleventh of the period during which it was at rest, so the customary shutter was dispensed with.[4] When a film of average length (about 40–75ft at that time) was to be shown, the roll of film was placed on the bobbin situated on the upper part of the door, but if a number of films were joined together, then the large spool on the top of the machine was employed instead[5] (see illustration).

To lace the projector, the loose end of the film was first passed between the guides and then under the cam and over the sprocket-wheel;[6] the film then issued freely through an opening in the bottom of the cabinet, as no take-up spool was provided.

Not many early projectors have survived in a complete state, or in working order, which means that considerable labour and expense would be entailed putting them to rights. This has precluded us from carrying out our own tests and so we are largely dependent on contemporary sources regarding their performance. Such is the case with the Moto-Photoscope, and indeed with other machines discussed in this history. Concerning the Moto-Photoscope, we must turn to the *Optical Magic Lantern Journal* for a comment upon its performance:

> The motion is very smooth, and the mechanism is made with such exactitude that the pictures present a perfectly steady appearance upon the screen. . . . During some recent trials with this apparatus, we were well pleased with the results attained.[7]

Within the year, Hughes brought out three different models of the Moto-Photoscope. Model 1, just described, cost £35.10s complete, or £27 without the lantern; and Model 2 cost £24.10s. complete, or £20 minus the lantern.[8] The two models probably varied from one another in quality rather than in principle, as seems to be the case regarding the lanterns where there is a difference of £4 in the price. The difference in the price of the two mechanisms may be partly due to the quality and type of lenses fitted, for we know that provision was made for either short or long focus lenses.[9]

*At that time, films seldom, if ever, carried a main title.

21　Hughes' Moto-Photoscope, 1897. Made for W. C. Hughes by the Moto-Photo Supply Co, later known as the Prestwich Manufacturing Company (*Barnes Museum of Cinematography*)

The Moto-Photoscope was also available for taking larger gauge films, one for film 2½ inches wide and the other 3 inches wide, the price being £45 and £75 respectively.[10] A third model was introduced in October called the Exhibition Portable Moto-Photoscope No 3 @ £15.15s. It was stated as being 'precisely the same in principle as the others'.[11] The original price of fifteen guineas [£15.75'] was soon reduced to fourteen guineas [£14.70p][12] and eventually to twelve guineas[13] [£12.10p].

One other machine bearing the Hughes label has yet to be described and that is the Moto Bijou Living Picture Camera (22). In actual fact, this apparatus could also be used as a printer and projector,[14] the conversion in each case being quite simple. But it was obviously more suitable for photographic purposes and it is in this role that it has been more particularly recommended. It was hardly larger than an ordinary hand

(a)

(b)

22 The Prestwich Camera, or, Moto-Photograph, 1897. Made by the Prestwich Mfg Co (formerly the Moto-Photo Supply Co). This camera was also marketed by W. C. Hughes as the Moto Bijou Living Picture Camera. (a) The camera as advertised by Hughes; (b) as advertised by Prestwich. Note the absence of the view-finder in illustration b (*Barnes Museum of Cinematography*)

camera, measuring $7\frac{1}{2} \times 4\frac{1}{2} \times 7\frac{3}{4}$ in., and weighing 6 lbs.[15] The film was driven by an eccentrically mounted sprocket-wheel (to be described later) and the take-up spool by a friction gear. A view finder was also fitted on the top of the mahogany case. The price of the apparatus was £15. Other models were also available for taking films of larger gauge than the Edison standard. One model was made for $2\frac{1}{2}$ in films [64mm] and another for 3in films [76mm]. The price in each case being £35 and £56 respectively.[16]

The Moto Bijou has a particular significance as it provides the clue to the origin of all Hughes' cinematographic apparatus discussed in this chapter. The Bijou is illustrated in one of Hughes' advertisements (22a) and is identical to a machine known to have been made by Prestwich, called the Moto-Photograph. The Prestwich Manufacturing Company was formerly known as the Moto-Photo Supply Co, a name which immediately suggests a connection between this firm and Hughes' Moto-Photoscope. The two terms Moto-Photo and Moto-Photoscope are too alike not to have a common origin. Bearing in mind therefore that the Moto Bijou and the Prestwich Moto-Photograph are one and the same instrument, we cannot help but draw the conclusion that the Moto-Photo Supply Co, as its name implies, was the firm which also supplied the Hughes Moto-Photoscope. Before pursuing this matter further we will first conclude our discussion of W. C. Hughes with a brief note on his career.

William Charles Hughes (1844–1908) (23), optician and lantern manufacturer, was the successor of William Parberry Hughes, chemist and druggist, of 151 Hoxton Street, London. From 1879 to 1882 W. C. Hughes carried on his trade from the Hoxton Street address, but in 1883 the business was transferred to Brewster House, 82 Mortimer Road, off the Kingsland Road. Here he built up a considerable trade in optical lantern equipment and slides, and took out several patents in this field.[17] Hughes was born about 1844 and before becoming a manufacturing optician, he had ventured on the stage as an entertainer, both in the capacity of an amateur and professional, receiving high praise for his dramatic readings, humorous songs and performances of magic and mystery.[18]

From the beginning of 1897, if not before, Hughes took an active interest in cinematography, adding both apparatus and films to his line of business. An advertisement published in November offers 'hundreds of special films, all subjects, from £1.10s [£1.50] each.' Included was a 'magnificent film of the Jubilee Procession, price £4.10s.' [£4.50][19] Although at first dependent on Prestwich for his cinematographic apparatus, Hughes was later to design his own, for which he was to hold several patents. His business survived into the present century, by which time he had earned himself an honourable place among the pioneers of the British film industry, both as an inventor and manufacturer. He died on the 7th August 1908, aged sixty-four.[20]

Prestwich Manufacturing Co.

The Prestwich Manufacturing Co, of 744 High Road, Tottenham, was destined to become one of the most important manufacturers of cinematographic equipment in Gt. Britain. The founder of the firm appears to have been W. H. Prestwich, an able, if undistinguished portrait photographer, with studios at High Road and 155 City Road.[27] (24) Also associated with the firm was J. A. Prestwich, whom we have already had occasion to mention in connection with a rather bizarre cinematograph patented by himself and William Friese Greene in August 1896.[22] J. A. Prestwich's profession is stated in the patent specification as that of engineer. He was clearly the brains behind

23 William Charles Hughes (1844–1908), optician and lantern manufacturer (*Barnes Museum of Cinematography*)

the whole Prestwich enterprise and his technical brilliance is further demonstrated by his subsequent development of the JAP motorcycle engine.[23] The relationship between W. H. and J. A. Prestwich has not been determined, but it seems likely that they were father and son. In the course of our investigation we shall also come across E. P. Prestwich, who may be yet another son of W. H. I hope at some future date to be able to delve more fully into the personnel of this firm, but for the present I am obliged to leave personalities aside and concentrate instead on the apparatus made by the firm.

An advertisement published in November 1897, under the name of the Prestwich Manufacturing Co, carries the following statement: 'Late the Moto Photo Supply Co.'[24]

24 Reverse of carte-de-visite photograph by W. H. Prestwich, advertising studios at Warmington House, High Road, Tottenham, near White Hart Lane; and 155 City Road, London (*Barnes Museum of Cinematography*)

Thus there is no problem in establishing a connection between the two firms. My first encounter with the company under its former title is in the Supplement to the *British Journal of Photography*, dated 16 April 1897. Here however a slight variation in the name occurs. It is given as The Moto-Photograph Supply Co, with an address at 3 Brushfield Street, Bishopsgate.[25] This is the only instance I have found where this particular title and address are mentioned. A few weeks later, *The Photogram* for June, lists among its new advertisers, The Moto-Photo Supply Co, 744 High Road, Tottenham,[26] the same address in fact, at which we later find the Prestwich Manufacturing Co. Apparently the trading facilities of the firm were somewhat unsettled and in a state of flux to begin with, and hence the decision to sell their products through the older and more established firm of W. C. Hughes. By November however, the situation had obviously changed and a more independent course had been taken, the firm now confident enough to trade henceforth under the Prestwich name. Not surprising really when we come to examine the wide range of new apparatus which the firm had to offer.

The first apparatus openly associated with Prestwich was the Moto-Photograph, that very same apparatus which Hughes put on the market as the Moto Bijou Living Picture Camera. It is illustrated and described in the Supplement to the *British Journal of Photography*, dated 16 April, from which the following transcription is taken:

The Moto-Photograph

The Moto-Photograph Supply Co., 3 Brushfield-street, Bishopsgate, E.C. This, one of the latest instruments devised for taking animated photographs, has been shown to us. It is very small and compact, and, besides being used as a camera, answers also, with a little adaptation, for either projecting the positives or printing from the negatives in contact. The essential movement, that for passing the film behind the lens, appears to be simple, novel, and effective, and a brief trial of the machine as well as an inspection of the results convinces us that the instrument is a thoroughly good one—it is comparatively noiseless, does not tear the film, and in size is not much larger than many hand cameras. Moreover, it is extremely well made and finished, and is cheap. An adjustable focal plane shutter is fitted to the camera admitting of exposures ranging from the tenth to the 1500th of a second![27]

The illustration accompanying this description (22b) is almost identical to one shown in Hughes's advertisement which appeared in *The Magic Lantern Journal Annual 1897–8* (published in October, 1897)[28] and which we reproduce as illustration 22a. The only difference being that Hughes shows a view-finder mounted on the top of the instrument, an appendage probably added some time after the apparatus first appeared and consequently not shown in the earlier illustration.

W. C. Hughes probably received supplies of the new apparatus almost immediately, for he advertises it in *The Era* for 1 May.[29] A few days later, the apparatus was demonstrated by its designer 'Mr. Prestwich' at a meeting of the Hackney Photographic Society, held on 11 May;[30] but unfortunately the published account of the meeting failed to mention either the christian names or initials of 'Mr. Prestwich' and we are at a loss to know to whom of the Prestwichs the statement refers.

In the June issue of *The Photogram*, the apparatus is advertised by the Moto-Photo Supply Co, as 'The "Prestwich" Camera', and a paragraph in the same issue gives a description of the apparatus:

'Another new apparatus which seems to combine in a marked degree many useful characteristics, has been named the Prestwich. It is light, compact, and very smooth in its working. On the screen it ought to give a very steady picture, and its price is low. The whole of the working parts are contained in a mahogany case of small size, which makes it an easily portable machine and one in which the mechanism is well protected. . . . The main sprocket wheel is excentrically pivoted so that while it is making a part turn around its main axis it makes a complete turn round the excentric axis, thus rapidly drawing off the length of film equal to one picture. The take-up reel is driven by a friction-gear so that it gathers the slack of the film which has passed the sprocket wheel, but cannot subject it to any strain.'[31]

The Prestwich camera was also advertised by Marion & Co, one of the leading photographic establishments in the country:

'Marion & Co., are agents, and have in stock the 'Prestwich' Camera, which is the most efficient and most portable on the market. It weighs only 6lbs. It is a beautiful (sic) finished piece of mechanism, made entirely in London of the best materials. The intermittent movement of the film is obtained by an epicyclic motion which runs smoothly and silently without causing any vibration or jerking. It is fitted with an adjustable focal plane shutter, admitting exposures varying from 1/10 to 1/1000 of a second. Fitted with Dallmeyer special lens f/4, with iris diaphragm and focusing index, and for Edison perforation (if desired Voigtlander's special lens may be fitted).'[32]

The 'epicyclic motion' refers of course, to the action of the sprocket-wheel and was the means by which the film was intermittently driven or advanced. Another notable feature of this camera was the variable focal plane shutter which was probably the first of its type to be applied to a movie camera. It certainly pre-dates the one used in the

25 The Prestwich Camera, 1897 (Exterior and interior views). Also known as the Moto-Photograph and the Moto Bijou Living Picture Camera (*Jones-Frank Collection*)

Darling-Wrench camera, if only by a few weeks. The price of the Prestwich camera was £18,[33] but a more expensive model, costing £38, was also made, which was fitted with daylight loading exterior film boxes taking 500ft of film.[34] Examples of both these cameras are to be found in the Jones-Frank Collection (25 and 26).

One of the highlights of the photographic calendar was the Photographic Convention, which in 1897 was held at Great Yarmouth from Monday, 12 July to Saturday, 17 July. It was attended by many of the leading photographers in the country, as well as the representatives of photographic journals and well known persons connected with the trade. Among those present was W. H. Prestwich, who, 'after the official group had been photographed . . . arranged for the members to file along in front of his Moto-photoscope (sic), and secured a very fine and interesting result.'[35] (27) The film was taken at midday on Wednesday, 14 July, and shown on the screen in Yarmouth Town Hall the following evening.[36] The resultant negatives were later used for a photomontage published in *Photograms of '97* together with a key to those represented.[37] The programme presented at the Town Hall had also included films of Queen Victoria's Diamond Jubilee procession,[38] which had previously been taken with the Prestwich camera.[39]

This camera also distinguished itself at the Glasgow International Photographic Exhibition, which was held during September and October. Here it won the highest award for excellence in the section devoted to apparatus, receiving the Silver Medal.[40] The illustrated catalogue to the Exhibition contains an article on the apparatus by William Goodwin, under the heading: 'The Moto-Photoscope (An Improved Cinematographe)', but unfortunately, the author does not give any information which is not already available from other sources. However, elsewhere in the catalogue, we learn that a display of living pictures by the Moto-Photoscope was given each evening by Mr. E. P. Prestwich of the Moto-Photo Supply Co.[41] E. P. Prestwich is thus the third member of the firm to come to our notice.

The Royal Photographic Society's Exhibition was also to be favoured with a demonstration on Monday, 18 November, and *The Amateur Photographer*, in a notice of the coming event, informed its readers that 'Mr. E. P. Prestwich has kindly promised to show some animated photographs by means of his "moto-photoscope", including "members of the Convention leaving the Town Hall after the taking of the official group." '[42]

On 1 October, the following announcement appeared in *The British Journal of Photography:*

> The Prestwich Manufacturing Company is the name under which the Moto-Photo Supply Company of 744, High-road Tottenham, N., will in future trade. Their specialities are cameras, projectors, perforating machines, developing outfits, and every accessory connected with cinematography.[43]

Without access to the company's records, which I fear no longer exist, it is impossible to describe all the equipment made by the firm at this period, but we do have some information on three Prestwich Projectors, known as models 1, 2 and 3. It will be more convenient to describe them in the reverse order.

Prestwich's No 3 Model Projector (28) cost £35 complete. It was fitted with spool boxes of the modern type for carrying 2000ft of film. The mechanism was contained in a boxed compartment so that the machine was practically fireproof, an important factor

26 The Prestwich Camera, 1897. Fitted with daylight loading exterior film boxes; capacity: 500ft (*Jones-Frank Collection*)

27 Photographic Convention, Great Yarmouth. Members of the congress parade in front of the Town Hall. Photographed by W. H. Prestwich with the Moto-Photograph, or Prestwich Camera, on the 14th July, 1897. From frame illustrations published in The Practical Photographer, vol 8, no 93 (September 1897) p 281 (*Barnes Museum of Cinematography*)

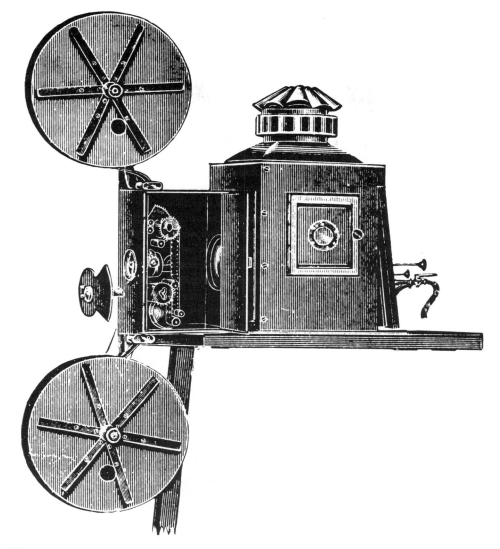

28 Prestwich No 3 Model Projector, 1897. A special fireproof machine, with metal film boxes (*Barnes Museum of Cinematography*)

since many local authorities were beginning to tighten up their fire regulations regarding cinematograph performances. The machine had an exterior single-blade shutter mounted in front of the objective and the film was advanced by an eccentric cam or 'dog', with a sprocket-wheel situated above and below the picture aperture.

Prestwich's No 2 Model Projector (29) cost £25. This was a modification of the machine known as the Hughes Moto-Photoscope, and had a very similar mechanism which too was mounted on the inside panel of the main door. Facilities also existed for showing slides when the film was being changed. The design of the cabinet was a little different and a film box of 75ft capacity was provided in place of the open bobbin employed on the Hughes machine. It also had a single-blade shutter whereas the

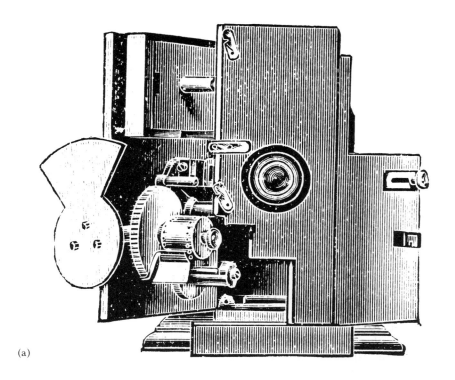

(a)

(b)

29   Prestwich No 2 Model Projector, 1897. A modification of the Hughes Moto-Photoscope (*Barnes Museum of Cinematography*)

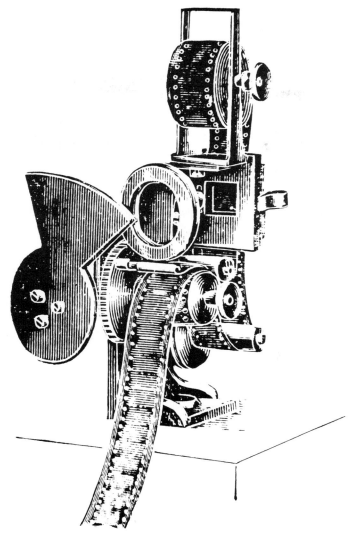

30   Prestwich No 1 Model Projector, 1897. Intended ostensibly for amateur use (*Barnes Museum of Cinematography*)

former had none. An example of the Prestwich Model 2 in an incomplete state, is in the Barnes Collection (29b).

Prestwich's No 1 Model Projector (30) had a similar mechanism to Model No 2, but was openly mounted on an iron casting, with an open frame at the top on which the roll of film was suspended. The casting also supported the lens mount for the objective, in front of which, a single-blade shutter revolved. It was a small instrument intended ostensibly for amateurs and was considerably cheaper than the other two models, costing only £15.[44]

A few general remarks about the Prestwich apparatus are to be found in the *British Journal Photographic Almanac for 1898* and are worth quoting:

The Prestwich cameras and projectors are made entirely of gun-metal and steel, and are fitted to best mahogany polished cases. For the longer lengths of film the automatic feed is fitted, so the film runs evenly all through. Detachable shutters are also an advantage, as some films show very much better without. Detachable sprockets made in several different gauges to suit the varying gauges are essential to perfect registration, the operation of changing taking but a few seconds.

The movement of all these projectors is a six to one, i.e., the film is stationary five-sixths, and is being changed in the remaining one-sixth, so that the shutter used is but a very small one, and only one-sixth of the light obstruction (sic), which reduces flicker to a minimum.[45]

The leading light behind the Prestwich enterprise had always been J. A. Prestwich, who combined a remarkable talent for mechanical engineering with a keen business sense. Under his guidance the firm rapidly expanded until it was soon engaged in a wide range of engineering products, most notably connected with the motorcycle industry. John Alfred Prestwich was born in Kensington on the 1st of September 1874, and educated at the City and Guilds School and the City of London School. At the age of sixteen he started work with S. Z. de Ferranti, the well-known maker of electrical apparatus and scientific instruments. After two years, he was articled to a firm of engineers and then at the age of twenty he left to start his own business, making electrical fittings and scientific instruments in a glass house in his father's garden. For nearly two decades he invented, designed and manufactured cinematographic equipment including cameras, printers, projectors, and cutting and perforating machines, as well as penny-in-the-slot Mutoscopes.[46] He died in 1952. The firm he had founded later became known as J. A. Prestwich Industries Ltd, and was eventually absorbed in 1964 by the Villiers Engineering Company.

Noakes & Norman
Early in 1897, the firm of D. Noakes & Son was taken over by G. P. Norman and a notice to this effect was published in February:

> The well-known business of D. Noakes and Son, Photographic Apparatus Makers and Dealers, of Greenwich, S.E., has been taken over by Mr. G. P. Norman, and the name of the firm will now be Noakes and Norman, retaining the services of Mr. D. W. Noakes as practical adviser. Lanterns, cameras, lenses, and all accessories are stocked in great variety. Messrs. Noakes and Norman are the makers of a well-known kinematograph, and a patent compound mixed chamber jet, which on account of its high candle power is specially suited for use with the kinematograph. Also one may mention as among this firm's specialities an intermediate gas regulator which can be fitted to jets of all descriptions.[47]

D. Noakes was primary a dealer in animal feeding stuffs and had never taken a very active part in the optical side of the business which was largely run by his son D. W. Noakes. The son had shown an early interest in optical projection and had fitted up a workshop in one of his father's wholesale forage warehouses, close to the riverside at Greenwich. Here the business of a manufacturing optician grew to such an extent that space could not be found for a showroom and a workshop, so in about 1889, this department of Noakes & Son's business was removed to larger premises in Nelson Street.[48]

Under D. W. Noakes' able management the business prospered and in addition to making all kinds of lantern equipment, it undertook certain small scale engineering work. Noakes Jnr. besides running the optical works, also attended to a section of his father's forage business and even found time to give lantern lectures with one of his magnificent triple lanterns, which he termed the Noakescope. At the time of G. P. Norman's take over, old man Noakes had reached the age of retirement and his son decided to relinquish the optical side of the business and step into his father's shoes as head of the forage business.[49]

The new firm of Noakes & Norman occupied the same address as its predecessor, 2 Nelson Street, Greenwich. Here the same line of business was continued, but cinematograph equipment and films were now included among its products. G. P. Norman had formerly been many years with Messrs Watson & Sons, of Holborn,[50] and it was there that he probably gained his experience of cinematography. Indeed, the cinematograph brought out by the new firm was not unlike Watson's Motorgraph in appearance. It was a small compact machine which served as both camera and projector and was named the Invicta[51] (31). It had no sprocket wheels and the film was advanced solely by means of a double-claw mechanism, the film being held in place by a spring plate. Since the period of rest was very much longer than the period of movement, there was the minimum of flicker.[52] The absence of a rack adjustment meant that the registration of the frame in the picture aperture had to be effected by pulling the film into place whilst the teeth of the claw were disengaged. The complete outfit, with lantern, lens, and limelight jet, cost £22.[53]

I do not know whether Noakes & Newman were engaged in film production, but an extensive selection of films was available, which included 500 Lumière subjects with Edison perforations, @ £3 each, as well as other films priced from £1.10s. [£1.50][54] Coloured films and Eastman and Blair film stock ready perforated, were also available.[55]

31   The Invicta Cinematograph, 1897. Introduced by Noakes & Norman, Greenwich. A combined camera and projector (*Barnes Museum of Cinematography*)

Haydon & Urry Ltd

Haydon & Urry Ltd, of 355 Upper Street, Islington, were one of the few manufacturers of cinematographs who had not been connected previously with the optical magic lantern trade. In 1896, the firm had produced a coin-operated moving picture device called the Autocosmoscope,[56] but it was not until February of the following year that a regular cinematograph was produced. It was called the Eragraph and at least two different models seem to have been made. Unfortunately, details of only one of these are known for certain, although a very incomplete mechanism in the Barnes Museum may be a relic of the earlier model (32). It has some characteristics of the regular Eragraph, having an identical Maltese-cross movement, with the mechanism similarly assembled on a brass plate.

The regular model Eragraph has survived almost intact and examples are to be found in the Science Museum, London,[57] and in the Barnes Museum (33). The Apparatus consists of two parallel brass plates 1/8in. and ¼in. thick, which are connected at their corners by steel rods with brass sleeves, so that they stand about 4 inches apart. The thicker back plate carries the film mechanism, comprising a Maltese-cross and cam for imparting the intermittent movement to the sprocket wheel which is situated below the picture aperture. The roll of film is suspended between two uprights at the top, and issues freely from the bottom of the instrument as no take-up spool is provided. The objective lens is mounted between the two brass plates and travels backwards and forwards on a screw for focusing, a suitable aperture being provided in the front plate to allow the image to pass. The shutter is situated immediately behind this aperture and is revolved by means of a pinion geared to the main drive and supported at its other end by a bearing in the front plate. The machine, together with its lantern, are mounted on a wooden baseboard, the forward section of which slides back and forth so that the distance between the two units can be varied to suit the requirements of the illuminant.

Haydon & Urry's first cinematograph, which we shall call the Eragraph No. 1, was probably the subject of patent application No 3572 of 10 February 1897. The application received provisional protection only so consequently was not printed. It almost certainly relates to the apparatus advertised in *The Era* for 20 February referred to as 'The New Kinematograph'.[58] This was advertised again in the same paper on 6 March, as 'The Latest Kinematograph'.[59] However, an advertisement in the issue for 24 April names the machine as the Eragraph.[60] As has already been suggested, this apparatus is probably the one represented in the Barnes Collection by the incomplete mechanism shown in illustration 32. The advertisement for 6 March quotes the price of the apparatus as £36, complete,[61] but a few weeks later it is being offered, with one film, for £25.[62] The same advertisement also mentions a 'Home Student's Cinematograph', complete with one film, @ £3.[63] A further advertisement of 14 August informs us that the Eragraph was 'now being shown at upwards of twenty principal theatres and music halls in the country.'[64]

The regular Eragraph, or Model No 2, is probably the subject of patent application no 20296, dated 3 September. This too was granted provisional protection only and so of course, not published. But it obviously relates to the machine advertised in *The Era* on 4 December, as the 'New Model Eragraph',[65] and which we have already described. Both the patent applications mentioned were submitted under the names of George Haydon and Haydon & Urry Ltd., which suggests that it was Haydon who was chiefly responsible for the technical side of the partnership. According to an advertisement

66

32 Projector mechanism, with Maltese-cross movement (Incomplete) ca 1897. Possibly part of the 1st model Eragraph made by Haydon & Urry Ltd (*Barnes Museum of Cinematography*)

33 The Eragraph Projector (2nd model?) 1897. Made by Haydon & Urry Ltd, of Islington (*Barnes Museum of Cinematography*)

published in October 1898, the Eragraph was the recipient of several awards, including a gold medal at the Trades & Arts Exhibition, Wigan, 1897; and Dumfermline Scientific Exhibition of the same year.[66]

Like many manufacturers of cinematographic equipment in the early days of the cinema's history, Haydon & Urry Ltd also engaged in film production. In April preparations were going ahead for the installation of a film processing plant and the firm announced that it would 'shortly be abel to supply English subjects at prices hitherto unheard of.'[67] By the 1st of May the plant was completed,[68] and it was not long before the first successful film was issued. This was a film of the Derby which was run on the 2nd of June. The film was 75ft long and priced @ £3.10s. [£3.50].[69] Next followed 'a grand series of six films' of Queen Victoria's Diamond Jubilee procession, each 75ft long and costing £4 each.[70] In July, events connected with Royal Henley Regatta were filmed, *The Era* commenting: 'an unique position on the umpire's boat has enabled the operator to get some splendid results.'[71] These were shown at the London Pavilion for the first time on 16 July.[72] The Pavilion was one of several theatres in London and the provinces, where the Eragraph projectors had been installed.[73]

The films taken at Henley Regatta by the Eragraph camera, were fully described in an advertisement published in *The Era*,[74] and is worth quoting as it may be useful to archivists for identification purposes:

1 Henley Regatta. Scenes at Henley taken at the umpire's landing stage. The Grand Challenge Cup. Exciting finish between the Leander and Dutch (eight oar boats).
2 Ladies Challenge Plate. Also an exciting finish between the Emanuel boat (Cambridge) and Christ Church (Oxford). This scene shows about half a mile of course, with magnificent display of boats, with Umpire's launch following.
3 Review of boats, showing a quantity of boats unable to get clear on account of the enormous traffic, forming one of the most picturesque collections of boats ever seen at Henley.
4 This scene shows boats passing under Henley Bridge going to the Regatta.
5 The Grand Challenge Cup. The New College (Oxford crew) landing at the boathouse after winning their race against Trinity Hall, Cambridge.
   The scene shows the crew leaving their boat to place the paddles in the tent, and returning taking their boat out of the water, carrying it to the boathouse.
6 Arrival of the Eton crew at the landing-stage after winning their race against Kings College, Cambridge.

J. W. Rowe & Co.

Another firm not previously connected with the lantern trade was J. W. Rowe & Co, of 15 and 16 Aldermanbury, E.C. Early in March they advertised three cinematographs under the rather awkward name of Pictorialograph.[75] Unfortunately, I have been unable to find an illustration of any one of these. Model No 1 was a miniature version intended for amateurs and cost £7.10., [£7.50] complete with 4in condenser, 4-wick paraffin oil lamp and one film. The projector was said to throw a fair-sized picture even with lamplight, but with a more powerful light a larger picture could be produced. An adjustable stand was also available for £1.10s [£1.50] extra.[76] Later, a very cheap camera was placed on the market, costing only £4.10s.[77] [£4.50].

The Pictorialograph No 2 was a much more substantial machine intended for theatrical use. It was said to be well made and to work without inordinate vibration.[78] The intermittent movement was of the maltese-cross variety,[79] but the feature of the machine which received most attention from the photographic press, was the unique form of shutter employed. This was of the fan type, but each blade was pierced by three radial slots so that the screen was never entirely dark and the flicker was thus somewhat reduced.[80]

The Pictorialograph No 3 was a combined camera/projector, priced at £15 and included 'two lenses of the best quality.'[81] Incidentally, the prices quoted for these machines, are those current at the time of their first introduction. Later, they underwent substantial reductions.

Rowe made a speciality of films, producing a London series showing such scenes as the Mansion House, Cheapside, Ludgate Circus, Oxford Circus and Rotten Row. The company also made a special feature of the Jubilee procession and was reported to have had six operators stationed at different points along the route. Other films included 'a number of very good scenes at Continental fairs, and some humorous subjects, such as a boy washing a dog, etc.'[82]

Fuerst Brothers

Before passing on to consider the rest of the London manufacturers who were active during 1897, this would seem a convenient place as any, to introduce Messres. Fuerst Brothers of 17 Philpot Lane, E.C. Although they were not manufacturers, they were nevertheless responsible for exploiting the Lumière films and Cinématographe in Gt. Britain. This aspect of their business will be described in chapter 6, but here it might be as well to examine their film making activities in this country. One of the brothers, Jules Fuerst (34) was reputed to be a very able cinematographer.[83] It was under his direction that the firm was able to secure several successful films of Queen Victoria's Jubilee procession.[84] The following month, using the Cinématographe-Lumière, he photographed two of the main events at Royal Henley Regatta, the race for the Diamond Sculls, and the Grand Challenge Cup. The latter was described as one of the most exciting races that Henley had ever seen, when New College beat Leander Club by two feet.[85] At the Aldershot Jubilee Review which took place on 1 July, Jules Fuerst 'also succeeded in securing no less than five admirable films, thereby testifying not only to his own skill but also to the excellence of the Lumiere machine.'[86] It seems quite likely that Jules Fuerst shot a number of the English subjects listed in the Lumière film catalogues.

E. G. Wood

Sometime during 1897, a cinematograph called Wood's Movendoscope appeared on the market, but I have not been able to find a description or illustration of this machine. It was made by E. G. Wood, of 74 Cheapside, a well known firm of manufacturing opticians, which specialised in optical lanterns and slides. The business had been established in 1855 by Edward George Wood (1811–1896), who had previously been a partner in the firm of Horne, Thornthwaite & Wood, chemical and philosophical instrument makers of 123 Newgate Street, London. After the partnership was dissolved in 1854, Wood carried on his own business, first at 117 Cheapside from 1855 to 1862, then at 74 Cheapside, where the firm remained until 1899, when it removed to 1 & 2 Queen Street. At his death in 1896, E. G. Wood was succeeded by his son A. A. Wood, who carried on the business until within a few days of his decease on 10 September 1900.[87] Thereafter, until 1920, the proprietor was F. S. Horsey.

Wood's Movendoscope projector was advertised as 'simple in its mechanism and smooth in working,' and cost twelve guineas [£12.60]. A camera was also available at ten guineas [£10.50]. This was called Wood's Movendoscope Camera, and was said to be a modified form of the projector.[88]

Levi, Jones & Co

Another machine which does not appear to have been widely publicised in England was the Rollograph, a combined camera/projector put on the market by Levi, Jones & Co, of 71 Farringdon Road. According to Cecil M. Hepworth, its chief point of originality was the clockwork drive applied to the take-up spool when the instrument was used as a camera. He also informs us that the apparatus was self-contained in a neat leather-covered box or case and appears to be both well made and efficient.[89] This

34   Jules Fuerst, of Messrs Fuerst Brothers, the English agents for the Cinématographe-Lumière and Films. He also acted as the Lumières' cinematographer in England. From an illustration in The Optician (7 October, 1897) p (*British Library*)

35   Robert Royou Beard (1856–1932), inventor and manufacturer of limelight apparatus, and maker of the Beard Cinematograph (*Barnes Museum of Cinematography*)

description so exactly fits a French apparatus patented by Bunzli and Continsouza, that I have no hesitation in believing the two machines to be one and the same. The apparatus will be found fully described in Chapter 6.

Levi, Jones & Company (Samuel J. Levi and Alexander S. Jones) was formed in April or early May, 1897, for the purpose of taking over and carrying on the business of S. J. Levi & Co. which had been established about seven years previously. They are described as wholesale opticians and manufacturers of photographic cameras, optical lanterns, leather cases, and accessories.[90] These goods were marketed under the trade name of Leviathan. In October the firm issued a lengthy catalogue of optical lanterns and accessories, comprising more than 100 pages, with a section devoted to cinematographic apparatus and films.[91] Unfortunately, no copy of this catalogue seems to have survived. In the following year, the firm introduced a cinematograph called the Cynnagraph and an optical toy called the Amateur Kinematodor which was a form of projecting phenakisticope using lithographed designs on a disc.

R. R. Beard

A famous name in the lantern world at this time, was R. R. Beard (10 Trafalgar Road, Old Kent Road, S.E.). His fame chiefly rested on a patent compressed gas regulator of his own invention, which became an essential piece of equipment for lantern exhibitors when using cylinders of compressed oxygen and hydrogen gases for the limelight, then extensively employed in optical lanterns and cinematographs as an illuminant. But he was also noted for other lantern appliances, such as gas pressure gauges, jets, and slide-carriers.[92]

Robert Royou Beard (35) was born on the 10th of March, 1856, at Royal Palace, Commercial Road, Peckham, and died in February, 1932. He had received his training in the engineering firm of T. J. Oakley & Co, and after developing a keen interest in optical projection, left the firm to set up his own business in order to specialise in this particular field.[93] With the increasing popularity of the cinematograph among lantern exhibitors, Beard was not slow in realising the growing demand for this class of apparatus and accordingly in 1897 brought out his own projector, which was known as Beard's Cinematographe. He also manufactured a high power limelight jet specially designed for film projection. This he advertised as 'too powerful for ordinary lantern work.[94]

Beard's Cinematographe (36) was mounted, together with its lantern, on a stout wooden base board with a large mangle-wheel crank on the side, connected to the main drive by a belt. The film was advanced by a single sprocket-wheel below the gate, which received its intermittent movement from a cam and 8-point star wheel based on the principle of the Maltese-cross. The general design of the apparatus, as can be seen from the illustration, was somewhat archaic in appearance even for that time, but no doubt, its simplicity of design was ideally suited to that class of itinerant exhibitor who served the smaller halls in country towns and villages. The price of the apparatus was £20.[95]

An imperfect example of the Beard Cinematographe is to be found in the Will Day Collection (Cinémathèque Française). It is listed as item No 145 in the Catalogue[96] and illustrated in plate 20a. Here the spool bracket is missing from the lantern body, revealing the holes where it was originally fixed. In its place, a rather crude film carrier has been fitted to the top of the projector mechanism. Incidentally, the caption to plate 20a in the Catalogue is incorrectly given as Edison's Kinetoscope.

It is interesting to note that the firm of R. R. Beard is still in business and is carried

36   Beard's Cinematographe, 1897. Made by R. R. Beard, London. Fitted with 8-star wheel Geneva Cross movement (*Barnes Museum of Cinematography*)

on by relatives of the original founder, who had established the firm as long ago as 1886. Although no longer concerned with optical projection and cinematography, the present business is still connected with the photographic trade.

F. Brown

Also engaged in a similar line of business was F. Brown, of 13 Gate Street, Holborn (est in 1890), who is described as a manufacturer of limelight apparatus and cinematographs, & c.[97] Like R. R. Beard, he too was noted for a limelight jet specially designed for cinematographs. This was known simply as the F. B. Jet, and was calculated to give from 1500 to 2000 candle power.[98] The only cinematograph known to have been handled by Brown, was Rosenberg's[99] an apparatus which dates back to July 1896 and which was invented and patented by William Routledge of Newcastle-upon-Tyne. This apparatus has already been described in the first volume of this history, so need not detain us further. But it is well to note that this little machine retained its popularity and continued to be manufactured throughout 1897, and indeed, 1898.[100]

Brandon Medland

In February, Brandon Medland, of 13 York Street, Walworth, was advertising a machine called the Vit-Autoscope.[101] According to the advertisement, he had formerly been an operator for R. W. Paul. An optician by the name of John Brandon Medland is listed at Borough High Street for the years 1876 to 1893 during which time he was engaged in the optical magic lantern trade. If this is the same person, then he was well fitted for his new occupation as a maker of cinematographs. Unfortunately, I have been unable to find any information about his machine or his activities during the period under discussion.

E. P. Allam & Co (Formerly Allam & Calvert)

Information is also lacking concerning an apparatus called the Photo-Vivant, advertised in July by Allam & Calvert of 14 Hatton Garden and priced at £25.[102] It was evidently the subject of a patent application for 'improvements in apparatus for projecting photographic and other pictures', filed on 29 July 1897 under the names of E. P. Allam, G. C. Calvert and J. Fleming (No 17803). The patent was never granted and unfortunately no record can now be found of the contents of the said application. The same is also true of an application filed on 11 March 1897 by the same persons, for 'improvements in or connected with apparatus or machines for taking and projecting animated photographs' (No 6439).

The Photo-Vivant was supplied with a 'Swift' lens and was advertised as 'the latest and best machine for showing animated photographs'.[103] A portable stand for use with the machine, plus a special frame (or Spool bank) for holding 'endless films' were also available at an extra cost of £5.[104] Allam & Calvert also made films, as well as acting as agents for Edison, Lumière and other noted makers. Exhibitions too were undertaken and supplied with skilled operators.[105] By August of 1897, the name of the firm had been changed to E. P. Allam & Co,[106] but the address remained the same and the same line of business was continued. First and foremost they were electrical engineers and they are listed as such in the trade directories. Like their neighbour R. W. Paul, who was also an electrical engineer, cinematography seems to have been to them no more than of secondary consideration.

J. Theobald & Co

Likewise, nothing is known concerning apparatus sold by J. Theobald & Co, of 19 Farringdon Road, the well known makers of chromo-litho lantern slides. In October of 1897, they advertised 'cinematograph films from 20/- and all apparatus in connection therewith,'[107] but it is doubtful whether these goods were of their own manufacture.

The Ludgate Kinematograph Film Co

The Ludgate Kinematograph Film Company is another firm about which little is known. They were not manufacturers of equipment, but seem to have been actively engaged in film production. One of their films was of the procession which accompanied the Prince and Princess of Wales to the opening of the Blackwall Tunnel on 22 May and was taken from the vantage point of the offices of the *Sydney Morning Herald* at 78 Queen Victoria Street, London, E.C.[108] The make of camera used on this occasion is not known, but it was one which had been specially constructed for 'a well-known and famous war correspondent' who had hoped to use it during the Greco-Turkish war, but found at the last moment that he could not take it with him 'as it made excess of the luggage allowed on the frontier.'[109]

The correspondent referred to was probably Frederic Villiers (1852–1922) who claims in *Who's Who* (1899) to have been the first to use a cinematograph camera during the campaign. In his book *Pictures of Many Wars* (London, 1902) p 76, Villiers mentions a cinematograph and films being in his possession during the Greco-Turkish War, but no mention is made of their being put to any use. It was not until many years later that he wrote in any detail of his war-time exploits with the movie camera (see *Villiers: His Five Decades of Adventure* (New York, 1920) pp 164, 170, 181–2). In the same book (ibid, pp 259, 260, 263–4) he also recounts his abortive attempts to film the Battle of Omdurman.*

The Ludgate Company also laid plans for filming the Jubilee procession on 22 June, and intended to have three cameras at the ready to ensure continuous filming of the event. The cameras were to be specially constructed for them by W. Watson & Sons,[110] but whether or not the project was successful has not been revealed.

Stafford-Noble & Liddell

There is an interesting piece of apparatus in the Barnes Collection, which was patented by Cecil Stafford-Noble and Francis Liddell[111] (37), but whether it was ever commercially produced remains doubtful. Stafford-Noble was an engineer of 15 Theobalds Road, London who in 1898, patented another apparatus in association with H. C. Newton,[112] which was put on the market as the "English" Cinematograph by the well-known opticians, Newton & Co. of 3 Fleet Street.[113] Without going more fully into this latter apparatus, which is outside the scope of the present volume, suffice it to say that it incorporated some of the features found in the former patent. We might say, the one served as the prototype for the other. It is this prototype which we shall be examining here.

The apparatus as it survives, will be found to differ in certain respects from that described in the patent. But this is often the case when a comparison is made between the patent and the finished article. A striking feature of the instrument was the method employed for driving the film. Instead of the normal sprocket-wheel, a perforated drum was used, which interacted with a spiked wheel, the spikes or pins of which, entered holes in the drum. This pin-wheel was mounted on a pivoted lever so that it could be locked against the drum by a thumb-screw. In this way, the film was held in contact with the drum which then performed the function of an ordinary sprocket. The patent specification states that this arrangement could also serve as a film perforator.

The intermittent movement used in the apparatus, consisted of a looping roller, or 'dog' which remained in constant contact with the film, thus avoiding the sudden blows normally inflicted on the film when more conventional *movements* of this type are employed. A further feature of the machine, not specified in the patent, was the double cylindrical shutter, one within the other, either one of which could be used independently or in unison. The outer one was of the normal opaque segmented barrel type, but the inner one had translucent mauve gelatine segments to act as an anti-flicker device when desired.

In the machine as described in the patent specification, the spool axles were prolonged in order to allow one film to be rewound while another was being shown, but this

*The reader is directed to an interesting article on Frederic Villiers by Steve Bottomore, published in *Sight & Sound*, vol 49, no 4 (Autumn, 1980) pp 250–55.

37 Projector Mechanism, 1897 (Incomplete). Patented by C. Stafford-Noble & F. Liddell. This apparatus has several distinctive features, including a barrel shutter incorporating an anti-flicker device; a special interlocking pin-wheel and drum sprocket; and an intermittent movement supplied by a looping roller or 'dog' which remains in constant contact with the film and so reduces strain (*Barnes Museum of Cinematography*)

part of the mechanism is missing from our example. The whole apparatus was neatly constructed, and consisted of two brass triangular side frames with cross bars, adapted to carry the mechanism. The patent application (No 14,861) was made on 19 June 1897 and the complete specification left on 19 March 1898, but it was not until 11 June 1898 that the patent was finally accepted.

Auguste Rateau

Henry V. Hopwood in his book *Living Pictures* names two machines associated with Auguste Rateau, of 27 Great Russell Street, viz: Rateau's Chronophotograph and the Rateaugraph.[114] The first is the subject of patent number 5026 of 24 February 1897.[115] In this machine the film is moved through the gate by spring-teeth and governed by rather complicated driving and tension devices. Evidently Rateau was not satisfied with this arrangement for he soon after took out another patent, no 18,014 of 31 July 1897.[116] The spring-teeth were now carried at the end of a lever, which received a rocking motion from a cam-groove. Other features included a pneumatic shutter-

77

regulator and clockwork drive. Rateau may already have been connected with the film business, probably as an importer, his stated occupation in the patent specifications, but information concerning him and his business is sadly lacking.

Miscellaneous Patents

There are three patents issued to inventors in the London area for which there is no evidence of commercial exploitation and the only information I have found concerning them is that contained in the patent specifications themselves. The first to be examined is an apparatus in which the intermittent movement of the film is achieved by means of a ratchet gear. The patentees were John Henry Duncan, chartered accountant of 39 Coleman Street, and Theodor Reich, a photographer of 63 Maitland Park Road. We have had occasion already to mention the latter in connection with a patent of 1896 in which he describes two types of movement, one employing a ratchet and pawl device, and the other a claw-type mechanism.[117] In the patent of 1897 (no 7628 of 24 March)[118] the ratchet form of movement is favoured and provision is also made for a cam-operated punch for perforating the film as it passes through the machine when being used as a camera, but which is thrown out of action when projecting, the same machine serving both purposes.

A combined camera/projector mechanism was also the subject of a patent issued to Roland Hugh Edwards, a draughtsman of 37 Queen's Road, Brownswood Park, Highbury (no 24,273 of 20 October).[119] The novelty of the invention lies in its method of imparting the intermittent movement to the film. This is described at some length in the complete specification, along with several variations, but in order to be brief we can do little better than to quote Hopwood's neat and succinct description:

> The continuously moving film is led over two rollers, the reciprocating motion of which periodically neutralises the proper motion of the film. This reciprocation may be vertical or horizontal, and several arrangements are shown.[120]

A machine in which the film is moved by teeth mechanically inserted and withdrawn, was patented by Ernest Francis Moy and Gilbert Howard Harrison (no 25,625 of 4 November).[121] Harrison was co-patentee of the Grand Kinematograph already described in our previous volume and again briefly referred to in the previous chapter. Moy, on the other hand, is new to our history, although later he was to be a big name in the cinema industry as a maker of cinematograph cameras in association with Bastie.[122] In the patent under review, a cam-groove is used for the double purpose of inserting the pins and also raising and lowering them, the pins being four in number.

Although applications for the three patents just mentioned were received by the Patent Office in 1897, it was not until the following year that the complete specifications were lodged and accepted. Any practical results therefore, which may have materialised from them is not likely to have been immediately apparent and so their true worth cannot be evaluated at this stage.

Manufacturers of Cinematograph lenses

Not every manufacturer of cinematographic apparatus had the necessary skills or facilities for making lenses and these were generally obtained from outside sources Already in 1897 there were several firms specialising in lenses for cinematographs among the principal being J. H. Dallmeyer; Perken, Son & Rayment; W. Wray; and J. Swift & Son.

J. H. Dallmeyer (25 Newman St, Oxford Street) was an internationally renowned optician of long standing, and recipient of the Royal Photographic Society's Progress Medal for the development of the telephotolens.[123] The cameras used by Edweard Muybridge for some of his electro-photographic studies of animal locomotion were equipped with lenses supplied by Dallmeyer,[124] as were many first class still cameras of the period. It is not known how extensively they were used for cinematography during 1897, but we do know that a Dallmeyer short focus projection lens was supplied for the Velograph.[125]

Perken, Son & Rayment were well-known manufacturing opticians of 99 Hatton Garden, who specialised in photographic and optical magic lantern equipment, and whose goods were marketed under the trade name of 'Optimus'. The business had been founded in about 1852, and until 1888 was known as Lejeune & Perken. Although makers of optical lanterns, Perken, Son & Rayment do not appear to have made cinematographs, but their special projection lenses seem to have been much in demand according to the following statement published in October 1897:

The "Optimus" cinematograph lenses (series of three foci) have been in great demand lately, and promise to be more so as they give a large image at a short distance from screen, with brilliant illumination and crisp definition.[126]

J. Swift & Son (81 Tottenham Court Road) announced in January 1897, that they had constructed a special series of lenses for film projection with foci of 2½, 2¾, 3, 3½ and 4 inches.[127] W. Wray of 59 North Hill, Highgate, shortly followed suit with a series of two lenses, one of 2-inch focus, with an aperture of f2, and the other of 3-inch focus working at f3. These were provided either with a spiral-slot focusing adjustment, or in a separate jacket with a rack and pinion.[128] Wray provided the lenses for Appleton's Cieroscope.[129]

The famous optical firm of Ross Ltd (11 New Bond Street) also advertised lenses suitable for cinematographic purposes.[130] The firm had been established as long ago as 1830 and was still in existence until quite recently. They manufactured a wide range of optical goods, but it was not until about 1918 that a cinematograph projector was produced by them.

Foreign lenses were also being advertised in England by Voigtländer and Sohn, of Brunswick,[131] and A. Darlot (L. Turillon) of Paris.[132] How widely they were used in this country during 1897, I do not know, but purchasers of the Prestwich camera had the choice of a Voigtländer lens,[133] and Levi's Rollograph, a French importation, was fitted with a lens by Darlot.[134] Wolff's cinematograph camera was supplied with two Zeiss lenses.

4 Brighton

There were two regions outside London where important developments in cinematography were taking place. One was in the north-east, at Bradford and Leeds, in Yorkshire, and the other on the south coast, at Brighton in Sussex. For the sake of convenience the two regions will be dealt with separately, the Brighton area being considered first.

The seaside town of Brighton seems a most unlikely place to figure in the early history of the British cinema, yet it was here, or in its immediate vicinity, that a small group of pioneers was beginning to take an active part in cinematography which was to have important consequences for the future development of the film industry. This small but influencial group comprised A. Esmé Collings, G. Albert Smith, James Williamson, and Alfred Darling.

Of the four, A. Esmé Collings was the first to take up cinematography, and although his actual achievements in this field were inconsequential compared with the other three, he nevertheless may have had some influence in their decisions to take up the subject in the first place, for apparently all four were known to one another.

Esmé Collings is an elusive figure, who has left little trace of his activities. Primarily a portrait photographer in Brighton (38), he turned his attention to film production sometime during 1896. Formerly he had been in partnership with William Friese Greene and together they had presided over a considerable photographic business, which had three studios in London, at 69 New Bond Street, 92 Piccadilly, and 100 Westbourne Grove, as well as a studio in Brighton, at 67 Western Road, and two in Bath, at 34 Gray Street, and 7 The Corridor[1] (39). It is quite likely that Friese Greene's early obsession with the photography of movement had some influence on his partner and was the cause of Collings' subsequent interest in cinematography. But undoubtedly it was Collings' association with the engineer Alfred Darling which was of greater significance from the practical point of view. Whilst wrestling with the problems of film production, it was to Darling that Esmé Collings went for technical assistance. Darling's work-book for the latter half of 1896 shows that he repaired a perforator for Collings, constructed a new one and also made him a new printer and projector. During January and February of 1897, Darling also undertook other work for Collings which seems to have comprised a new model projector and a new camera — the entries in Darling's work-book are scribbled in pencil, often mis-spelt, and not always easy to decipher[2] (see illustration 51). We shall have more to say about Alfred Darling later on in this chapter.

Apart from the work-book just mentioned, Collings' name appears twice in G. A. Smith's cash book for 1897, but I have not found a single reference to him in any of the photographic journals for that year. What little is known about his previous film work has been noted already in the first volume of this history; his 1897 production however, remains a complete blank and only the entries made by Darling and Smith testify to the fact that he continued to be active in the field of cinematography at this time. The trade directories list him as a photographer of 120 Western Road, Hove.

G. Albert Smith's career on the other hand, is comparitively well documented. He likewise first turned his attention to cinematography in 1896. His name first appears in connection with a patent application made in December, in association with A. S.

38 Portrait of a child. Tinted opaline photograph (22×27cm) signed and dated: A. Esmé Collings, Brighton, 1892 (*Barnes Museum of Cinematography*)

Friese Greene & Collings

SPACE FOR AUTOGRAPH

69, NEW BOND STREET
92, PICCADILLY &
100, WESTBOURNE GROVE. LONDON

39   Cabinet photograph, taken in one of the studios jointly controlled by W. Friese-Greene and A. Esmé Collings, during their partnership in the 1880s (*Barnes Museum of Cinematography*)

Frazer, which is headed 'Improvements in Apparatus for the Exhibition or Projection of Photographic Moving Objects' (No. 28152). This received provisional protection only and was not printed, so regrettably we are unable to learn the nature of the said invention, the original document having since been destroyed. It does reveal however, his inventive turn of mind which was later to lead to his discovery of the first successful colour process for cinematography, known as Kinemacolor. Although the patent applied for by Smith and Frazer was never issued, there is reason to believe that the apparatus to which it referred was in fact constructed, and that the man entrusted to carry out the work was Alfred Darling. Entries in Darling's work-book for December (the month when the patent application was made) show that work on Smith's behalf was begun on a 'new taker' [camera/projector (?)] and other entries reveal that it was completed by 9 January 1897, the sum of £17.4s.0d. [£17.20] subsequently being paid for it.

By the time he first entered the film business, George Albert Smith (1864–1959) (40) was already a keen astronomer and a Fellow of the Royal Astronomical Society. He was also known for his lectures on this subject and was well acquainted with the optical or magic lantern, which he used for showing the slides that supplemented his talks. Like many other lantern lecturers of the time, his attention was inevitably directed to the projection of 'animated photographs', and like his colleague Esmé Collings, he soon became involved in their production.

The tranquil setting of Smith's surroundings were no doubt condusive to creative and inventive persuits, for he was the lessee of St. Ann's Well and Gardens (41) 'a quiet leafy retreat,' comprising 'six acres of refreshing foilage and shady walks,' situated at Furze Hill, Hove, quite close to Brighton. Here afternoon teas were served under trees, with plenty of swings for the children and where the celebrated gipsy fortune-teller, Mrs. Lee, was also in attendance. The famous Chalybeate water was drawn free from the Well, and ferns, flowers and grapes, &c. were on sale in the glass houses. Admission to this Garden of Eden was 3d on weekdays, and 6d on Sundays.[3] Here Smith established his 'film factory' as he termed it, and in 1900 was to build his first film studio.

By May 1897, Smith had already converted part of the pump house standing in the grounds, for use as a film laboratory[4] (42). A respresentative from the *Hove Echo*, who interviewed him at this time, reported that he had already 'earned a high reputation as a producer of "animated photographs",' and had exhibited them 'with the greatest possible success in various parts of the country.' The reporter, in the course of his interview, was shown around the new laboratory, by which he seems to have been completely baffled. His interview was published on 8 May, under the heading, ' "Animated Photographs." A Chat with Mr. Albert Smith,'[5] but its rather facile manner precludes it from being the ideal source of information which one might be led to expect. We can however, glean from it a few concrete facts. For instance, the rate at which Smith's films were photographed was about 20 frames per second and averaged about 75ft in length. Smith also claims to have taken the first successful football picture that had ever been exhibited,[6] explaining that such a subject presents great difficulties as the players almost invariably get beyond the range of the camera. He also speaks of the necessity for strong sunlight for the satisfactory taking of the films and adds that for this reason they are mostly taken in spring or summer.

After reading the article, one is left wishing to be told more and one cannot but regret this lost opportunity. Those who interviewed Smith in his later life had only an old

40   George Albert Smith (1864–1959) (*British Film Institute*)

(a)

(b)

(c)

(d)

41   St Ann's Well & Gardens, Hove, of which G. A. Smith was the lessee for eleven years, 1894–1904. (a) The Entrance. (b) Part of the Gardens. (c) The Old Cave. (d) The Well. From photographs taken by H. Bennett, Cowper Street, Hove (*Barnes Museum of Cinematography*)

85

man's reminiscences to rely upon, never a very satisfactory means for getting at the facts. Unfortunately too, the few contemporary instances when Smith is mentioned in the photographic press, the notices are brief and the facts equally scarce. A report in *The Optical Magic Lantern Journal* for July, states:

> Mr. Albert Smith, the well-known proprietor of St. Ann's Wells and Gardens, Brighton (sic), who takes special delight in giving atronomical lectures, has gone in for animated photographs with great success, and has lately fitted up dark-rooms in connection therewith.[7]

Of his films during this period, few are mentioned. In August he was granted permission to film the actress Ellen Terry,[8] and it was reported in the *Hove Echo* that he had 'obtained a number of extremely good pictures, which will probably find their way to all quarters of the globe.'[9] Indeed, we can be sure that he obtained at least one highly successful scene of the actress, for it was still current in 1901 and is listed in the Warwick Trading Company's catalogue for that year. By this time, Warwick had become the agent through which Smith sold his films. The catalogue entry reads:

> MISS ELLEN TERRY AT HOME. A charming half-length portrait of the popular actress. She appears at the casement window of her cottage, kisses her hand, throws a flower, etc. Beautifully sharp and clear.[10]

The cottage referred to was Tower Cottage in Winchelsea, Sussex, which she had acquired in 1896 from her friends the Comyns-Carr.[11]

G. Albert Smith was also present at Queen Victoria's Diamond Jubilee celebration in London on 22 June, where he took a successful film of the procession.[12] By October, the number of films completed by Smith was sufficient to warrant the publication of his first catalogue.[13] This was duly received by the editor of *The British Journal of Photography*, who reported that 'many attractive and amusing subjects are embraced in the list.'[14] No copy of this list is known to have survived, which is a great loss since it would provide us with the only reliable guide to his film output during the preceeding months. The *British Film Catalogue* (Newton Abbot, 1973) is not entirely reliable as far as Smith's films for 1897 are concerned. For example, *The Haunted Castle*, attributed to G. A. Smith for December, is in fact a film by Georges Méliès, and is listed as such in an advertisement of Philipp Wolff's, published in October, in *The Magic Lantern Journal Annual 1897–8*, p xcviii. Furthermore, the film had already been available in England for several months, and is mentioned as early as May.[15]

Among the films known to have been made by Smith during 1897, are several short comedies. One in particular is worth noting here since it was probably one of the first trick films made in England. It is called *Tipsy, Topsy, Turvey*. Compared with the trick films already being produced by Méliès at this time, Smith's film was very elementary indeed, and merely derived its effect from the use of reverse motion. At that time the easiest method of accomplishing this effect, without actually having to reverse the mechanism of the projector whilst the film was running, was to film the scene with the camera upside down; the positive print was then turned the other way up and all the action was seen reversed. The same effect could also be obtained by the use of a reversing prism in the camera or by means of an optical printer.[16]

Reverse motion effects were then still something of a novelty. A Lumière film called *Bathing at Milan*,[17] shown at Gatti's music hall in London, at the beginning of December, showed a diver emerging backwards from the water and resuming his

42 The Pump House, St Ann's Well & Gardens, Hove. Used by G. A. Smith as his film laboratory (*Barnes Museum of Cinematography*)

43 *The Miller and the Sweep* (G. A. Smith, 1897) Frame illustration from a contemporary print in the National Film Archive

position on the diving board; 'the effect is indescribable', noted the reviewer.[18] Smith's film at least showed a little more imagination and showed a drunk undressing only to find his clothes mysteriously returning to his body.

On 18 November, G. Albert Smith addressed a letter to the editor of *The Optical Magic Lantern Journal*, stating that all his films were now supplied with a protective covering of transparent celluloid on the emulsion side, much in the manner that an ordinary lantern slide is protected with a cover-glass. This was to prevent it from being

44 *Hanging Out the Clothes* (G. A. Smith, 1897) Frame illustration from a contemporary print in the National Film Archive

scratched and so prolong the life of the film.[19] Certain entries in Smith's cash book may refer to this practice. For instance, entries dated 2 September 1897 and 3 January 1898 record payments made to a Lizzie Shaw for cleaning and polishing films, which could be preparatory work carried out prior to the application of the protective covering mentioned. It is easy to see his reason for adopting this measure at this time, for one of the defects of many early film projectors was that the whole surface of the film came into contact with some part of the mechanism. Too often the sprocket-wheels and film-gate were made without the necessary rebate between the edges which would prevent all but the perforated edges of the film from surface contact. How long Smith adopted this protective measure is not certain, but it is unlikely that it was for very long since in the coming months new projector design had eliminated this defect.

The chief source of information on G. A. Smith's film activities for the year, is the cash book,* now preserved at the National Film Archive.[20] The entries date from 1 January 1897 and the first few weeks are mainly taken up with accounts relating to the installation and equiping of the film laboratory and dark room. The equipment acquired for this 'film factory' as Smith terms it,[21] included a film printer obtained from Jacob Bonn who had a business in High Holborn, and whom we have already had cause to mention in the course of this history. The accounts show that Smith had to pay Bonn's men five shillings for working overtime on the installation of the printer. Alfred Darling, who had supplied Smith with his camera, also provided a film perforator and winder. Later, Smith acquired a printer from Darling, which enabled him to sell the old Bonn printer to his neighbour James Williamson for £3.10s., Smith having originally paid £3 for it. He obtained his chemicals for the dark room, from F. W. Salmon, although some were supplied by Williamson. Film stock was mainly acquired from the Blair company, but Fitch film was also occasionally used. As for Smith's film making activities, the cash book shows that his first commercially successful production was the football film already mentioned, copies of which he was able to sell to several leading London dealers, who henceforth, were willing to buy other films of his as they became available. Among his regular customers were W. Watson & Sons; J. Ottway & Son; W. C. Hughes, Philipp Wolff and David Devant. Other customers named in his accounts were W. Heath & Co; Owen Brooks, and Wyndham of Poole. His local custom comprised Esmé Collings and James Williamson.

Smith's films included topicals and actualities, but he concentrated more especially on comic subjects. The first account that might be interpreted as referring to a film of this genre, is for 27 March, when 'Whiskers and Spirit Gum' were purchased. I have been unable to trace any film, made about this date, which might conceivably call for such a make-up, so I presume the intended film was a failure.[22] This also seems to have been the case with a film centered on a midget, for on 20 May a tip of two shillings was paid to the midget's coachman, and on the following day a similar amount is recorded in the book for 'expenses taking midget'. Another failure occurred on 24 July when Smith filmed *The Miller and the Sweep*. It is obvious that something went wrong because two months later he re-made the subject. It is probably this successful second version that is now preserved in the National Film Archive[23] (43). In the film, the miller is seen leaving his mill with a sack of flour when he bumps into a chimney-sweep carrying a bag of soot. In the ensuing encounter, the miller becomes covered in soot and the sweep in flour. The action takes place in a natural setting with the sails of the windmill revolving in the background. The actual mill used in the film was known as Race Hill Mill, which stood for many years on the hill north of Brighton Race Course, just west of the path leading down to Bevendean Farm. The mill was blown down on the 16th of May, 1913.[24]

Just prior to making *The Miller and the Sweep*, Smith had engaged a Mr and Mrs Tom Green to act in a series of little comedy sketches,[25] the first of which was *Hanging Out the Clothes*, referred to several times in the cash book simply as 'Clothesline'. A copy of this film has also miraculously survived[26] (44). This simple comedy is filmed in a single

*For a more detailed study of Smith's cash book see Appendix 1.

45 What the Missus Saw, by Orrin C. Dunlap. This photograph, published in Photograms of the Year 1896, may have provided G. A. Smith with the idea for his film Hanging out the Clothes (*Barnes Museum of Cinematography*)

camera set-up, in the open air. The master comes across the maid hanging out the clothes. Their amorous behaviour is rudely interrupted when the mistress comes on the scene and catches them kissing behind a blanket. The idea for this film may have been suggested by a recently published photograph in *Photograms of the Year 1896*.[27] It bore the title 'What the Missus Saw', and was by the American photographer Orrin C. Dunlap (45).

Hanging Out The Clothes was followed by *Comic Shaving* (also known as *The Lady Barber*) in which Tom Green appeared with W. Carlile. Next followed *Comic Face*, which probably showed Tom Green in close-up making grimaces. *Weary Willie* followed, with Tom Green and his wife playing the parts. Tom Green then appeared in *The X Rays* (also known as *The X-Ray Fiend*). On 2 October, a trip to Hastings resulted in a film called *Love on the Pier*. A Reverse-action comedy, also with Tom Green, followed, which is referred to in the cash book simply as 'Reversal'. This is without doubt, the film known later as *Tipsy, Topsy, Turvy*. The final comedy film of the year was probably *Making Sausages*, which showed live cats and dogs being fed into a machine to emerge as sausages.[28]

Apart from persons hired to take part in the films, Smith's film factory was essentially a one man affair, although he did employ an assistant during the initial stages. This was a man named Axel Holst, who was employed for 12 weeks at a salary of £3 per week. This was a reasonably good wage for those days, so Holst was no ordinary odd job man, but must have performed duties of some importance. We know that he was occassionally sent upon errands to London, on one occasion to fetch the Bonn printer. But it seems that once the plant was established, Smith no longer required his services and his name disappears from the records.

46   James A. Williamson (1855–1933) (*British Film Institute*)

47 Williamson's chemist and photographic shop, 144, Church Road, Hove (*East Sussex County Libraries: Hove Area Library*)

A close neighbour and colleague of G. Albert Smith was James A. Williamson (1855–1933) (46), who had a pharmaceutical and photographic business at 144 Church Road, almost opposite the old Parish Church at the top of St Aubyn's, Hove[29] (47). Here he sold various photographic equipment and undertook 'developing, printing, enlarging, mounting, retouching, &c. &c.'[30] He had also acquired X-Ray equipment which was then in its infancy and generally referred to as the Rontgen Rays. When the occasion arose, he was not averse to X-raying patients with broken bones.[31] There can be little doubt that Williamson's X-Ray machine was the inspiration for Smith's early comedy, *The X-Ray Fiend*.

Like G. Albert Smith, James Williamson also had a scientific bent, which stood him in good stead when he eventually abandoned film production to concentrate all his energies on the manufacture of cinematographic equipment, but this was still some little way in the future. In 1897 his film activities mainly consisted of giving cinematograph shows at various local functions and occasionally filming the odd subject as his fancy dictated. In this sense he was still much the amateur, although he did undertake some developing and printing of cinematographic film for his customers.

During October Williamson was interviewed by a representative of the *Hove Echo*,[32] and gave a brief account of his film career: 'I purchased a machine last year', he is reported as saying, 'and I spent a lot of time and trouble in adapting it both for taking and projecting on a screen, although I utilise the machine merely as a means of obtaining subjects which I could otherwise not get.' Williamson also informed the *Echo*'s representative that each of his films was 75ft long. Two films, very popular with

48 Alfred Darling (1862–1931), engineer and manufacturer of cinematographic equipment (*Kenneth & Philip Darling*)

his audiences, we are told, show his own children playing 'Ring-a-ring-of-roses' and 'Fox and Geese'. Another successful picture was one he took of naval cutlass drill by the Hove Coastguards. 'The latter portion of the scene is where they march round and then come forward as though they were about to march out of the picture, but turn aside suddenly.' This little incident, which obviously pleased Williamson's innate sense of cinematic composition, is most significant for it is our first intimation of his future concern for technical innovation, of which he was one of the first exponents and for which he is now chiefly remembered, along with his confrere G. Albert Smith. Their part in the development of film technique will be examined in a future volume of this history.

On the 25 November and the following day, the Hove Camera Club held its second annual exhibition at the Town Hall, during which James Williamson demonstrated the Rontgen Rays and the cinematograph.[33] It seems to have been his policy when giving film shows of this kind, to use films made by G. A. Smith and to intersperse them with a few of his own, and perhaps supplement them with one or two from other sources. This was certainly the case when he gave a show at 'A Grand Naval Entertainment' on behalf of the Royal Seamen and Mariners' Orphan Home, Portsmouth, which took place at the Town Hall on 24 November, the day before the Hove Camera Club's exhibition. We will quote the relevant part of the programme in full, since it provides a valuable means for dating some of his, and Smith's, films. After giving an account of the preceeding part of the entertainment, the *Hove Echo*, in which the report appeared, continues:

A series of Aminated Photographs were then shown by Mr. Williamson. They were as follows:- Seamen at Cutlass Drill; Flag Drill; An excellent reproduction of a rough sea; A game of football; A game of cricket, in the course of which the batsman was run out; Bull Fight; A comic incident, representing a pretty housemaid hanging out articles on a clothes line. Her master follows and is soon discovered by his irate better half embracing the housemaid. His wife revenges herself by plucking out his hair by the roots; The Jubilee procession: The Naval Brigade, Colonials, Queen's Carriage; sailing boat coming ashore in a rough sea; The electric car at Brighton; Rough sea at Hove; Sailing boats racing (rounding the buoy); Making sausages. This scene represented the machine at work, into which live dogs were placed, re-appearing at the base as sausages; Miller and Sweep (a dusty fight); a comic effect with the "X" Rays; Tipsy, Topsy, Turvy, showing a ridiculous effect by reversing the motion of a photo; The Nelson Column on Trafalgar Day. A scene at the railway station brought this wonderful display to a termination.[34]

The majority of the films mentioned were made by G. A. Smith and can be identified from references to them in Smith's account book, or from a list of Smith's films published in the Warwick Trading Company's catalogue for 1898,[35] for by that year Warwick had acquired the rights to Smith's films. Of the other films mentioned, *The Bull Fight* was a Lumière film, then very popular, and *The Naval Brigade* was a Watson film recently sold to Williamson by Smith.[36] Only the two films, *Seamen at Cutlass Drill* and *Flag Drill* can be attributed to Williamson himself.

Alfred Darling (1862–1931) (48), the fourth member of the Brighton group, was an engineer who undertook to make all manner of light engineering products. Williamson refers to him as having provided technical assistance to both himself and to Smith,[37] whereas Esmé Collings, who was probably responsible for introducing Darling to them

49   47 Chester Terrace. Alfred Darling's house in Brighton, in the back bedroom of which he set up his first workshop in 1894. His two grandsons, Philip and Kenneth Darling, pose outside the house in 1978 (*Barnes Museum of Cinematography*)

50 A corner of Alfred Darling's Workshop, 25 Ditchling Rise, Brighton, which he occupied until 1926 and where the greater part of his cinematographic work was carried out (*Kenneth & Philip Darling*)

in the first place, appears to have been the first to enlist his services. Thereafter, Darling developed a peculiar talent for manufacturing, and in some cases designing, cinematographic apparatus.

There is no doubt that Darling was a very able mechanician, and the cinematographic cameras he was later to make were probably among the best in the world for their time. In 1897, he was associated with the firm of J. Wrench & Son, and in July of that year took out a patent, with Alfred Wrench, for a claw-operated cine camera with a variable shutter (British Patent No. 17248).

Like so many inventors, Darling's achievements are mostly submerged in the commercial world in which he worked, the credit generally going to the firm that employed him. Thus a great deal of the credit for the success of Wrench's early cinematographic apparatus must surely belong to him, and there can be little doubt that he enjoyed considerable prestige within the trade. There is no evidence for supposing that Darling was ever engaged in film production, although he is likely to have taken 'test strips' during the period when a particular camera he had made was undergoing trials. That he undertook work for a large number of well-known firms connected with the cinematograph trade is apparent from a perusal of his ledgers and account books, many of which are still extant. For example, those for the period between 1900 and 1910 reveal that his customers included, among others, L. Gaumont & Cie; J. Wrench & Son; the Warwick Trading Co; G. A. Smith; the European Blair Camera Co; J. Williamson; Charles Urban; Deutche Bioskop Gesellschaft; the Alpha Trading Co, Ltd; W. Butcher & Sons Ltd; W. Friese Greene; Raleigh & Robert, Paris; S.J.C. Societa Italina Cinematografica, Torino; Romanet & Guilbert, Paris; Walter Tyler Ltd; the Williamson Kinematograph Co. Ltd; Lapierre Frères & Cie, Lagny,

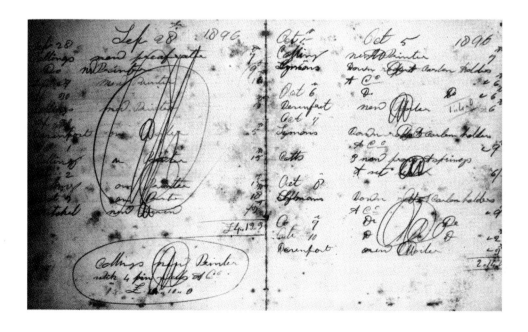

98

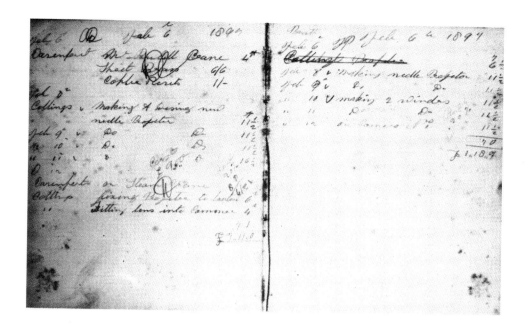

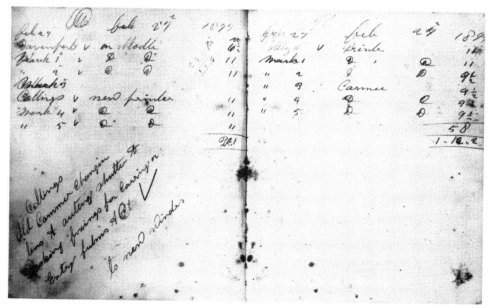

51   Eight pages from Alfred Darling's work-book, 1896–7, showing entries relating to cinematographic work carried out for A. Esmé Collings (*Alfred Darling & Sons*)

France; and E. H. Kemp of New York. The work done for some of these firms was quite considerable; for example for the Warwick Trading Co he manufactured their famous Biokam, and for Urban the well-known Bioscope Cameras. On the other hand, he was prepared to undertake quite minor work, such as that for the Alpha Trading Co Ltd, of Bedford Park, St Albans, which entailed 'overhauling rotary perforator (18 September 1906), ditto (9 February 1907), and supplying 'one pair of perforating wheels' (10 January 1908). It seems that Alfred Darling kept a fairly complete photographic record of the cinematographic apparatus he manufactured and an extensive collection of glass photographic negatives still exist. An examination of a number of old prints from these plates shows that Darling made a wide variety of equipment during his lifetime including cameras, printers, winders, measurers, tripods and projectors. Many of these prints are captioned and so provide an excellent pictorial record of Darling's cinematographic work.

According to Kenneth and Philip Darling, grandsons of Alfred Darling, their grandfather was from London, but his exact place and date of birth were unknown to them. They also informed me that Alfred Darling's first workshop was the back bedroom of his house at 47 Chester Terrace, Brighton (49) where he installed a metal-working lathe and other machine tools. At first, I was inclined to take this story as one of those romantic tales that are apt to be told about early inventors and which generally turn out to be more apocryphal than true. However, when I called at the house, the present owner, Mr Trangmar, informed me that after he had acquired the house and was doing some re-wiring in the back bedroom, he came across traces of metal swarf underneath the floor boards and remembered being puzzled by its presence, not knowing until my visit, of the room's former use, nor, until a few days prior to my visit, the occupation of the former owner.[38] So the story told me by Darling's grandsons was thus happily confirmed.

Such was his talent that Darling's back bedroom could not serve his needs for long and he soon moved to more commodious premises at 25 Ditchling Rise, where his workshop was set up over some stables belonging to a builder by the name of A. Dean[39] (50). Here he remained until 1926, when the business was transferred to new engineering works at South Road, Preston Park, Brighton, where the firm functions still, under the name of Alfred Darling & Sons. But it was at the former works that the bulk of the cinematographic work was done.

Darling's engineering business was established in 1894, but the earliest record we have of cinematographic work being undertaken by him is an entry in his work-book dated 18 September 1896, when work was begun on repairing a film perforator for Esmé Collings (51). The work was spread out over a period of four days and cost £2. On 23 September Darling began work on a new perforator for Collings, but we cannot be sure that it was to his own design, only that it cost £8. Prior to this work, the same work-book shows that Darling constructed an electric arc lamp for Simmens, Simmons, Simons, or Symons (the name appears with all four spellings), but it is impossible to be sure that this was intended for film projection purposes.

Apart from the work carried out for Esmé Collings during 1896–7, the only other customer of Darling's at this time, for whom cinematographic work was done, and for whom we have records, was G. A. Smith. On 11 December 1896, work was begun on a camera/projector, which was probably the apparatus referred to in the patent application filed by Smith and Frazer as No. 28152. Unfortunately, Darling's records for the early years of his career are incomplete and the work-book mentioned covers only the

52 Film perforator (Incomplete) Made by Alfred Darling of Brighton, ca 1897 (*Science Museum, London*)

53 A Combined Cinematograph Camera and Printer, ca 1897. Made by Alfred Darling, of Brighton (*Science Museum, London*)

TRADE

MARK

54   Trade Mark of Alfred Darling, mechanical engineer and manufacturer of cinematograph mechanisms, Brighton (*Alfred Darling & Sons*)

period from 31 August 1896 to 5 March 1897. So it is only fair to state that our knowledge of Darling's early cinematographic work is far from complete. For instance, we know from Smith's account book that the goods manufactured for him by Darling during the period under discussion included a complete camera outfit together with four extra aluminium reels; a film perforator; a film winder and two printing machines. Nor must we forget the work that must have been done on the cinematograph camera patented by himself and Alfred Wrench in July 1897.

The Science Museum, London, has on loan, two pieces of equipment by Darling, which seem to date from this period. One of the items is part of a film perforator which is designed to punch eight holes on both edges of the film at each operation[40] (52). The second item is a combined camera and printer[41] (53). Our illustration shows the apparatus with the cover removed. When operating as a camera, the unexposed negative is placed on the forward top spool and laced between the guide rollers, down through the gate and over the sprocket wheel to the lower take-up spool, the latter of which is driven by a spring belt from the main driving shaft. The segmented front shutter allows the aperture to be adjusted for variations in exposure. The mechanism is then placed inside the cover and secured. It is the back of the cover which is shown in the illustration, with the sight-hole for the focusing tube visible centre-left of the panel. The objective lens was attached to the front panel at the other end of the cover, but in this case, both components are wanting. When in use as a printer, the focusing tube is removed and the negative is placed on the forward top spool and the unexposed film on the spool behind it. Both these spools are governed by a tension spring so that the film does not over-spill when being payed out. The two films are then placed in contact and laced together through the machine, the lower take-up spool receiving the negative and the rear upper spool the newly exposed film. This latter spool also being driven by a spring belt attached to a pulley on the main driving shaft. The apparatus is then enclosed in its case and the film exposed in front of a suitable light source.

Farther along the coast from Brighton, at Southsea near Portsmouth, the well-known yachting and marine photographers, G. West & Son, were established. Here Alfred J. West (1858–1937) was just beginning a successful career as a cinematographer and exhibitor of naval subjects which, from 1898 onwards, were to achieve a considerable reputation in England under the general title of *West's Our Navy*. This series comprised a number of films dealing with various aspects of life ashore, and afloat, in the Royal Navy. In 1897, West carried out his first experiments with cinematography with the assistance of the Royal Naval Torpedo School, Portsmouth,[42] but his film career more properly belongs to the succeeding years, so will be left to a future volume.

5 Bradford and Leeds

Bradford and Leeds can each boast an early association with the cinema, beginning in 1896. In both towns cinematographic apparatus and films were being made in that year; in Leeds by John Henry Rigg of 43 Skinner Lane, and in Bradford by Riley Brothers of 55 & 57 Godwin Street. The former produced a machine known as Rigg's Kinematograph (55), which remained on the market throughout the following year, whereas Riley Bros produced a machine known as the Kineoptoscope, which was to be replaced in 1897 by a modified version.

The new version of the Kineoptoscope was first advertised in January,[1] and was subsequently mentioned in several photographic journals. *The Photogram* for March states that it 'works with great smoothness, so that the picture (with a true standard film) is wonderfully steady on the screen'.[2] *The Optician* also was 'greatly struck with the extreme steadiness of the pictures.'[3] This apparatus employed a four-toothed claw mechanism which engaged two perforations on each side of the film, advancing it by

55 Rigg's Kinematograph, 1896–7. Patented and manufactured by J. H. Rigg, of Leeds, in association with E. O. Kumberg of the Anglo-Continental Phonograph Company (*Barnes Museum of Cinematography*)

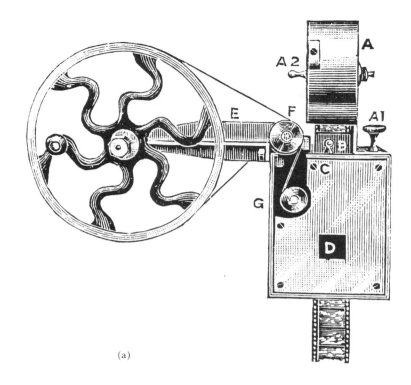

(a)

(b)

56 Riley's Kineoptoscope (Revised Model) 1897. Made by Riley Brothers, of Bradford. This machine was designed to fit into the slide-stage of any ordinary magic lantern. (a) Front elevation. (b) In position in the lantern (*Barnes Museum of Cinematography*)

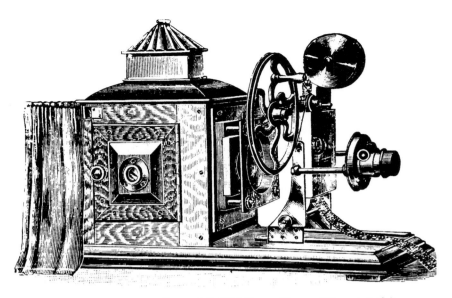

57   Riley's Kineoptoscope (Free-standing model) 1897 (*Barnes Museum of Cinematography*)

one frame at each downward stroke. This was the sole means of advancing the film since no sprocket-wheels were provided.

The projector was available in two forms, either as a single unit for insertion in the slide-stage of an ordinary magic lantern (56), or as a free-standing model for mounting on the baseboard in front of the lantern (57). The prices in each case were £10 and £19. 10s. (£19.50) respectively.[4] The London stockists for the Kineoptoscope were O. Sichel & Co, 20 Berners Street, Oxford Street.[5] An example of the free-standing model is to be seen in the Science Museum, London (Inv. No. 1948–278) (58).

In June, Riley Brothers introduced their Kineoptoscope Camera, which was simply an adaptation of the projector and employed essentially the same mechanism[6] (59). Both instruments owe their inception to Cecil Wray, under whose patent they were covered (British patent no. 19181). This patent has already been described in the previous volume of this history, where a description of Rigg's Kinematograph is also to be found.

Both manufacturers were engaged in film production during 1897, but little is known at present concerning this aspect of their trade. Riley Brothers for example, issued a catalogue in July which was said to include a number of films.[7] It seems likely that some of these were made by Riley, since another source specifically states that 'the Kineoptoscope is used by its inventors for taking their own films.'[8] Rigg likewise made his own films. In a report published in March he is said to have 'a series of his own subjects, including some very effective groups of skaters during the recent frost'. It is also said that he makes 'a special point of supplying Kinematographs synchronised with the loud-speaking phonograph, giving words or music to suitably accompany the kinetograms'.[9] A thorough investigation of the films made by these two producers has yet to be made, but will ultimately depend upon the discovery of their printed catalogues, which until now have not come to light. We know that Riley Brothers, in addition to the catalogue issued in July, issued another in October, comprising 250 pages.[10] Moreover, that part of the catalogue devoted to cinematography was also

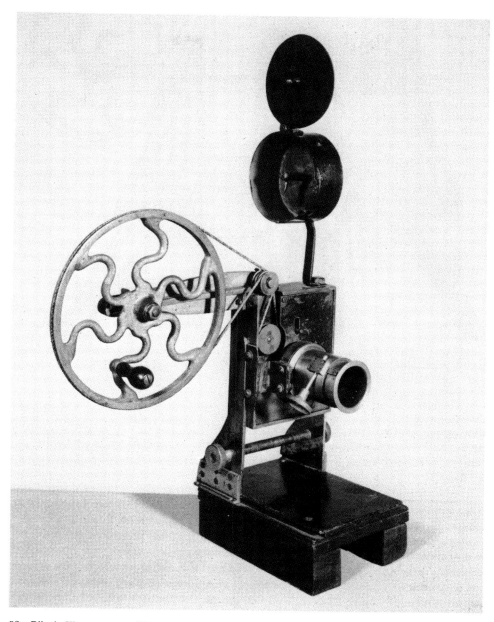

58　Riley's Kineoptoscope (Free-standing model) 1897 (*Science Museum, London*)

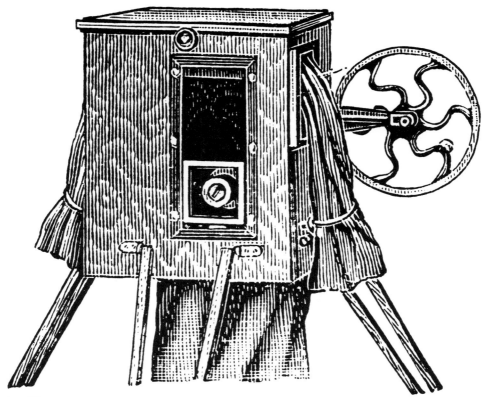

59   Riley's Kineoptoscope Camera, 1897. This instrument was modelled on the Kineoptoscope Projector
and employed the same type of double-claw mechanism (*Barnes Museum of Cinematography*)

available in French and German editions. An American catalogue was also issued from
their establishment at No 16 Beckman Street, New York.[11] This American branch of
the business was under the management of H. J. Riley, whilst the senior partner in the
concern, J. Riley, was resident in Bradford, where he was assisted by another brother,
W. Riley.[12]

After his initial success with Riley Bros as the designer of their Kineoptoscope, Cecil
Wray went into partnership with Cecil William Baxter and together they functioned as
'Baxter & Wray', with an address at Borough Mills, Manchester Road, Bradford.[13]
Their partnership however was of short duration and by 1899 Wray was trading on his
own account as Cecil Wray & Co, from the same address.[14] During the brief period
when they were together, Baxter & Wray produced two machines which seem to have
met with a fair measure of success. The first was introduced in April or May, 1897, and
was known simply as the 'B & W' cinematograph.[15] It was a combined camera and
projector, specifically designed for the foreign market. It had several features which
made it particularly suitable for use in unequitable climates and according to a report
published in September, several examples were already in use in remote parts of the
world.[16] It also had the distinction of being the first cinematographic apparatus
imported by Japan, and can thus be regarded as forming the first step towards the
establishment of the Japanese film industry.[17]

108

60   The 'B & W' Cinematograph, 1897. Made by Baxter & Wray, of Bradford. A combined camera and projector, specifically designed for use in unequitable climates (*Barnes Museum of Cinematography*)

61 The 'Perfection' Cinematograph, 1897. Made by Baxter & Wray. This projector had a claw mechanism for imparting the intermittent movement to the film (*Barnes Museum of Cinematography*)

The particular features of the 'B & W' cinematograph were its robust construction and simplicity of design, which combined to make it the ideal instrument for use under difficult circumstances. The working parts were enclosed in a stout mahogany case, with exterior film boxes also made of the same wood. The film was advanced by a single sprocket-wheel which was intermittently driven by a pegged-wheel actuated by a slotted disc, and the main drive was applied by an exterior hand-cranked pulley wheel. This latter was also connected by a driving belt to the take-up spindle of the lower film box. The only example of this apparatus known to be extant is that in the Barnes Museum of Cinematography (60).

The second apparatus produced by Baxter & Wray, was patented by them on the 6th May 1897, in association with a Bradford clockmaker named Joseph Oulton*

---

*J. Oulton is briefly mentioned in the previous volume of this history in connection with a patent filed on 4 April 1896 (British patent no 7817).

(British patent no 11273) and manufactured under the name of the 'Perfection' cinematograph. It was totally dissimilar from the 'B & W', being entirely of brass and steel and employing a claw-type mechanism. It was not unlike the Riley Kineoptoscope in appearance and clearly reflected the hand of the same designer (61). It was placed on the market probably late in July at the earliest, since a report published in *The Photogram* for that month speaks of it as still in an incomplete state.[18] Bearing in mind that the report was probably written the previous month to meet the deadline for July publication, the apparatus is not likely to have been ready for several weeks from the time the report was written. When eventually placed on the market, it sold for as little as £15 and, if we are to believe the claims of its makers, as of November, over 200 of these machines had already been sold.[19]

Baxter & Wray also offered films for sale, including those of Georges Méliès (Houdin).[20] The latter were priced from £3, which shows the high esteem in which these films were held, English films at that time were normally selling for about thirty shillings [£1.50]. It is not known whether Baxter & Wray were engaged in film production, but the evidence, or rather the lack of it, makes this seem unlikely. A catalogue of cinematographic equipment was issued in June which contained a list of 'some hundreds of subjects'.[21] Perhaps, if a copy of this catalogue could be found we might be able to learn the source of some of these films and so determine whether any of them were produced by the firm.

Another Bradford firm specialising in cinematographic equipment, was R. J. Appleton & Co, Photographic and Lantern Outfitters, of 5 Manningham Lane.[22] The date

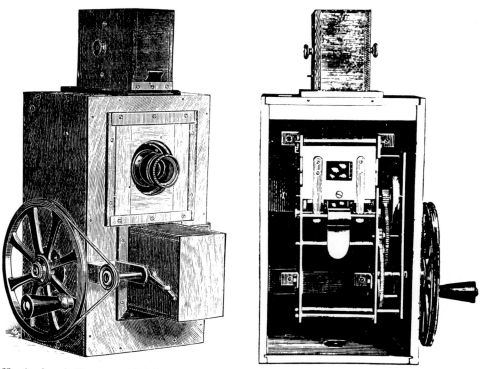

62   Appleton's Cieroscope, 1896–7. A combined camera, printer and projector. Made by R. J. Appleton & Co, Bradford (*Barnes Museum of Cinematography*)

when this firm was first established has not been determined, but a photographic business trading as Appleton & Co was active in the 1870s, with a studio in Horton Lane, Bradford. This studio is pictured on the backs of several surviving *carte-de-visite* of the period.[23] Two books published in London in 1876 and 1877, are each illustrated with four Woodburytypes from photographs by Appleton & Co, the books being *The History and Antiquities of Morley, in the West Riding of York*, by William Smith, and *Sir Titus Salt, Baronet. His Life and its Lessons*, by the Rev R. Balgarnie. Appleton & Co must therefore have been photographers of some repute and it seems likely that R. J. Appleton & Co, the subject of our present study, has a direct link with that establishment.

The apparatus with which the name of R. J. Appleton & Co is connected was called the Cieroscope and combined the three functions of camera, printer and projector (62). It was introduced on the market not later than February[24] and sold for £15.15s. [£15.75], or £17.17s. [£17.85] when fitted with W. Wray's special cinematograph lens.[25] No patent applicable to this machine has been found, so precise details of its mechanism are unknown. Neither have I been able to locate an existing example of the instrument from which an accurate description can be made. The illustration shows a pattern not unlike the 'B & W' cinematograph mentioned above. It has an exterior hand-cranked pulley-wheel supplying the main drive and which is also connected by a band to the take-up spindle. The mechanism is enclosed in a wooden case, with exterior film boxes for daylight loading. If there was some plagiarism here, the onus must rest with Baxter & Wray since their apparatus followed the Cieroscope by several months.

Appleton also made a machine for projecting purposes only, which was known as the Cieroscope No 1 (63). The price was £15.15s.0d. [£15.75], but the complete outfit with mahogany lantern and alum trough cost £21.[26] Again, information is wanting concerning the mechanism, but the general design was similar to the combination camera/projector model.

The Cieroscope Camera was used by its makers to produce their own films, a fact which elicited special praise from Cecil M. Hepworth:

> I always feel predisposed towards a machine that is regularly used by its inventor for the production of successful films that are good enough to be put upon the market . . . The fact that Mr. Appleton uses his instrument for the production of his own successful films should be sufficient recommendation for his compact Cieroscope.[27]

Among the most notable of his films was a series of Queen Victoria's Diamond Jubilee procession. By an amazing feat of organisation, these were shown in Bradford on the night of Jubilee day, being developed and printed en route (see page 189). Not much is known about other films by this producer, but a few may have been included in a programme organised by the Wakefield Photographic Society, presented at the Mechanic's Hall on the 2nd and 3rd of September. The following is a shortened account of the programme published in The *British Journal of Photography*:

> The great attraction was, most undoubtedly, a first class set of about a score [of] cinematographic views, obtained by Messrs. R. J. Appleton & Co., of Bradford, with an instrument of their own invention, and cleverly exhibited by them on a screen, whilst the band executed appropriate selections of music. The marvellous animated photographs created much

(a)

(b)

63   Appleton's Cieroscope No 1, 1897. For projection purposes only. (a) General view. (b) With Lantern ready for projection (*Barnes Museum of Cinematography*)

amazement and amusement, provoking hearty applause and roars of laughter. A street scene was followed by a representation of a duel, and a ghost scene, a skirt dance, bathing at sea, acrobats, &c. A representation of high tide on the rocks at Flambro' Head was realistic, and so also was a steeplechase, a kissing performance, a railway station platform, and an unfortunate fisherman. Five views, illustrating sections of the recent Jubilee procession in London, were very greatly admired . . . [28]

Without the aid of supplementary material, it is difficult to know which of these films were actually produced by Appleton. The Jubilee films almost certainly were, and probably also the representation of high tide on the rocks at Flamborough Head, this being too local in character not to be otherwise. The street scene mentioned, may also have been his.

R. J. Appleton & Co's involvement with the exhibiting side of the industry had begun late in 1896, and Mr R. Brown of Bury, during a search of the *Bradford Observer*, has come across several references to their activities in this respect.[29] For example, an advertisement in the issue for 14 November, 1896, reads:

APPLETON'S CIEROSCOPE
Exhibition of Animated Photographs at
BAZAARS, PRIVATE PARTIES, AT HOMES, ETC.
For terms and particulars apply to
R. J. APPLETON & CO 58 MANNINGHAM LANE, AND
23 CHARLES STREET, BRADFORD T.N.4659[30]

In the same year, for the week commencing 14 December, performances were given by Appleton at the Mechanics Institute,[31] notice of which, duly appeared in the local paper:

EXHIBITION OF ANIMATED PICTURES — Messrs R. J. Appleton & Co, Bradford, are giving a series of exhibitions during the present week, at the Bradford Mechanics Institute, illustrative of the wonderful powers of their 'Cieroscope' an apparatus for presenting to view animated photographs or living pictures. The effects are produced by presenting in rapid succession, hundreds of instantaneous photographs such as street scenes, with moving pedestrians, etc; the arrival and departure of railway trains, and pourtraying (sic) in a vivid manner, all the bustle and commotion usual on such occasions, sailing vessels and steamers at sea, showing breaking and foaming of the waves, military manoeuvres, and many others. Every movement of real life is depicted on the screen. Two exhibitions are being given each afternoon, consisting of animated photographs only, with a further exhibition each evening, comprising in addition, a number of choice lantern slides.[32]

The source of Appleton's films is not stated and it would be impossible to identify any of them with certainty from such meagre descriptions as the above. They are unlikely to have been supplied by Birt Acres or R. W. Paul, since at that date, their films were not freely available on the open market. Most probably they were of French make and supplied by Philipp Wolff. One or two may even have been taken by R. J. Appleton as we know the Cieroscope also operated as a camera.

Mention must also be made of another leading Yorkshire photographic firm by the name of C. C. Vevers, with an address at 163 Briggate, Leeds. In addition to photographic equipment they also dealt in magic lanterns and accessories and later in the year turned their attention to cinematography. On 30 September, C. C. Vevers applied for a patent for 'improvements in apparatus for exhibiting, taking, or printing moving or animated photographs (No 22423). The patent never issued so consequently the provisional application was not printed, but it probably referred to an apparatus called the Vivograph, which was advertised in *The English Mechanic & World of Science*, for 10 December:

Animated Photographs. The "Vivograph" projector fits any lantern, £5, films, accessories. Catalogue 1d. — Vevers, Briggate, Leeds.[33]

An advertisement in the *British Journal Photographic Almanac for 1898*, refers to it as 'Vever's Patent "Vivograph". £5. The latest, cheapest and best Cinematograph for projecting, taking and printing Animated Photographs.'[34] Hopwood, in his book *Living Pictures* (London, 1899) lists the apparatus by name without describing it.[35] So far, no further information about this machine has come to light, but judging from its price, it must have been rather inconsequential.

Nothing is known of a Leeds camera maker named Charles Grayson, of 30 Elmwood Street, who patented a cinematograph camera of a rather peculiar design (No 12,052. 15 May, 1897); but whether it was manufactured commercially has not been determined. According to the patent specification, the lens was set back in a sliding box compartment in order to exclude the light from surrounding objects, acting like a lens hood or shade. The box in which the lens was fitted was adjustable by a rack and pinion for focusing. At the back of the camera was another opening through which the image on the film could be seen, and a frame, glazed with ruby glass, could be fitted to the opening when very sensitive film was employed. A slot in the bottom of the camera allowed the exposed film to pass through. This opening was surrounded by a flange to which a light-proof bag was secured to receive the film.

Neither Vevers nor Grayson seem to have figured very prominently in the film business and in this respect were probably more of regional significance. Not so the other four manufacturers discussed in this chapter; they each established a national reputation, and in at least one case, an international one. Nor were they to be the only firms engaged in the film business in this part of the country. In 1899, they were joined by James Bamforth, of Holmfirth, a firm which specialised in 'life model slides' for the optical lantern, and which had a profound influence on the early film makers. Bamforth's work falls outside the scope of the present volume, as does that of A. Kershaw, of Leeds, who, at a very much later date, established a fine reputation as a manufacturer of projection equipment and whose Kalee projectors were known to projectionists throughout the world. But it was those pioneer firms afore mentioned, which made Yorkshire such an important centre of the film industry during the last years of the 19th century.

Outside the main centres of the film industry (viz: London, Brighton, Bradford and Leeds) there is little to report; but mention should be made of a Birmingham inventor by the name of Walter John Hubert Jones. He patented a cinematograph which he named the Excelograph (No 19,278. 20 August 1897).[36] Jones' occupation is not stated in the specification, but his address is given as 105 Vyse Street. The mechanism of the Excelograph has little to recommend it and the movement by which the film is moved is rather awkward to say the least. Hopwood gives the following account of its working:

The film is drawn down by the grip of two rubber-faced rollers. One of these rollers is periodically revolved by the stroke of a toothed quadrant gearing with cogs on the same axle as the roller. The latter is prevented from turning backward on the return of the quadrant by a ratchet. The quadrant is caused to make intermittent strokes by the action of a stud on a revolving disc, such action being direct or through intermediate levers.[37]

6. The Foreign Influx

By the end of 1896, and at a time when a very vigorous native film industry indeed was growing up in Great Britain, Cecil M. Hepworth, writing in *The Amateur Photographer*, was obliged to pose the question: 'What do you say to the fact that all the best kineti-projection films are "made in France"?' He then continues:

> Certainly, the English weather is rather against us just at present, but that is not sufficient to account for the state of things, besides Englishmen might easily go abroad in search of their subjects. Of course, there are films being made in England, and very good ones too, but nearly all of the immense demand is being met with goods of French manufacture. Here is a case which shouts aloud for reformation, and there is no doubt it will get it very shortly, but why was it ever necessary to import foreign films for our home-made cine-projectors, and thereby introduce a competitor it will be very difficult to oust?[1]

Hepworth was in a favourable position to judge the market trends of the times, for he wrote a regular column on lantern matters for *The Amateur Photographer*, which constantly took note of new developments in the trade, of which cinematography was a subject then very much to the fore. He also contributed articles of a like nature to other periodicals, notably *The Optical Magic Lantern Journal*. He can be regarded therefore as somewhat of an authority on contemporary film production and his opinion respecting the superiority of French films ought not to be ignored. From my own examination of the evidence there seems to be ample justification for Hepworth's conclusion.

One of the largest importers of French films was Philipp Wolff, who had entered the film business late in 1896. He very soon became the dominant supplier of foreign films in Great Britain, with offices in London, Paris and Berlin.[2] Thus he was well placed as regards the acquisition of new subjects. As one commentator wrote: 'he has an immense stock of all the films that are worth having from all parts of the film-producing globe.'[3]

It is a pity that none of Wolff's published film catalogues seems to have survived. We know that at least three were issued during the period 1896–97, for they are recorded as having been received by editors of photographic journals. The first, which was probably issued at the end of December 1896, is described as 'a lengthy list in three languages of titles and prices of up-to-date films'.[4] A second list appeared in March,[5] and a further one is recorded as having been issued in July, which was said to include 'scenes from many lands'.[6] This comprehensive list prompted an editor to add, 'It seems as if, before very long, the available variety of kinetograms [films] will be as great as the variety of ordinary lantern-slides.'[7]

We are fortunate in having a five-page advertisement of Wolff's in *The Optical Magic Lantern Journal Annual 1897–8* (published October 1897).[8] The absence of the official catalogues makes this advertisement of particular importance as it provides much useful information not otherwise available. It is reproduced, in part, on pages 118 and 119. (64)

Other films issued by Wolff are mentioned in various periodicals, but seldom, if ever, with the name of the producer or country of origin. In common with some other agencies, such as Maguire & Baucus Ltd. and Fuerst Bros., Wolff handled the Lumiére films as perforated to the Edison gauge. In addition, he acted as the British agent for the films of Georges Méliès, which at that time, were advertised under the name of Robert Houdin.[9]

Méliès was then producing simple 'actualities' as well as the 'made-up' films for which he became famous. Both types are to be found in Wolff's list, although it was the 'made-up' subjects which naturally attracted the most attention. These latter were then, as now, considered technically advanced for their time and exceedingly well staged. Indeed, the Méliès films reveal a very personal stamp and a creative talent almost entirely lacking in other films of the period. *Photograms of '97* had this to say about his Graeco-Turkish War series:

'Another series, which has some artistic claims, is produced by the same publisher [Philipp Wolff], and consists of three scenes from the Graeco-Turkish war. A fight on a man-of-war, ending with the explosion of a shell and the partial burning of the ship; the defence of a small walled courtyard; and the defence of a garret room, in which one of the defenders is wounded and tended by a nurse, are wonderfully realistic and extremely popular. The "art" steps in with the fact that all these scenes, including that upon the unstable deck of the man-of-war, are kinetographed in a Parisian garden, and owe their attractiveness to good scene-painting and realistic actors.'[10]

Some of Wolff's other French importations received notoriety for other reasons, as is evident from the following account in the same publication:

'Kinetography has hardly claimed, and certainly has not been recognised as having any artistic pretensions, and yet it has revived, in a very practical manner, the old question of how far the public exhibition of the nude is admissible. The question arose out of certain subjects published by Philipp Wolff, of Paris, Berlin, and London. Four of his subjects, at least, viz.- *The Temptation of St. Anthony*, *The Artist's Model*, *A Bride Unrobing*, and *A French Lady's Bath*, although popular in certain Parisian circles, were received with scant favor in Britain. In one of them, at least, the separate subjects are such as would be accepted at an exhibition of paintings, calmly viewed by all classes of society, and reproduced in our strictly moral illustrated weeklies. But when the subjects are projected in rapid succession, giving a certain illusion of life, their eligibility for public exhibition becomes very doubtful. Other subjects in the series are distinctly unsuitable (according to ordinary British ideas) for public show. Here comes a very curious point, for though when first introduced there was no sale for these subjects in this country, there is now a very brisk and considerable demand. And it may be said for them that they are technically, and even artistically, immensely superior to the bulk of the kinetograms on sale'.[11]

These films had also provoked similar comment in *The Photogram* for March:

'Even now, many of the most popular films are specially-arranged "set pieces" with more or less trained actors; and a series of new subjects of a domestic or humorous interest, recently placed on the market by Philipp Wolff is being wonderfully well taken up. A few of these, such as "A Lady's Bath," "The Sculptor's Model," and others on similar topics can hardly be shown to the average British audience, though we believe they are immensely popular in their native France. Certainly they are amongst the very best films, technically, that come to Britain. Another section of the same series will most surely, ere long, give rise to considerable

PHILIPP WOLFF for FILMS.

Special Terms to Dealers.

THIS List is composed of 4 Series (A, B, C, D), in which the subjects are numbered.

By giving an order it must be kept in mind that though the names of some subjects are similar, they differ in price and quality.

Concerning the length mentioned in the headings, no guarantee can be given as to the exact length indicated.

All my Films are after the Edison perforation system (4 holes) and can be worked on any machine.

SERIE A—Between 60 and 75 feet long, clear.

1 A dispute with a coachman
2 The drunkards
3 Menuett Louis XV.
4 The sentinel (comic scene)
5 Feeding an elephant at the Zoo
6 The Czar in Paris

7 The Czar in Paris (4 lengths)
8 Bath of a Parisian lady
9 A bride retiring to bed (dbl. length)
10 Assault of arms between the champions, Pini and Kirshoeffer (1½ lengths)

New Serie : Scenes of the Life of Christ. These pictures of great artistic value, varying in length according to the subject they represent—their prices are in proportion.

11 The birth of Christ, the Shepherds and Magi (about 53 ft.)
12 Jesus in the Temple (about 40 ft.)
13 Jesus restoring to life the Widow's son (about 43 ft.)
14 Let the little children come unto Me (about 69 ft.)
15 Entry into Jerusalem (about 40 ft.)
16 The Last Supper (about 26 ft.)

17 Gethsemane, the Agony, the Treason (about 92 ft.)
18 Before Pilate, Condemnation, Ecce Homo (about 32 ft)
19 On the way to Calvary (about 56 ft.)
20 Golgotha, the Cross (about 56 ft.)
21 The descent from the Cross (about 24 ft.)
22 The Resurrection (about 19 ft.)

The whole Serie (11-22)—Price on application.

ROBERT HOUDIN.

SERIE B—About 75 feet long, clear.

1 A wedding party leaving church
2 A terrible night (comic scene)
3 Lightning cartoonist (drawing M. Thiers)
4 Lightning cartoonist (drawing Mr. Chamberlain)

5 Lightning cartoonist (drawing Queen Victoria)
6 Lightning cartoonist (drawing Prince Bismarck)
7 The vanishing lady
8 Ladykillers

LONDON.   PARIS.   BERLIN.

9, Southampton Street, Holborn, London, W.C.

Telegraphic Address—" INFILMED, LONDON."

PHILIPP WOLFF for FILMS.

Special Terms to Dealers.

SERIE B—*Continued*.

9 The haunted castle
10 The haunted castle (3 lengths)
11 Leaving a workshop
12 The clown
13 On board a steamer (between Calais and Dover)
14 Mont Blanc, a dangerous passage
15 On the roof (exciting scene)
16 Nightmare
17 Mr. Devant, "the famous conjuror"

SCENES IN THE GRAECO-TURK WAR.

18 Mohammedan inhabitants of Crete massacring Christian Greeks
19 Turks attacking a house defended by Greeks (Turnavos)
20 The Greek man-of-war "George" shelling the fort of Previsa
21 Execution of a Greek spy at Pharsala

SERIE C.

LUMIERE

FILMS

COMPLETE LIST OF THIS SERIE WILL BE

FURNISHED ON APPLICATION.

LONDON. PARIS. BERLIN.

9, Southampton Street, Holborn, London, W.C

Telegraphic Address—" INFILMED, LONDON."

64   A list of films published by Philipp Wolff in The Magic Lantern Journal Annual 1897–8 (October 1897)
Two pages only of a five-page advertisement (*Barnes Museum of Cinematography*)

controversy, and probably awaken afresh the most heated discussion on the question of "the nude." A typical subject is "The Temptation of St. Anthony." In the earlier pictures the saint is seen devoutly adoring the figure on the crucifix. Suddenly, the crucified Saviour is replaced by a nude woman, who proceeds, as the film unwinds, to display her charms, and endeavor to withdraw the good saint from allegiance to his principles. The film in question is technically excellent, the models are good, and probably every single picture, if copied by a painter to life-size, and colored (sic) with the tints of life, would be hung in one of the picture exhibitions, frankly accepted by the public, and reproduced in the illustrated weeklies. The question then arises – if each of the pictures, separately, is acceptable, is life-size projection of the whole series entirely inadmissible. Frankly, we think it is; but then, we have a difficulty in giving a logical reason, unless we turn back and re-consider the decision with regard to the single picture. Perhaps some enterprising showman will try this particular subject (say in Glasgow) with the certainty of either scoring a great popular success, or a great free advertisement – or possibly both.[12]

The Temptation of St Anthony is the title of a film made by Georges Méliès, which is generally believed to have been made in 1898.[13] One might be led to suppose that the description quoted above, refers to this film, but a contemporary frame illustration shows it to be otherwise[14] (65). Whether or not this earlier version was also made by Méliès is open to question. The film is not listed among the Houdin films in Wolff's advertisement (64), but he may have deliberately omitted the title in defference to public opinion.

Wolff also issued a series of twelve films on the life of Christ, which shown together would comprise a film of about 550ft in length. Although the production company and country of origin are not stated, this is almost certainly the remarkable film made by the Frenchman Léar. Other films in Wolff's list are probably also by the same producer and such films as *The Czar in Paris*, *A Bride Retiring to Bed*, *Bois de Boulogne*, and *Manoeuvres of Artillery*, may be attributed to him.[15]

The Passion film was probably the second longest* on a single subject since Robt. W. Paul's *Tour in Spain and Portugal* (600ft) made in September 1896, and as with that film, may sometimes have been shown in its entirety at a single performance. A suggestion to this effect is put forward in a review of the film published in the June issue of *The Photogram:*

'Another very important novelty, "The Passion Play," is by far the greatest effort yet made in the way of arranged pieces. It consists of no less than twelve films, representing twelve principal scenes of the Passion Play, and giving an exhibition of about twenty minutes' duration. Such a subject, so treated, seems sufficient for a complete performance; and, fortunately, it is unusually good from the technical, as well as the artistic or dramatic point of view.'[16]

Philipp Wolff probably held the finest stock of films to be had anywhere, and it certainly included some of the most notable films of the period. Cecil M. Hepworth, who had expressed his regret at the dominance of French films in England, nevertheless had to admit that they were well made, as the following appraisal testifies:

*It was exceeded in length by the Veriscope Company's film of the Corbett-Fitzsimmons fight of 17 March, 1897, which lasted 1 ½ hours.

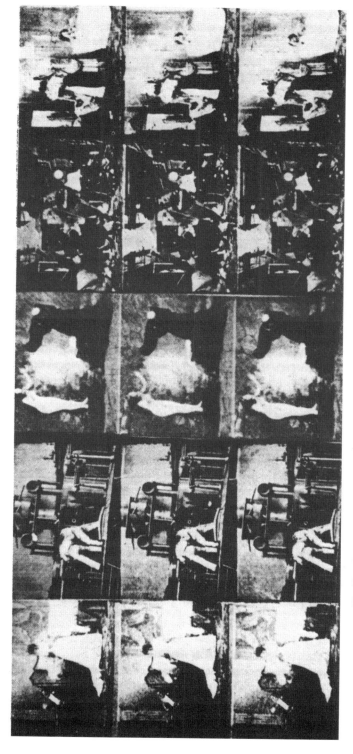

65 Five French films issued by Philipp Wolff in 1897. Left to right: A Bride Unrobing; Graeco-Turkish War, Afloat; Temptation of St Anthony; Graeco-Turkish War, Ashore; French Lady's Bath. From frame illustrations published in Photograms of the Year 1897, p 37 (*Barnes Museum of Cinematography*)

'I was trying a short time ago some pictures which may to described as being of an episodal nature – far more interesting than the interminable street scenes of which there are so many about. These were little comedies in one short act, as arranged for the cinematograph by Philip Wolff (sic). Well acted and well staged, so to speak, they were calculated to please the most exacting, and did it too.'[17]

Of the numerous films on offer from Philipp Wolff, during 1897, the most successful were probably those which he made a special point of publicising. Nearly all were French, and included the following films by Georges Méliès: *The Haunted Castle (Le Chateau Hanté), Nightmare (Le Cauchemar), On the Roofs (Sur les Toits), D. Devant, Conjuror (D. Devant, Prestidigitateur), The Greco-Turkish War* films *(La prise de Tournavos; Exécution d'un Espion; Massacres en Crète; Combat Naval en Grèce),* and *Clowns* (Auguste et Bibb (?)). Other French films given particular notice were *The Passion Play*, and *Carnival in Paris*. A film called *Poor and Rich* is also advertised, but its origin has not been determined. Of the 100 English subjects which Wolff offered, only the following received special publicity: *Party at Buckingham Palace, Death of Nelson, The Indian Mutiny*, and, of course, the Jubilee films.[18] Some of Wolff's other offerings as we have seen, created a sensation of another kind, due to the salacious nature of their subject matter. This caused a good deal of comment in the photographic press and helped to give the films a certain notoriety, although Philipp Wolff himself appears to have refrained from subjecting them to undue publicity. The films in question were, of course, *The Temptation of St. Anthony, The Artist's Model, A Bride Unrobing*, and *A French Lady's Bath;*[19] See illustration 65.

If French films held a dominant place in the English market, the same cannot be said of French apparatus, although there were several machines of French make which were highly esteemed and widely used in Great Britain. Even so, there is nothing to suggest that they were in any way superior to the British product.

The first French apparatus to appear in England was of course, the Cinématographe-Lumière, but it was not until May of 1897 that the machine became available for the first time on the open market.[20] For over a year it had enjoyed an almost exclusive run, under the sole management of Mons. Trewey, at the Empire Theatre, Leicester Square, after being transferred from the Royal Polytechnic, Regent Street. The ending of restrictions on the open sale of the apparatus probably influenced the decision to terminate the performances at the Empire and by July its place had been taken by Professor Jolly's Cinematographe,[21] another French importation. The British agents for the Lumière machine and films, were Fuerst Brothers, who already handled the firm's other products, such as the Limière Dry Plates.[22]

The Cinématographe-Lumière has already been described in the first volume of this history and no further comment is needed, except to note the introduction of a safer form of condenser (66) which came into use in July. We can do little better than quote the official description:

THE BALLOON CONDENSER

The lens which has hitherto been used for projecting, and which served to concentrate the luminous rays, also concentrated the heat very strongly upon the film, and the film was liable to be damaged if exposed too long to this heat. Arrangements have therefore been made to avoid this, and it is now replaced by a so-called balloon-condenser (a glass globe filled with water) . . .

With the balloon globe replacing the condensing lens; the rays of light are concentrated

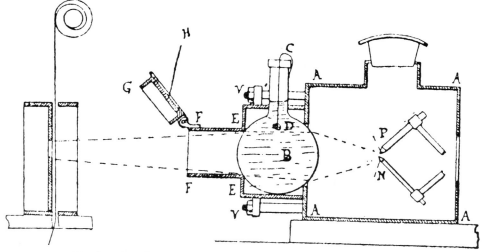

AAAA, Projecting lantern.
B, Condensing balloon.
C, Wire suspending a
D, Small piece of coke.
EEFF, Black enamelled metal box to fix the balloon up against the lantern by means of the bolts and nuts, vv.
G, Stop valve provided with a movable ground glass screen, H.
PN, Electric carbons.

66   Safety Condenser for the Cinématographe-Lumière. A glass globe, filled with water, was substituted for the ordinary condenser lens in the lantern, so as to absorb the heat from the illuminant (*Barnes Museum of Cinematography*)

without any appreciable loss of lighting power, and it absorbs the greatest part of the heat rays. During an hour of continued projection the water comes to a boiling point without the least inconvenience. The temperature remains constant and rises very little. The light by this arrangement is whiter and the effect of the greenish colouration of the light caused by the condensing lens is altogether suppressed.

If the balloon globe has to be removed for any reason, or if the water runs away or evaporates, no condensation of light rays takes place, and consequently the operator need not be afraid of any heat on the film. Thanks to this arrangement it becomes impossible to commit serious mistakes, the whole concentration being produced by the neutral body which absorbs the heat rays.

To avoid projecting when the water is at boiling point it is sufficient to suspend a small piece of coke, attached to a wire, into the globe, and the evaporisation of the water then goes on with the greatest regularity.[23]

The principle of the water-filled glass globe condenser was nothing new. It dates back at least to the 17th century[24] and was often referred to as a lace-maker's glass, although it was used by other craftsmen, who needed a strong concentration of light when exacting work had to be carried out at night. It was then of course, used with a candle or oil lamp.

The belated appearance of the Cinématographe-Lumière on the open market proved to be to its own disadvantage, for now it had to compete with dozens of machines, many of which were technically more advanced. It had too, the further drawback of taking only films perforated in the Lumière fashion, that is to say, with two round holes to each

123

frame. As the Edison perforations were now the ones generally adopted throughout the trade, the Lumière machine fell out of favour with exhibitors who did not wish to restrict themselves in this way. Such a state of affairs however, was soon resolved and a new Lumière projector, to take films of the Edison gauge, was put into production. In the meantime, the stock of Lumière films was made available with a choice of either Lumière or Edison perforations. A catalogue, issued by Fuerst Bros., in May, lists over 300 Lumière films available with either type of perforation. The catalogue received a very favourable review in *The British Journal of Photography:*

> The subjects of the views are very diversified – amusing, instructive, and interesting. Besides the general and comic series, there are numerous views, taken in all the European countries, of notable events and scenes, as well as a selection made from negatives obtained in America. An infinity of delight is included in this catalogue.'[25]

The notice ended on a moral note, having in mind the rather risqué subjects available from other importers of French films at that time:

> There is one point upon which Messrs. Lumière and their agents are to be congratulated and that is, the exclusion from the catalogue of any subjects at all approaching riskiness of character. It has come to our knowledge that animated photographs of a by no means unobjectionable kind are available in certain quarters, but we trust that they will not be suffered to obtain currency in this country. One of the causes that led to the decline in public favour of stereoscopic photography is said to have been its abuse in the direction hinted at, and we are sure we have the concurrence of our readers in expressing the hope that the popularity of animated photography will not be menaced in a similar way.[26]

Another edition of the Lumière film catalogue was issued by Fuerst Bros., in September, this time listing some 600 different subjects, again of course, with a choice of either type of perforation.[27] By December 1897, they were claiming that there were now over one thousand titles to select from.[28] Whether or not, the type of subjects offered was falling out of favour with English audiences, or some other factor was involved, the price of Lumière films gradually decreased during the year. To begin with, the price had been £3 10s each [£3.50].[29] But in June the price was reduced to £3 2s [£3.10],[30] and from 25 August a further reduction was made to £2 10s each [£2.50].[31]

Most of the Lumière films have been preserved, and many have since been shown on television. They are already well documented and there is little point in discussing them further. But a brief comment published at the very end of 1897 may not be amiss:

> '. . . the Lumiere films, as everybody knows, who knows anything in this connection, are still entirely unrivalled for the most important characteristics of a cinematograph film.'[32]

Before the year ended, the Cinématographe-Lumière had been largely superseded by a new machine called the 'Triograph'. Unlike the former, which had served as a projector, printer, and camera combined, Lumière's Triograph was solely designed for projection and used film perforated to the Edison gauge. It still retained some features of the original machine, but in several respects it was substantially remodelled, and when eventually put on sale on the open market it became known as the Lumière

124

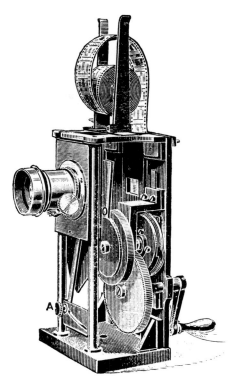

67   The Lumière Triograph Projector, 1897. Designed to use film with Edison-type perforations. Placed on the open market in 1898 as the Lumière Cinématographe Model B (*Barnes Museum of Cinematography*)

Cinématographe Model B (67).[33] As the Triograph, it had its English début at the Washington music hall in London on 26 July, 1897, under the direction of George Francis.[34] During August it was also exhibited at the Queen's, Poplar,[35] and in September at the Bedford.[36] During October and December it played at Gatti's two music halls.[37] But before we follow in more detail, the successful launching of the new Lumière machine, let us see what had become of the famous Felicien Trewey and the original Cinématographe-Lumière.

As the day approached when the Cinématographe would be readily available on the open market, Trewey's engagement at the Empire Theatre, Leicester Square, was at last drawing to a close and by May his long association with that theatre had ceased,[38] after fulfilling a continuous engagement lasting some 59 weeks. It speaks well for the Cinématographe that it should have lasted so long and was able to hold its own against the numerous machines that had been introduced since its début, especially as it had not itself undergone any modification throughout this period, save for the addition of a safer form of condenser. The reason for Trewey's departure is not stated, but one suspects that recent improvements in projection apparatus generally and the introduction of the Triograph in particular was at last rendering the Cinématographe obsolete, at least so far as its theatrical life was concerned. This, coupled with the fact that Trewey was no longer to enjoy exclusive rights to the machine probably all helped to bring about the end of the engagement. Perhaps too, Trewey sensed that his performances could no longer satisfactorily compete with those of his now numerous rivals.

There is a hint of this to be found in the space alloted to the Cinématographe in the pages of *The Era*. The review published on 9 January reveals that the audience was still enthusiastic at this time:

'Several new views, we believe, have been added to the list of those exhibited by the aid of Lumière's Cinématographe, under M. Trewey's management; but the most popular are still the Fire Brigade Call, the Charge of Cavalry, the Water Chute, and the Dragoons swimming their Horses across the River. Several of these views are enthusiastically encored.'[39]

This was followed by another favourable review at the end of the month:

'. . . Monsieur Trewey does not allow Lumiere's Cinématographe to fall in favour for want of judiciously-introduced novelties; and, amongst the pictures which seem less familiar to us in the present series are one of Hyde-park-corner with various vehicles; another of Brooklyn-bridge with trains passing each other; a third showing M. Trewey's adroit manipulation of the piece of felt which he twists into so many hat-shapes; a fourth in which a procession of Chicago policemen is depicted; and a view of the Grand Canal, Venice. The charge of cavalry and the fire brigade call are still great favourites.'[40]

Thereafter, a period of almost three months elapses before the Cinématographe is mentioned again. On 24 April it is accorded the very briefest of notices; after the other music-hall turns have been duly noted and commented upon, the piece concludes: '. . . and the always interesting Cinematographe.'[41] This is the last we hear of the renowned Trewey and the amazing Cinématographe at the Empire.

With the end of its exclusivity in the hands of Trewey, the Cinématographe-Lumière now became available to all, but to what extent the machine was in demand is hard to tell. By this time it was obviously past its prime, but it was certainly to enjoy a measure of popularity with photographic societies. It was exhibited by Jules Fuerst at a meeting of the Royal Photographic Society on 19 October,[42] and again at the Society's Exhibition at Pall Mall on 1 November.[43] At a meeting of the same society on 14 December 'Mr. Jules Fuerst, on behalf of Messrs. Fuerst Brothers, presented the Society with one of Lumiere's cinematographs',[44] this gift probably heralding the end of the machine's commercial life.

Returning to our discussion of the Triograph, this new projector was not available at first on the open market, but was reserved for special exploitation at leading theatres. Its English début at the Washington Theatre of Varieties on 26 July was amazingly successful and was reported with remarkable enthusiasm by *The Era*:

'To procure crowded houses at a suburban hall just now is a task of extreme difficulty, and it can only be achieved by providing some extra powerful attraction. This is just what Mr. R. Rhodes, the proprietor of the Washington, has done, and the name of the magnet that has drawn such large audiences to the York-road establishment this week is the Triograph (Lumière's). With the numerous variations of the Cinématographe that are now on the market, and the improvements that are constantly being made, there will soon be no need for the lover of spectacle to brave the squeezing and the jostling, the dust and the noise that at present have to be faced. He will simply wait a day or two, then repair to one or other of the halls, and from a comfortable seat witness at his ease what used to cost hours of trouble and inconvenience to see. The Triograph is a wonderful machine, and the series of pictures it presents will bear favourable comparison with any set that we have seen. The whole opening of the proscenium is occupied with the screen, and the entire surface thus offered is filled. The advantage thus gained is enormous, for with increased size comes increased clearness of outline, and lookers on are enabled to see distinctly what in many other cases is blurred and uncertain. Then again the pictures are strikingly steady, the flicker having been reduced to a minimum. Some of the views are especially good, and we may select for particular notice a Panorama of La Rochelle Harbour, with a sailing vessel running up to anchor; Cornish Coast and Sea, a fine photograph of an ironbound shore, with the waves throwing themselves in all their fury against the frowning rocks; Cavalry Regiment Jumping Hurdle, the horsemen coming round with a graceful sweep and clearing the obstruction in fine form; a view taken from the rear of a train, in which the illusion is perfect, the station platform and its occupants gradually receding and finally vanishing; a Fire Call, a splendid reproduction of the headquarters of the Brigade, showing how quickly the men and horses can be sent out (encored); and four instalments of the Jubilee Procession. There are various other fine pictures; in fact, the difficulty is to say which are the best, and Mr G. Francis, under whose direction the series is presented, well deserves the enthusiastic call that brings him to the front to bow his acknowledgments. With such favour has the Triograph been received that Mr Rhodes has decided to retain it in the bill for the holidays.'[45]

The report in the *Sunday People* was equally enthusiastic:

The Washington. – This famous hall of Battersea folk is crowded nightly by an audience attracted principally by the animated photographs now being presented under the direction of Mr Francis. Lumière's Triograph, or Macrocosm of Manifold Marvels, gives some of the most finished and steady pictures that have yet been thrown upon a screen, and the photographs are considerably more than life-size, filling nearly the whole of the frame of the proscenium, 27ft. by 24ft. Amongst the most popular of the pictures are cavalry regiment jumping hurdle, the sack race, the musical lunch, and the Jubilee scenes. The most clever of the pictures, to those who know the difficulties of photographing scenery from a railway train or the deck of a steamer, is the panorama taken from the rear of a train – the illusion is perfect. Several fresh pictures are promised during the period of the engagement of the Triograph.[46]

The theatrical paper *Entr'acte* also spoke well of the occasion:

A remarkably good series of animated pictures are on view at the Washington, projected by Lumière's Triograph, under the direction of Mr G. Francis. They occupy the whole of the proscenium opening, 27ft. by 24ft., and embrace several good and novel views. Business at the Washington is very brisk.[47]

It was never the intention to give the Triograph an exclusive run at any one particular theatre in London, as had been the case with the original Lumière Ciné matographe. Indeed, the exploitation of the new machine was to be much more broadly based, catering more particularly to the less affluent members of society. There was to be no West End showing, with the attendant glamour of an Empire Theatre, or the added attraction of a world celebrity such as Trewey. George Francis, as 'director' of the Triograph, performed quite a different function. His role seems to have been entirely technical, no doubt being responsible for the proper installation of the machine and screen and seeing to it that the films were correctly projected and an appropriate choice of subjects made. The sole representative and business manager of the concern was Aspinal Thiodon, who happened also to be the manager of the Washington. It was to him that all enquiries and bookings regarding the Triograph were to be addressed.

Advertised as 'Lumiere's Triograph, and Macrocosm of Manifold Marvels, the perfection of all Cinematographs',[48] its engagement at the Washington lasted ten weeks,[49] with performances every evening at 10.15,[50] supported of course, by a full programme of music-hall turns. When, on 23 August, the representative of *The Era* again visited the theatre, he found that several new pictures had been added to the programme since his previous visit. Unfortunately, a slight breakdown occurred towards the very end of the performance, but this did not deter him from writing another favourable report of the show:

"The Batterseasider is like the hero of a certain popular song – "He knows a good thing when he sees it," and what is more he patronises it. Mr Rhodes, the proprietor of the York-road variety house, has found this out, and is not only providing a good thing, but a succession of good things. The Triograph is one of these, and so successful an engagement has this proved that, though it was in the programme when we last visited this house some weeks ago, we found on Monday a crowded audience enjoying to the full the fine series of pictures projected on to the screen by Lumiere's machine. As we have before stated, these photographs are of unusual size, occupying the whole proscenium opening – in actual measurement, 27ft. by 24ft. This, of course is an immense advantage, as it brings into prominence many details which are lost in smaller views. Some fresh films have been added since our last notice, and the collection now comprises Turkish Infantry, Train Arriving at Station, Venice Panorama, a view of the city of canals, with stately palaces lining the waterway, along which glide various gondolas; Musical Drill (Scots Guards), Arab Market, A Trick on the Gardener (always popular), Scots Guards Marching Past in Hyde-park, Receding Train, a marvellously illusive picture; French Artillery Rear-limbering up, a fine view of a portion of the ironbound coast of Cornwall, Fire call at the Headquarters of the M.F.B., Southwark-bridge-road; Royal Horse Artillery, the Marines, Household Troops and the Queen. The last two, unfortunately, could not be shown on Monday owing to a little difficulty with the electric light, but so satisfied were the audience with what they had already seen that they took the limitation very good-naturedly, and heartily cheered Mr G. Francis when he came forward to make a little apology.'[51]

In the meantime, the Triograph had also opened at the Queen's, Poplar, where it played for four weeks.[52] Although some of the films duplicated those already being shown at the Washington, this item on the bill was still regarded as one of the major attractions and was duly reported as such in *The Era*:

'. . . . A specially interesting item is Lumière's Triograph, which is under the able direction of Mr G. Francis. The splendid views include clowns doing the hat trick, panorama of La Rochelle Harbour, squad drill (Scots Guards, Wellington Barracks), Cornish coast and sea, comic scene, "Teasing the Gardener," cavalry regiment jumping hurdle; panorama view taken from rear of train, the illusion being so perfect that one imagines that one is moving away from the picture; Queen's Guard, St James's Palace, better known as "Musical Lunch;" fire call. Queen in Hyde-park and the crowd following. Pictures of the Jubilee procession include Marines dragging guns, Colonial Governors and respective troops, foreign envoys, and Her Majesty the Queen.'[53]

Other theatres where the Triograph was shown during 1897 included Gatti's, Westminster Bridge Road and Gatti's Charing Cross; the Bedford, Camden Town, where it played for four weeks; the Grand, Clapham Junction, for three weeks; Palace, Croydon, two weeks; Empire, Brighton, two weeks; and the People's Palace, Bristol, for two weeks. In Ireland it was specially engaged for the opening of the Empire Theatre, Dublin, and ran there for two weeks. It was also engaged for three weeks at the Empire Theatre, Belfast.[54] The show at the Bedford was written up in *The Era*, and among the fifteen or so films shown, the following are mentioned:

:. . . a comic incident in which a soldier and a nursemaid figure; a duel fought in France, the tragic ending to which being most realistic; the Scots Guards in Hyde-park; a musical drill; the Queen entering London on June 21st, 1897, and the crowd following; a laughable scene, "teasing the gardener;" La Rochelle Harbour; cavalry jumping hurdles; a fire call; and the Jubilee procession, showing her Majesty and escort.'[55]

The Triograph had its longest run of the year at Gatti's, Westminster Bridge Road, known for short as Gatti's (Road), where it ran for several months. The most memorable event during this period was the visit to the theatre of A. Promio, the distinguished operator employed by Lumière. Promio had witnessed the first performance of the Cinématographe at Lyon in June 1895, and from that moment was determined to enter the services of Auguste and Louis Lumière. His wishes were soon granted for by the beginning of 1896 he was in their employ. Almost immediately, he became one of their ace roving cameramen and operators, and was the first to introduce the Cinématographe to Spain, where he was also responsible for filming the many Spanish subjects to be found listed in the Lumière catalogues. He subsequently visited many other countries in a similar capacity, including England, Belgium, Sweden, Turkey, Italy, Germany and the United States. It was during his visit to Venice, he claims, that he first got the idea of taking 'panoramic views' as they were then called, and which we would now more properly refer to as 'travelling shots'. Mounting his camera in a gondola, he took passing shots of the palaces and buildings lining the canals, as he glided smoothly by.[56] Panoramic views of this kind quickly became popular and thereafter cameras were mounted on a host of moving vehicles such as trains, trams, ships and cars, etc.

Promio's visit to Gatti's (Road) music hall therefore, did not go unnoticed, since he was now somewhat of a celebrity. He was there for the opening night of the Triograph's first appearance at this theatre and for the occasion ceremoniously operated the projector himself.[57] The films were greeted with loud applause and those singled out for special favour were the Swimming Bath, the Fire Alarm, the 13th Hussars and 'a fight between four girls, a man, and a dog.'[58] The following Thursday, 21 October, Promio gave a private performance at Gatti's, of a number of English and Irish subjects, but it is not clear whether these films were actually photographed by him. Quite likely they were, and the chief reason for Promio's visit to the British Isles was probably in pursuit of such subjects. Since so little is known at present about Promio's eventful career, it may be as well to quote the details of this performance as they are related in *The Era:*

'The possibilities of animated photographs would seem to be endless, and this fact was impressed upon us by a private exhibition given by M. Promio, of the celebrated firm of Lumière, at Gatti's (Road), on Thursday, when a number of views of English and Irish subjects were shown for the first time. These photographs, we were given to understand by Mr George Francis, who acted as cicerone, were taken for Messrs Moss and Thornton, the eminent firm of music hall proprietors, and will be shown on their circuit in England, Scotland, and Ireland. Many of the scenes were panoramic, being taken from a moving object. In this way we were shown some capital views of the Mersey and Liverpool Docks, photographed from the Overhead Railway. Some good scenes in Dublin included the O'Connell Bridge and Sackville-street, and pictures full of fine animation and real activity were supplied by the Dublin Fire Brigade getting to work and a company of cavalry exercising over hurdles. The audience was also shown the scenery of Blackrock, the country round Drogheda, a street in Belfast, and other places of interest. A selection only of the numerous pictures will be given, and the exhibition should certainly be an attraction, as the vibration which has hitherto been the *bête noire* of animated photographs is conspicuous by its absence in the Triograph.'[59]

On another occasion, a special afternoon performance of the Triograph was arranged at Gatti's, Charing Cross, for Her Majesty's Regiment of Scots Guards, the show taking place at 2.30 on 23 December.[60] Meanwhile, the Triograph was continuing its successful run at Gatti's (Road), where it was still proving to be one of the most popular items in the programme:

'The Triograph still forms one of the strongest attractions in the bill at the popular little hall in Westminster-bridge-road. For weeks it has acted like a magnet, and has drawn crowds to see the fine series of pictures at the command of the operator. These "graphs" enjoy the immense advantage of being able to constantly vary their entertainment so that even the regular visitor always finds something fresh to admire, to interest, or to amuse. Among the pictures at Gatti's are a troop of Hussars jumping hurdles, a fine view of a body of well-mounted horsemen taking their timber in first-rate fashion; the always-popular Turn-out of the Fire Brigade; three clowns doing an acrobatic turn; a Steamboat on the Thames; the Snowball Fight, with an unhappy cyclist made the target for the icy bullets; a Bed Trick, in which a would-be sleeper is unceremoniously bundled on to the floor; Bayonet Exercise; and Bathing at Milan, a wonderfully realistic photograph, showing the natationists jumping, diving, and turning somersaults into the water. The startling part of the picture is when it is reversed and we see the whole thing backwards – the splash, then the bather emerging from the water flying through the air, and resuming his position on the diving board. The effect is indescribable.'[61]

Professor Jolly's Cinematographe, which replaced Lumière's at the Empire, was another French importation. It was patented by Joseph-Henri Joly and constructed by Ernest Normandin and originally known as the Joly-Normandin Cinématographe.[62] It seems likely that the name was changed for reasons connected with the tragic fire at the Charity Bazaar in the rue Jean Goujon, Paris, where on 4 May 1897, one hundred and forty people were burnt to death. The Joly-Normandin Cinématographe was not at fault, but the accident occured through the carelessness of the operators whilst recharging the oxy-ether saturator used as the illuminant in the projector.[63] The adverse publicity which the projector received in consequence of this calamity, was reason enough for the change of name, even though the machine itself was eventually exonerated.

The apparatus could be used either for projection, or as a camera (68) and employed an intermittent mechanism actuated by a ratchet and pawl device. Each revolution of a heavy flywheel, driven by gearing, caused the pawl to move the ratchet-wheel round to the extent of one quarter of a revolution. This ratchet-wheel was directly connected to the same axle as the sprocket-wheel which drove the film. The linkage was so arranged that the ratchet-wheel was at rest three times as long as the period of motion.[64]

The English début of Prof. Jolly's Cinématographe (as it was called in England) took

68 The Joly-Normandin Cinématographe. Patented by Joseph Henri Joly and constructed by Ernest Normandin. This machine was introduced into England as Prof Jolly's Cinématographe and received its première at the Empire Theatre, Leicester Square, on 19 July, 1897 (*Barnes Museum of Cinematography*)

place at the Empire Theatre, Leicester Square, on Monday 19 July, when a series of films of Queen Victoria's Diamond Jubilee procession were shown. These received very favourable comment in the *Era's* regular column devoted to the London music hall programmes, but little was said about the apparatus in general, the reviewer simply remarking that 'the pictures are for the most part surprisingly clear and distinct' and that 'Professor Jolly's cinématographe ought to prove a strong attraction at the Empire for some time to come.'[65]

On 23 November, Jolly's Cinématographe had the honour of being exhibited at a Royal Command Film Performance at Windsor Castle as part of the birthday celebrations of Prince Henry of Battenberg.[66] The performance was accompanied by a special selection of music performed by the Empire orchestra under its director Leopold Wenzel. To mark the occasion, a souvenir programme was produced, printed on

69 Souvenir programme printed on satin, commemorating the Royal Command Film Performance given at Windsor Castle on 23 November, 1897, by Prof Jolly's Cinematographe and the Empire Theatre Orchestra (*Barnes Museum of Cinematography*)

satin[67] (69). George Capel, the stage-manager of the Empire, announced the films shown, which included the Diamond Jubilee procession and the Naval Review. Also part of the programme was Taffary's performing dogs, and the royal youngsters present, were much interested in their performance.[68] The whole entertainment was under the management of H. J. Hitchins, manager of the Empire, who had the honour of being presented to the queen, and later received a most gracious message of approval, plus a diamond pin.[69]

The Joly apparatus was not for sale in England on the open market, but instead, was available on hire for limited engagements from the British Cinematographe Company, Limited, 36 Victoria Street, Westminster, the manager of which was George Manners.[70]

Another machine of French make which appeared on the English market during 1897, was the Cinéma Dom-Martin, a combined projector, camera and printer (70). It possessed a single spring escapement and took film of the standard Edison gauge, but the mechanism engaged only two perforations at a time.[71] It was also said to have 'no rubbing surfaces to scratch or tear the film.'[72] References to the apparatus in English are few, which seems to suggest that it was not widely used on this side of the channel. It was relatively cheap, the complete outfit, with lantern, costing £16 and the films £2 each.[73] It was advertised in England by the maker, Dom-Martin, a manufacturing engineer of 51 bis. Boulevard St Germain, Paris, who specialised in photographic apparatus and materials.[74]

A machine which is not identified by name, but somewhat similar in shape to the Cinéma Dom-Martin, although different in principle, was patented by René Bunzli and Pierre-Victor Continsouza, the latter a well known engineer who later constructed apparatus for Pathè Frères. Although patented on 14 November 1896 (French Patent No 261292) it seems unlikely that the apparatus was seen in England until 1897. It was a combined camera/projector, with a Maltese-cross and 2-pin cam movement, with a lens by Darlot of Paris. A special feature of the machine was the clockwork drive applied to the take-up spindle when used as a camera. An apparatus with these features

70   The Cinema Dom-Martin. A combined camera, printer and projector, manufactured by Dom Martin, Paris (*Barnes Museum of Cinematography*)

71 The Rollograph. A combined camera and projector, with Maltese-cross movement and lens by Darlot of
Paris. Patented by René Bunzli & Pièrre Victor Continsouza (French patent no 261292. 14 November, 1896)
Marketed in England by Levi, Jones & Co (*Barnes Museum of Cinematography*)

was sold in England by Levi, Jones & Co, under the name Rollograph, and there is no doubt that this was the apparatus designed by Bunzli and Continsouza. An example of the apparatus is to be seen in the Barnes Museum of Cinematography (71).

In addition to the apparatus already mentioned, there were three French machines, first introduced in 1896, which still remained on the English market. These were the Kinetographe De Bedts, the Vitagraphe of Clement & Gilmer, and the Demeny Chronophotographe produced by L. Gaumont & Cie. All three have been described and illustrated in the first volume of this history, and there is little to add except for a few remarks concerning their roles during 1897.

Of the three, the Kinetographe De Bedts is the one mentioned least. It was one of the few foreign machines included in 'A Review of Some Present Day Machines' by Cecil M. Hepworth, published in *The Amateur Photographer* for 24 September,[75] which indicates that the apparatus was not yet obsolete, although it was one of the very first to appear on the market. Clement & Gilmer's Vitagraphe is also included in Hepworth's survey, under its English name Vitagraph. It is reported as being well made and to have met with considerable favour in its own country. According to a report published in *The Photogram* for June, Clement & Gilmer had just issued a new catalogue 'descriptive of their Vitagraph and accessories, and giving complete list of their large series of

72   The Mutograph, or, Cinématographe-Griolet. A combined camera and projector made by Clement & Gilmer, Paris. Introduced into Gt Britain in 1897 (*Barnes Museum of Cinematography*)

135

73   60mm film. Example of the wide gauge film used in the Gaumont-Demeny Chronophotographe (*Barnes Museum of Cinematography*)

films. Amongst the novelties which they announce is a special apparatus intended for both photography and projection which is so arranged that the films can be changed in daylight.'[76] The special apparatus referred to was the Mutograph, which was intended chiefly for amateurs[77] (72). It was not unlike the Kinetographe de Bedts in appearance, but with a different intermittent movement. Eug. Trutat in his book *La Photographie Animée* (Paris, 1899), refers to this apparatus as the 'Cinématographe-Griolet'.[78] This is a far better name for it because the name Mutograph had already been used by the American Mutoscope Company for their camera. Moreover, J. N. Maskelyne, of Egyptian Hall fame, had also used a very similar name for the apparatus he invented, viz: Mutagraph. Such nomenclature can lead to a great deal of confusion. Clement & Gilmer's Mutograph, or Cinématographe-Griolet, was actually the invention of Raoul Grimoin-Sanson, of Cinéorama fame. In his autobiography *Le Film de ma Vie* (Paris, 1926) page 79, he gives an illustration of the apparatus, plus a key to the principal components, but does not describe it or provide any facts regarding its history. Moreover, the illustration he uses is identical to the one found in Trutat's treatise, which is the official one taken from the manufacturer's block, and the one we reproduce in this book.

The Gaumont-Demeny Chronophotographe, also mentioned in Hepworth's survey, had first been demonstrated in London late in 1896, but does not appear to have been used for public exhibition until early the following year. Its success was immediate for, according to a report published in March, the demand already exceeded supply.[79] The apparatus was a combined camera/projector, which used a large gauge film, 60mm wide (73). Hepworth's report states: 'All the operators that I have met who use the Gaumont machine speak well of it, both as regards its simple working and the excellence of the results.'[80] Yet despite its obvious merits, the size of the film was against it for commercial purposes and in December it was replaced by the Gaumont Chrono, which used film of the standard Edison gauge.[81] The Chrono was also a combined camera/projector and retained the Demeny 'dog' movement for its intermittent motion (74). To launch the new Chrono, L. Gaumont & Cie, had taken a temporary office at 7 Hills Place, Oxford Circus, London, W., but during the following year moved to a more permanent address at 25 Cecil Court, Charing Cross Road. They were soon to play a very prominent part in the British film industry.

There is reason to believe that the French were almost as prolific as the English in the manufacture of cinematographic equipment, and it seems reasonable to assume that many more machines of French make found their way into England than have been accounted for in this survey. A detailed examination of French apparatus manufactured during this period, has yet to be made – a study best undertaken on the other side of the channel.

In connection with L. Gaumont, a rather curious device must be mentioned called 'La Grille', for which a British patent application was made on 19 March, under the heading, 'An Open-work or Perforated Screen for Obviating the Effects of Scintilation experienced in Viewing Projections of Animated Photographs' (No. 7214). It was a simple anti-flicker device which took the form of a little perforated paper fan designed to be held in the hand and waved gently in front of the eyes whilst watching the screen (75). It might be said that Gaumont had issued this device to counteract the flicker in their Chronophotographe, since it was introduced when that apparatus was still on the market. Of course Gaumont never admitted that it should be used in connection with their own apparatus, but the fact remains that no more was heard of "La Grille" after

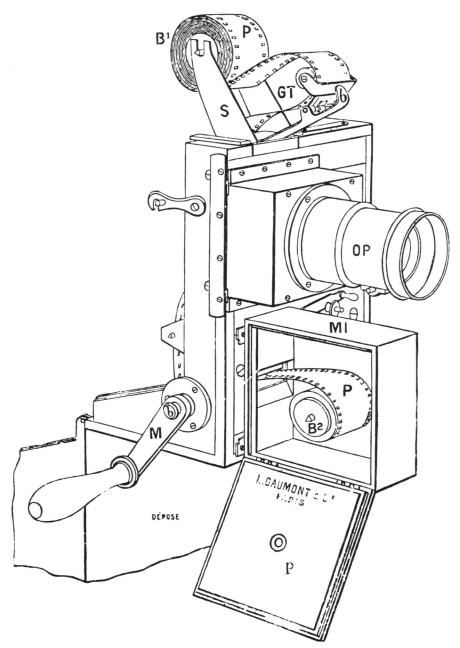

74 The Gaumont-Demeny 35mm Chronophotographe, 1897. A combined camera and projector made by L. Gaumont & Cie, Paris. Fitted with Demeny's patent beater or 'dog' movement (*Barnes Museum of Cinematography*)

75 La Grille. 'An open-work or perforated screen for obviating the effects of scintilation experienced in viewing projections of animated photographs.' Introduced by L. Gaumont & Cie, Paris. This simple anti-flicker device was held in the hand and waved gently in front of the eyes whilst watching the screen (*Barnes Museum of Cinematography*)

the departure of the Chronophotographe from the scene. We know that a flicker problem had existed in that apparatus because an attempt had been made to overcome the defect by the use of a special shutter consisting of a circular glass plate on which several thicknesses of tissue-paper were pasted, each shorter than the other. By this means the change from dark to light was gradual, and even where the tissues were most dense, the screen was partially lighted.[82] This was not the only apparatus in which a semi-opaque shutter had been used in an attempt to eliminate flicker; other examples have already been noted, such as Wolff's Vitaphotoscope for instance. Of course the defect in the Chronophotographe was exagerated owing to the extra large gauge of the film employed, but one obvious factor contributing to flicker in those days, and this applies equally to other makes of projector, was the manual method of operation. If the operator failed to crank the handle fast enough, flicker was bound to arise. The whole crux of the matter however, was in establishing the correct ratio between the period during which the film is in motion and the period when it is at rest. In other words, the amount of time it takes for one frame to succeed another should be appreciably less than the period during which the film is stationary. This simple fact was not at first grasped by some manufacturers, and even when it was, they evidently did not possess the mechanical expertise to put it into practice.

Gaumont's explanation of 'La Grille', as recounted in *The Photogram*, is worth quoting in full, if only for its absurdity:

'The prevention of flicker has been the great problem of kinetographic projectors, and the simple apparatus by which M. Gaumont claims to have completely overcome the difficulty is full of interest. It is merely a light, black fan, pierced, as is indicated by its name, La Grille, with a complete network of small holes. By waving this gently to and fro, and viewing the screen through the grating, M. Gaumont assures us that the most unsteady kinetogram can be seen with pleasure and without strain to the eyes. Not only so, but he further claims that the very quick running which has been adopted by most kinetographers in the effort to secure a smooth appearance of motion, becomes unnecessary. It becomes possible to give longer exposures to each section of the film in making the original negative, and by working more slowly to represent a much longer phase of action with a given length of film. La Grille is made in an exceedingly cheap from, selling in France at 25 francs a hundred, so that as M. Gaumont points out, it might almost be given away to spectators, especially if it were used for advertising purposes.'[83]

The account in *The Optical Magic Lantern Journal* states that the device can be sold for about £1 per 100.[84] But *The Amateur Photographer* sounded a satirical note in their approach to the problem:

'The "Kinedodgescope" is the latest invention relating to applied animatography. Even the best exhibitions of animated photographs are to some extent painful to witness, owing to the dancing and flickering of the projected image. The "Kinedodgescope" is designed to mitigate these sufferings, and happily the contrivance is practically within the reach of all, though whether it will be adopted except by those strong-minded individuals who will do or dare anything in the cause of science is problematical.
,And what is the "Kinedodgescope"? According to Mr. Appleton, of Bradford, it simply consists of the human hand, which, extended fan-like, is held close to the eye and moved

76 Dr Smith's Patent Cinematograph. Manufactured by Dr J. H. Smith & Co, Zurich, and distributed in Gt Britain by Archibald Rider, 83 Mortimer Street, London (*Feroze Sarosh Collection*)

quickly from right to left so as to break up the field of vision. The device is said to be as effective as it is simple and cheap; but it is to be hoped that variations of the prescribed movement will not be indulged in.'[85]

The Swiss firm of Dr. J. H. Smith & Co, of Zurich, established a foothold in England during 1897, and became noted for its high quality cinematograph film. Its negative stock was said to be 'much faster than usual,' and that for positive prints. 'beautifully transparent and of good quality.'[86] The firm's English agent was Archibald Rider (83 Mortimer St, Regent St, London, W.),[87] who had recently commenced business on his own account, having formerly been manager of the Kinetographe Company which

77 A section of 70mm Biograph film (positive). A special wide gauge film used by the American Mutoscope & Biograph Syndicate Ltd. Paper prints from the negative could be used in the Mutoscope (*Kodak Museum, Harrow*)

handled the Kinetographe De Bedts in this country. Reports published in July[88] and September[89] speak of his plans to sell Dr. Smith's patent cinematograph and camera, which suggest that the apparatus was not available as yet. However, a more definite statement made in November seems to indicate that the apparatus was indeed ready by that time.[90] Smith's cinematograph had been patented in England on 12 January 1897 (British Patent No 886) and was of a most unusual design. The mechanism was contained in a drum-shaped casing, pierced with equally spaced openings and the whole drum acted as a muliple shutter. The feed was accomplished by a revolving eccentric which struck the film.[91] The patent specification states that the apparatus, with a little adaptation, could be used as a camera, printer, and projector. A specimen of this machine is in the Feroze Sarosh Collection (76).

142

The first American apparatus to make an impact in England was the Biograph, owned by the American Mutoscope Company (837–841 Broadway, New York). Like the Chronophotographe, this too took a large gauge film (77), but unlike the Demeny machine, was never sold on the open market. Instead it was leased out under contract with its own specially trained operators, since the apparatus was rather complicated to run. The films for use in the projector were photographed with a special camera called the Mutograph which was also company controlled. Both the camera and projector were largely the brain child of W. K. L. Dickson, who had previously been responsible for the invention of the Edison Kinetograph and Kinetoscope.

Dickson, after his departure from Edison, had joined forces with Elias Koopman, Harry Marvin, and Herman Casler to form the K.M.C.D. combination, the object of which was to exploit the Mutoscope, a machine for viewing a series of picture-cards, flicked over by cranking a handle (later commonly known as 'What the Butler Saw').[92] The venture soon came to embrace the Biograph and the K.M.C.D. was officially incorporated as the American Mutoscope Company, subsequently to become the American Mutoscope & Biograph Co.

The Biograph had its American debut on 14 September 1896, at the Alvin Theater, Pittsburgh. Gordon Hendricks has already written an authorititive history of the beginnings of the Biograph in America,[93] so we need only concern ourselves here with its activities in England.

The English debut of the Biograph took place on 18 March 1897 at the Palace Theatre, London,[94] and immediately created a sensation by the immense size of the projected pictures. The screen completely filled the vast proscenium area of the theatre[95] 'with really wonderful results.'[96]

The films were taken and projected at about 40 pictures per second, with the result that rapidly moving objects were photographed without the usual blur.[97] The size of the picture area too, about 70 × 55mm, made it possible to fill a larger screen than was obtainable with films of the standard Edison gauge. Both these factors naturally required an extremely efficient illuminant in the projection apparatus, a feature which was not lacking at the Palace, since the pictures were specifically described as being 'wonderfully well lighted.'[98]

The Palace Theatre had previously abstained from including 'animated photographs' in its programmes,[99] so it speaks well for the Biograph that this policy was changed. It was so successful in fact, that the Biograph ran at this theatre for over three years, the performances finally coming to a close in September 1899.[100]

A preview of the first programme to be presented at the Palace by the American Biograph, was held on 18 March, and received a lengthy review in *The Era*:

THE BIOGRAPH AT THE PALACE

The American Biograph, introduced to a select audience at the Palace Theatre on Thursday afternoon, is the invention of Mr Herman Casler, of New York, and is very similar in the effects it produces to the numerous other "graphs" which have become the vogue in every music hall programme during the past twelve months. The blurring and indistinctness that often mar other graph views have been entirely conquered by Mr Casler, and there is less of the "flickering" or vibration that is often a common drawback to such shows. The pictures, too, are larger, and form a most interesting series. To numbers of English playgoers Mr Joseph Jefferson, the admirable American actor, is only a name; but now one will be able to see him moving and acting in the part he has made his own – Rip. We are introduced to Mr Jefferson in

143

the famous toast scene from Washington Irving's wonderful story. So realistic is the effect produced that one seems to hear Mr Jefferson say "Here's to your health and your family's may they live long and prosper." The ability of the Biograph to reproduce the most rapid motion is shown in the picture of the Empire State Express, New York Central Railway, going at sixty miles an hour. This is one of the fastest long distance trains in the world. The locomotive, while running, is seen taking water from the track tank, the spray sent out from both sides of the engine being distinctly visible. The Chicago Limited Express in the Alleghany Mountains gives the untravelled a capital idea of some of the most beautiful American scenery. In the distance this express can be seen winding in and out around the bases of the heights. On the right hand side the Juaniata River glides tranquilly by. A rush and a roar and the express is rushing by before us and is gone. We were introduced to President M'Kinley at his home in Canton, Ohio, and there were no less than three views of Niagara – as seen from Luna Island, showing the suspension bridge in the background, the Whirlpool Rapids, where Captain Matthew Webb lost his life, and the Upper Rapids. A really droll picture is the piccaninny's bath, in which an unwilling Negro "kiddy" is being washed with remarkable vigour. The mother evidently will have no nonsense, and the boy is soused again and again in the tub. A sequel to this picture is "Pussy's Bath," in which the process of bathing is imitated by a child with a kitten. All goes well till pussy resents the treatment with a scratch. The rapid change from joy to grief on the features of the little girl is very clearly shown. Another comic picture is that representing the "Prodigal's Return." The humour of this is accentuated in the next scene, in which the same actions are reversed, the ludicrous effect of the hat, coat and garments flying up from the floor on to the wearer's person being heartily laughed at. Still another comic picture is "Boys will be Boys." Herein are seen a couple of mischievous urchins placing a brick under a hat. No sooner have they hidden round the corner to watch developments than a tipsy passer-by kicks the hat and the brick and rolls over in the snow. The series also includes a coloured representation of the kissing and smoking episode between Trilby and Little Billee; the Stable on Fire; the New York Fire Department responding to an alarm, the scene being the corner of Thirty-fourth-street and Broadway; a full dress parade of the 14th United States Infantry, the firing of the 10-inch disappearing gun – an interesting view obtained by special permission of the U.S. War Department at the testing grounds off Sandy Hook; Broadway and Madison squares, New York; Sandow's muscular exhibition; a New England winter scene entitled "Ye Merrie Sleigh Bells;" and several others. The Biograph will be introduced into the Palace programme in place of the Tableaux Vivants, and Mr Charles Morton is to be congratulated on having secured such an interesting and attractive exhibition.'[101]

A matter of particular interest was the innovation of exhibiting 'stills' of the programme outside the theatre, an entirely novel idea for the times, which did not escape the attention of that indefatigable commentator, Cecil M. Hepworth:

'The management has hit upon an attractive method of advertising this new "turn." Outside the theatre there are four enlargements of considerable size, each labelled, "One of a series of several thousand Mutoscopic Photographs, taken at the rate of forty per second for the American Biograph by the American Mutoscope Company." One of these represents the firing of a 10-inch disappearing-carriage gun, and if the rest of the film is as wood (sic) as this particular photograph it should mark a step in the direction of utility as well as of general interest. Anyway, the subject is a distinct departure from the general run of these things, and as such should be welcome.'[102]

The Biograph programme seems to have remained virtually unchanged for several weeks, and when the *Era's* reporter again visited the Palace in May, he found little new to report:

'. . . A strong attraction here is the American Biograph, the views in which are wonderfully distinct and large. The stable on fire, with the grooms hurriedly bringing out animals and carriages; the fine view of Niagara Falls; the sleighing scene, showing the snow as it is dashed up by the runners and the feet of the horses; Mr Joseph Jefferson delivering the well-known speech in *Rip Van Winkle* about "your health and your family's health, and may they live long and prosper;" the bath of a "piccaninny," and that of a pussy-cat; the pillow-fight between little children, and the motor fire-engine and express trains in motion are items which always evoke enthusiastic approval.'[103]

In a subsequent programme, a Biograph film of a completely different character was introduced, which later had many English imitators. It was taken from the front of a locomotive with the Mutograph camera mounted on the cattle-guard of a West Shore express, travelling at full speed.[104] The film was first shown at the Palace Theatre on Monday 25 October and the novelty of the scene singled out for special mention in *The Amateur Photographer*:

'Here we have a rapid change of scene, the spectators in spirit flashing past object after object. The entrance of the Haverstraw tunnel [New York] is seen in the distance, and it widens until the dark area covers the screen. The white speck next seen expands as the train travels on until the train emerges from the tunnel, and new scenes appear'.[105]

Equally enthralled by this cinematic experience was the reporter for *The Era*:

'The Biograph, which originally came to the Palace for a month, has now become one of the most popular attractions at the Shaftesbury-avenue establishment since its inception as a music hall. The most recent addition to the pictures is a series of panoramic effects produced, so we are informed, by the placing of a camera in the "cab" of the locomotive of a West Shone (sic) express. Instead, therefore, of looking on at a scene, the spectator now participates, so to say, in the movement – becomes, as it were, part and parcel of the picture. With a very slight stretch of imagination he can fancy himself tearing along at express speed on a cow-catcher, with the landscape simply leaping towards him. He sees the stretch of metals before him, just as if he were travelling with the train, which rushes into the tunnel, seen looming ahead long before the train enters the darkness, from which it emerges into a beautiful country, bathed in sunlight. A more exciting and sensational piece of realism has never been presented to an audience.'[106]

When one remembers the immense size of the picture projected on the screen at the Palace, it will be realised what an impact this simple subject had on contemporary audiences, who hitherto had been accustomed to subjects recorded with a static camera. This type of subject came to be known as a 'phantom ride'. The first English film of this kind was probably one called *The Phantom Ride Through Chislehurst Tunnel on the S.E.R.* [South Eastern Railway], and advertised by Chard's Vitagraph on 9 April 1898, as 'the only English Phantom Ride on sale'.[107]

Commenting upon the Biograph film, *The Photographic News* recalled a somewhat similar effect in a film of Birt Acres:

'Some months ago Mr. Birt Acres showed us a series of animated photographs of the Cambridge University Boat Club practising on the Thames in preparation for the annual contest with Oxford. Mr. Acres followed the crew in a small boat, making his exposures on the

145

78   Programme of the Palace Theatre of Varieties, Cambridge Circus, London, for the week commencing September, 1897. Item 14 on the bill consists of a number of films presented by the American Biograph including several English subjects (*Barnes Museum of Cinematography*)

journey, and the effect in (sic) the screen was a realistic representation of the oarsmen as they rowed over the course, the bridges and river banks, "passing by you," at it were. We at once saw that there was something in the idea which lent itself to great effect for projection purposes, and it appears to have been adopted by the shrewd people who are showing the biograph at the Palace Theatre. The spectator, it is said, can imagine himself on the "cow-catcher" of an American locomotive as it tears along at the rate of sixty miles an hour. This effect has been obtained by placing a camera on the "cab" of a locomotive. The long track of shining metals stretches out in front, the lever is pulled full over, and the engine dashes on at topmost speed. For a time the run is in the open day. Then a dark spot looms ahead; this is the mouth of the tunnel, and towards it the spectator is carried, as it were, on a phantom train. The spot grows larger and blacker, then suddenly the tunnel is entered and the train is overwhelmed in gloom, but a speck of light shines in the darkness; it broadens out, and with a rush the tunnel is passed, and once more the train is flying on past fields and hedges in the sunlit country. We have borrowed this piece of vivid description from a contemporary. We also note that at the Empire Theatre a photographic panorama taken from a train in motion is shown. Remarkable to note how frequently great minds think alike!'[108]

The Birt Acres film referred to, was taken from the stern of the *Hibernia* whilst steaming at between twenty-two and twenty-three knots per hour.[109] The film was probably shot some time in March, that is, prior to the race which took place on 3 April. The film does not seem to have been widely shown, but we know it was screened at a meeting of the London & Provincial Photographic Association on 22 April.[110] Acres also attempted to film the actual race itself, from the umpire's launch, but owing to bad weather the results were unsatisfactory.[111] As we have already noted, Lumière's operator, A. Promio, claims to have discovered the moving panorama or travelling shot whilst filming in Venice, an assignment that can be placed in the year 1896. The following January, one of the Lumière films shown by Trewey at the Empire, was 'a view of the Grand Canal, Venice',[112] which may very well have been the so called 'panoramic' scene taken by Promio from a gondola. It is impossible to say whether or not Birt Acres was aware of this film when he boarded the *Hibernia* to film the University crew, but his film is evidently the first English example of the genre. It is interesting to note that the list of Lumière films published by Maguire & Baucus Ltd in September 1897 (see Appendix 2) includes no less than twenty-two examples of moving 'panoramic' views (or travelling shots) some of which are specifically described as 'taken from moving train', or 'taken from a boat' as the case may be.

Gordon Hendricks informs us that W. K. L. Dickson left for Europe on 12 May 1897, where he continued to supply foreign subjects for the American Mutoscope Company.[113] Most probably his first assignment was centered on London and it was he who was responsible for some, if not all, of the English subjects which began to be included in the Biograph programmes. Among the English subjects listed in a programme for the week commencing 13 September 1897 (78) were the following:[114]

Henley Regatta
The Eclipse Stakes, Sandown Park
The Diamond Jubilee Procession
The Naval Review at Spithead
The Military Review at Aldershot
Afternoon Tea in the Garden of Clarence House
H.R.H. The Prince of Wales Leaving Marlborough House

The last two films were singled out for special mention in the *Era's* regular review of the London music halls, on 4 September:

'In our last notice of the Palace we omitted to mention in our account of the American Biograph two interesting views, one showing H.R.H. the Prince of Wales proceeding from Marlborough House to St. James's Palace to hold the investiture on behalf of the Queen, and the other depicting members of the Royal Family at afternoon tea at Clarence House – a pretty and interesting picture of an informal gathering of a number of the Royal visitors brought to England to take part in the Jubilee celebrations. At the extreme right may be observed H.R.H. the Duke of Saxe-Coburg-Gotha (Duke of Edinburgh), and near him H.R.H. the Duchess of York and the Grand Duchess of Hesse, to the left being H.R.H. the Duchess of Coburg. T.R.H. the Duke of Hesse, the Duke of York, and the Grand Duke of Hesse are shown at the left. The baby Princess is the child of the Grand Duke and Duchess of Hesse, and forms an interesting foreground to the picture as she plays with and teases her good-natured playfellow. Other personages in the scene are Prince Charles of Denmark and the Hereditary Prince of Saxe-Coburg.[115](79)

In 1899, *Pearson's Magazine* published an article on 'the wonders of the Biograph' with illustrations of both these films, along with others considered of historic interest. The author of the article, R. H. Mere, clearly realised the importance of preserving such films for posterity, and said of the Biograph: 'It brings the past to the present, and it enables the present to be handed down to the future'.[116]

79 Afternoon Tea in the Garden of Clarence House (Biograph, 1897) From a frame illustration published in Pearson's Magazine, vol 7 (London, 1899 p 195 (*Barnes Museum of Cinematography*)

Another Biograph film of special interest to English audiences at this time, was one showing the Gordon Highlanders. This famous regiment had recently distinguished itself by gallantly storming the heights at Dargai, which were being stoutly defended by the tribesmen of the North-West Frontier of what was then India. There were no official army cinematographers in those days of course, to record the action, so the Biograph compensated for this lack of foresight by quickly presenting a film to appeal to the patriotic fervour of the moment. Thus whilst the news of the action at Dargai was still fresh in the minds of the public, the film of the Highlanders received its first showing at the Palace on 22 November, barely a month after the actual battle took place. Here is the *Era's* account of the film:

'The noble work again done by the Gordon Highlanders has made this already long-distinguished regiment occupy a prominent position in the public eye; and their deeds of valour are on the tip of everyone's tongue to-day. Responding to the popular feeling, the management have arranged to exhibit on the Biograph, at the Palace Theatre, a series of views which will doubtless be of great interest to the public, showing the Gordon Highlanders in camp during their leisure hours, with diversions of song and reel. Another exciting and interesting scene is a bayonet assault between some members of the camp at Aldershot. These scenes present soldier-life with a startling reality and fidelity which few can ever hope to see. They are not made up by persons disguised as soldiers, but taken from life, the principals being veterans in active service, who have "smelt powder" many times. Suitable music has been composed by Alfred Plumpton, and the new pictures will be on view for the first time on Monday next.'[117]

Biograph films at that time were each about 250ft long,[118] but this does not represent such an appreciable increase in running time as at first appears, for it must be remembered that they were projected at more than twice the normal speed. Snippets from a few of these early Biograph films have been preserved in the reels produced for the Kinora, a miniature version of the regular Mutoscope. *The Burning Stable* for instance, is pictured in a reel preserved in the Barnes Museum of Cinematography. Other Biograph films have been preserved in the paper print collection at the Library of Congress, Washington. Many Biograph negatives, taken with the large gauge Mutograph camera, were also used to supply the paper prints for Mutoscope reels, but sometimes a particular subject was filmed exclusively for Mutoscope use and no regular projection print was made. After about 1905, the American Mutoscope & Biograph Company ceased to use the large gauge film for theatrical purposes and henceforth all their films were shot on standard 35mm film.

Besides the performances at the Palace Theatre, London, which were exclusive to the Metropolitan area, the Biograph was also exhibited in the provinces. For instance, it was booked at the Alhambra Theatre in Brighton, for the week commencing 15 November.[119] Its exploitation in Great Britain seems to have been closely guarded and the American Mutoscope company was not slow to prosecute any theatre which it thought made unauthorised use of its trade name. An action of this kind was brought against the Manchester Theatre of Varieties to restrain it from using the name Biograph or the American Biogram.[120] The original Biograph was so unlike any other machine being exhibited at the time, and so superior in many respects to most, that it is quite understandable that its reputation should have been so jealously guarded.

Indeed, the reputation of the American Biograph was such that the Prince of Wales

149

(later to become King Edward VII) arranged for a special performance to be given at St. James's Palace. The performance took place on 20 July and was given in Queen Anne's room where the audience consisted of His Royal Highness and the Grand Commanders of the Order of the Bath. Among the films shown were scenes of the Diamond Jubilee festivities, including the Jubilee procession, the Naval Review at Spithead, and the military review at Aldershot; also some views of members of the Royal Family at home which had recently been taken by special command.[121]

The need for larger and more permanent headquarters in London forced the American Mutoscope & Biograph Syndicate Ltd to look for a site on which to build new offices and studios, and in 1897 a suitable location was acquired at 18 and 19 Great Windmill Street.[122] Formerly, their offices had been located at 2 and 4 Cecil Court, off Charing Cross Road, which was rapidly becoming the centre of the budding British film industry. Biograph's move to the new premises probably took place towards the end of 1898, and it is interesting to note that today the building now forms part of the famous Windmill Theatre.

Apart from the Biograph films, very few American films seem to have made much impression in England during the year, but one in particular was of unusual interest and created something of a sensation over here. This was the film of the Corbett-Fitzsimmons fight, which was a special promotion of the Veriscope Company of America. The film used was about 55mm wide and several thousand feet in length.

The fight itself took place on 17 March 1897 at Carson City, Nevada, and was specifically staged with the film in mind. For this purpose a special camera had been built under the direction of Enoch J. Rector, who was also one of the promoters of the fight and a partner in the Veriscope company.[123] The successful exploitation of the film in America was followed by an equally successful run in London, where it opened on 27 September at the Royal Aquarium Theatre, Tothill Street, Westminster. This theatre had been built at the west end of the Royal Aquarium, hence its name, and was opened in 1876. It was later known as the Imperial Theatre and was finally closed in 1907.[124] The theatre had already figured in the history of the cinema as providing the venue for Rigg's Kinematograph, which has the distinction of being the third film projector to be commercially exhibited in England, taking third place to Lumière's and Paul's.[125] Now the same theatre enters film history again as the venue for yet another extraordinary event, a film lasting an hour and a half at a time when the average film lasted no more than 50 to 60 seconds.

The British Journal of Photography wrote that 'apart from the ethics of prize-fighting, the show is an extremely interesting one, for it is the most ambitious effort yet made in the animatographic line. The figures are life size; every movement is, as a rule, clearly defined'.[126] A film featuring the Cornishman Bob Fitzsimmons, was bound to attract British fight fans and no doubt they flocked in their hundreds to the Aquarium to see their idol defeat the great James C. Corbett. Here is *The Era's* detailed account of the performance:

THE GREAT FIGHT AT THE AQUARIUM

The "sensation" at the Westminster Aquarium on Monday last was a splendid cinematographe exhibition representing the fight for $50,000 between "Bob" Fitzsimmons and James J. Corbett. For some time before the commencement of the exhibition the pay-places of the Aquarium Theatre were besieged by hundreds of eager, pushing people, ready to pay their guinea or their five shillings for admission. When, at last, the audience was seated, Mr Ben

150

Nathan gave them a few necessary and valuable pieces of information. It did not – as it turned out – prove difficult to distinguish the tall figure of Corbett from the "stocky" shape of Fitzsimmons, but it was as well to know that the plump gentleman with his coat off, who hovered near the combatants, and occasionally drew them apart, was the referee, and that a personage in a soft hat, who took it off and waved it a few moments before the conclusion of each round, did so as a signsl to Corbett. The great fight, it will be remembered, was fought in fourteen rounds, and took three years in arranging, having been stopped in Florida, where a special law was passed forbidding it. The same was done in Texas. The Government of Arkansas called out the military and stopped the preparations, and the Senate of the United States Congress obtained the signature of the President to prohibit the conflict, thus stopping the contest in all the territories and neutral districts in the United States. The fight ultimately took place in Carson City, in the Nevada States, in the presence of 6,000 people, many of whom paid £10 a-head to see it, others further incurring upwards of £50 expenses a-head in travelling many hundreds of miles to witness it. The films used measured over two miles in length. Upon these were photographed upwards of 165,000 moving living pictures. Spectators with sharp eyes found on Monday that every line of the competitors' faces was clearly traceable, and that Corbett's awful look of despairing agony at his defeat was marvellously reproduced. After the fight was finished the beaten combatant, on his partial recovery, became frantic, broke away from his seconds, and rushed about after his conqueror, striking blindly right and left, his seconds having finally to carry him by force from the ring. This finale was truly depicted in the show at the Aquarium, which is said to have cost in obtaining and in production upwards of £5,000. The exhibition at the Aquarium supplies the spectator with much novel information. One's imaginations of a prize-fight are completely corrected. Instead of the savage and repulsive butchery, the mighty blows, and the liberal supply of "gore" which fancy depicts, the unscientific spectator sees an agreeable display of skill and activity. The knowing ones, however, well realised on Monday the terrible force with which Fitzsimmons "countered" Corbett's blows; and, frequently, some unusually spirited "rally" evoked a hearty round of applause. The exhibition, which lasted an hour and a half, was judiciously curtailed by the omission of some of the intervals between the rounds; and excitement was intense when Corbett, who appeared to have been already overmatched by Fitzsimmons's strength and experience, fell to the ground after receiving the now almost historical blow on the heart, which, by "knocking him out of time," concluded the combat. The fight for $50,000" is one of the biggest things ever secured by the energetic and indefatigable Mr Ritchie for his establishment. As an achievement of "animated photography" this representation of the Fitzsimmons and Corbett fight is remarkable for the elaborate manner in which the incidents of the combat are represented. First, the men are seen walking about the ring in their long overcoats. After certain preliminary delays, Corbett advances towards Fitzsimmons and offers his hand, which Fitzsimmons appears to refuse to take, or, all events, not to accept cordially. At first the non-sporting spectator will be puzzled by the frequent recurrence of embracements between the combantants; but this is explained by the necessity of parting them whenever they become locked, and the dread of each pugilist lest the other should get in a quick blow at the moment of separation. This fear is the reason of the extreme caution with which the pair come apart. As the fight proceeds there is more boxing which can be appreciated by the ordinary spectator, though, as most of the hitting is done at half-length, there are few of those sensational "slogging" blows which we read about in accounts of the old-fashioned prize-fights. Only once is Fitzsimmons's face disfigured by his blood; and towards the close both men appear to suffer more from exhaustion than from actual punishment. Of course, the scene to which we have alluded, when Corbett falls on the stage something in the attitude of the "Dying

80 The Edison Projecting Kinetoscope, shown with spool-bank attachment for carrying looped film for continuous projection. From an illustration published in The Optician, vol 13, 1897, p 176 (*British Library*)

Gladiator,'' and his subsequent attempts to get at his rival after the referee has declared them to be "up", are specially sensational. A large number of the sporting fraternity were present in the Aquarium Theatre on Monday; and they showed by their remarks that they fully appreciated both the marvellous fidelity of the reproduction and the skilful tactics of the combatants. The importance attached to the fight in pugilistic circles, the discussions to which it gave rise, and the deep interest which it excited on both sides of the Atlantic fully account for the eagerness to witness the cinematographic wonder which was shown on Monday night. It supplies, in fact, all the scientific interest of a prize-fight without any of the disgusting or brutal accessories which we are accustomed to associate with such conflicts.'[127]

Neither the veriscope nor the Biograph equipment was for sale and the only apparatus of American manufacture available on the open market in England was an Edison machine and the Urban Bioscope. The first projector associated with the name of Thomas A. Edison had been the Armat Vitascope, and during 1896 an unsuccessful attempt was made to launch the machine in England. In actual fact, Edison was connected with this machine in name only, for he had played no part in its invention. However, shortly afterwards he brought out one of his own design, which was called the Edison Projecting Kinetoscope. The first model appeared on the English market late in 1896[128] and like its progenitor the Kinetoscope, carried its film on a spool bank, so that it ran in an endless loop over a series of widely spaced pulleys situated on a framework behind the lamp-house (80). This proved somewhat unsatisfactory since only a relatively short length of film could be laced up at a time, to say nothing of the fire hazard which such an arrangement presented. Modifications were consequently called for, and a new model was produced in which the film was carried in the conventional manner with a top and bottom spool allowing lengths of up to 350ft of film to be carried (81).

81 The Edison Projecting Kinetoscope. Made by Thomas A. Edison, New Jersey, USA. With Maltese-cross and 2-pin cam movement (*Barnes Museum of Cinematography*)

The tension of the take-up spindle was governed by a friction roller connected to the top of the driving shaft. The projector mechanism was mounted on an oak board so that it was free to move up and down for racking the picture. The intermittent movement was supplied by a Maltese-cross and 2-pin cam.[129] Agents for the machine in England were Dolland & Co of 35 Ludgate Hill,[130] and Maguire & Baucus Ltd of Dashwood House, 9 New Broad Street, London, E.C.[131] The latter had been associated with Edison since the early days of the Kinetoscope and we shall have more to say about this firm further on in this chapter.

It seems that in May, Maguire & Baucus introduced the '97 Model' Projecting Kinetoscope to the English market, for in that month *The Optician & Photographic Trades Review* were able to publish an account of the apparatus after having witnessed a private demonstration given by Maguire & Baucus. The account, in part, is as follows:

'We had the pleasure of being present at a private Exhibition a few days ago of one of these machines and noted the absence of any vibratory or wavering motion on the projecting screen which, we learn, is accomplished by improved steadying devices.

A brilliant light without any unpleasant flickering is produced by a specially designed hand-feed arc-lamp, which is provided with a resistance coil and is suitable for use on any direct or alternating current of not over 200 volts.

It projects a picture even greater than life-size if desired, without distortion or indistinctness, and also without the use of special films.

It is fitted with wide angle objective lens giving a field ten feet high by thirteen and half feet wide at a distance of about forty feet to the screen. Proportionately larger or smaller pictures may be had by increasing or decreasing this distance.

Only one operator is required, and the objectionable perpendicular rays seen in the reproduction machines using a "pitman" or striker are entirely eliminated by a peculiarly constructed shutter, which at the same time allows more light to pass through than is usual.'[132]

The illustration which accompanies the article (80), shows the apparatus complete with spool bank attachment, but this could be dispensed with and the projector fitted up with 'reels for "feed" and "take up" each of which has a capacity of at least six fifty-feet films'.[133] Maguire & Baucus were also able to supply Edison films in various lengths.[134] Dolland advertised the machine for sale at £21 net and gave the picture size capable of being thrown by the apparatus as 11 feet by 13 feet.[135] In May, A. Rosenberg & Co were also advertising Edison machines and films,[136] so one must conclude that in England, like elsewhere, Edison goods were in demand. Shortly, a company by the name of Edisonia Limited appears, with offices at 3 Broad Street Buildings, London, E.C.[137] The name implies that this was an Edison subsidiary. It offered for sale phonographs and cinematograph equipment, as well as films, including one of the Prince of Wales on board his yacht Britannia.[138]

Among the first to exhibit the Edison machine in England, of whom we have a record, were the Barron Brothers, who introduced it at the Bedford music hall, Camden Town, on 4 January.[139] This would have been the first version. Later, the same exhibitors stated that their machine was obtained through Interchangeable Limited, of 57 St John's Road, Holloway,[140] which would seem to suggest that a different make of apparatus was then being used by them. There is a record of the Edison machine having been exhibited during November at the Peoples Empire, Bow, where it was billed as 'Edison's Latest Projecting Kinetoscope,'[141] but otherwise, information about its use in England is sadly lacking.

154

82 The Bioscope 35mm Film Projector (1st model) Introduced into Gt Britain in 1897 by Maguire & Baucus Ltd (*Barnes Museum of Cinematography*)

An American projector which met with far more success in England than the Edison machine, was introduced later in the year. In fact it was to have quite a phenomenal success, perhaps more so than any other machine for the next decade. It hailed from New York and was sponsored by the two veterans of the film industry, Maguire and Baucus, who had introduced Edison's Kinetoscope into England back in 1894. By 1897, they had long ceased to exploit that machine and were now best known in connection with their agencies for cinematograph films, of which they probably had one of the largest selections of any firm in the world.[142] They had the selling rights to the Edison films and also the famous Lumière films as perforated to the Edison gauge.[143]

It was in July that Maguire & Baucus Limited of Dashwood House, 9 New Broad Street, London, E.C. announced they would shortly be introducing to the English market a new cinematograph of American manufacture, said to be superior to anything as yet produced in the United States.[144] It was to be called the Bioscope. By September,[145] it had reached the market accompanied by such slogans as 'Absolute Steadiness' and 'Freedom from Flicker'.[146] *The Amateur Photographer* pronounced it 'a remarkably fine instrument,' and added 'the pictures are wonderfully steady, in which respect they cannot be beaten by any other machine on the market.'[147] *The Optician & Photographic Trades Review* likewise praised it:

'It does not tear or injure the film and so far as clearness goes, it may be said that the flickering is entirely eliminated. The definition is exceedingly fine, owing to the superior quality of the lens, and there is notable absence of any vibratory or waving motion in the projected scene.'[148]

The fact that the period during which the film was in motion was only one-eigth as long as that in which it was at rest, the customary shutter was dispensed with.[149] The machine employed the beater or 'dog' movement and had a continuous feed sprocket above the 'gate' and another below the eccentric having a continuous motion imparted

155

83   The Bioscope, shown with spool-bank attachment for continuous projection. From an illustration in The Optician, vol 13, 1897, p 422 (*British Library*)

84   4 & 5 Warwick Court, High Holborn, London, as seen today. The premises were once occupied by Maguire & Baucus Ltd (later The Warwick Trading Company) (*Uwe H. Breker*)

156

85 The private office of Joseph D. Baucus, Warwick Court. Left to right: Charles Urban (Manager), Herman Kimble (Director) and J. D. Baucus (Chairman) Note the portrait of Thomas A. Edison above the fireplace (*Science Museum, London*)

86 Main office of Maguire & Baucus Ltd, Warwick Court. Charles Urban is shown standing in the left foreground; his private office can be glimpsed beyond the doorway in the background (*Science Museum, London*)

87   Charles Urban's private office, Warwick Court (*Science Museum, London*)

to it by the handle by which the machine was operated (82). The Bioscope was supplied with a spool bank for showing endless films (83), but the machine could also be used in the normal way with reels. The lens regularly supplied with the projector allowed a projection throw up to 50 feet, but if a greater distance was required between the screen and the projector, a special lens could be procured. The regulation lamp house was fitted with a hand-feed arc lamp working on 110–120 volts DC or 52 or 104 volts AC, but limelight could easily be substituted if required.[150] The Bioscope was distributed in the North of England by Messrs Sharp & Hitchmough, photographic instrument makers of 101 & 103 Dale Street, Liverpool, the price of the machine being £26.[151]

In May, Messrs Maguire & Baucus Ltd entered into a contract with Messrs Antoine Lumière and Sons, of Lyons, France (inventors of the celebrated Cinématographe-Lumière) taking over their business in the United States and also obtaining the selling agency of their standard gauge films in Great Britain.[152] This did not include the agency for the Cinématographe itself, which, in England, remained in the hands of the Fuerst Brothers.[153] A reduction in the price of the films followed, from 62/- [£3.10] to 50/- [£2.50]. In September, a list of the films was published in *The Optician*, which took up six three-column pages (This list is reproduced in Appendix 2). The length of each film was given as about 55 feet and the running time as 50 to 60 seconds.[154] In December, 'a neat little pocket list' of Lumière films was issued and a larger illustrated catalogue was promised in the near future.[155] 'We have yet to see a better exhibition than that produced by the "Bioscope" with the Lumiere films', commented *The Optician*.[156] Maguire and Baucus must have been well content with the Lumière product for they decided to dispose of their stock of Edison films and these were offered to the trade at a specially low price.[157]

158

It is quite likely that the new driving force behind the firm was the young American, Charles Urban, who had recently been engaged as manager of the London branch.[158] At his appointment, the Agency certainly seems to have undergone a marked rejuvenation. During September the business removed from New Broad Street to more commodious premises at 4 & 5 Warwick Court, High Holborn. The building still stands and remains virtually unaltered (84). Joseph D. Baucus (Chairman) had his private office behind the arched window on the left of the building and Charles Urban's was situated in a little room leading off from the main office. All three rooms are shown in the accompanying illustrations (85–87) and are taken from original photographs in the Charles Urban Collection at the Science Museum, London.[159]

Charles Urban had been connected with the film industry since 1894, when he was manager of a Kinetoscope parlour in Detroit, and his first contact with Maguire and Baucus probably dates from that time. Moreover, Urban may have played some part in securing the Bioscope projector for them and may even have been connected in some way with its manufacture, if not its invention. He eventually claimed the invention as his own and later models of the projector bore his name as inventor on each casting. Not many months after the move to Warwick Court, the name of the firm was changed to the Warwick Trading Company, adopting the name of its place of business. Urban rose to be managing director, but in 1903 he probably felt he had reached a stage in his career when he needed to branch out on his own and he left the firm to found his own business which he named The Charles Urban Trading Company. This firm was subsequently to become one of the most important in the British film industry. He eventually retired to Brighton and resided in a flat at No 7 Clarendon Mansions, East Street. He died in a nursing home at 12 Dyke Road on 29 August 1942, aged 75 years.[160]

One other American import may be mentioned, although I have not found out much about it, except that it was some kind of street cinematograph which could be easily carried about by one man. It was advertised as coming from Chicago and available in England from the Eclipse Kinematoscope Office, 73 Ackham Road, London.[161] Another novelty to be seen in the streets at this time was the flip-book giving a miniature display of animated photographs. The idea was an old one, for in 1868, J. B. Linnett had patented a similar moving picture device called the Kineograph.[162] It consisted of a little book, on the pages of which a figure was drawn in different positions so as to represent a series of consecutive phases of movement. When the leaves of the book were flipped over by the thumb, the figure appeared to be animated. This idea now had a considerable revival of popularity in 1897 under the name of the Pocket Kinetoscope, but this time, half-tone photographs were employed instead of drawings.[163] The photographs used for the purpose were simply obtained by printing off the required number of frames from already existing negatives of cinematograph films. Most, if not all, of these Pocket Kinetoscopes emanated from abroad and sold for about a penny. A German supplier, S. Lubszynski of 4–6 Konigsstrasse, Berlin, issued a series which measured about $2\frac{1}{2} \times 1\frac{1}{2}$ inches and contained about fifty leaves each.[164] Others were issued by Thomas A. Edison. An example in the Barnes Museum of Cinematography depicts the famous Rice-Irwin Kiss, filmed in 1896 for the Vitascope. This book-form development of animated photography has been attributed to a colleague of Edison's named Colonel Gouraud,[165] somewhat absurdly it would seem, since the principle must have been known for a number of years. Even so, this did not prevent two weavers of Padiham, Lancaster, from obtaining a British patent for the self-same thing. Their names were John O'Neill and Robert McNally and the patent was issued as no 8572 of 3 April, 1897. Various mechanical contrivances for turning the leaves had also been devised, among the better known being the Mutoscope of Herman Casler,[166] and A. & L. Lumiere's Kinora.[167] A smaller and simpler device was of course Short's Filoscope, to exploit which, the Anglo-French Filoscope Syndicate (Limited) was registered in 1897, with a capital of £5,000 in £1 shares.[168] A 'miniature cinematographe' costing two shillings and sixpence complete with one subject, was advertised by the Cinematographe Company, Kenilworth. It was described as 'a marvellous little instrument, ingenious, and amusing, wonderful life-like effects.' Subjects included *Girl Skipping* and *The Czar* (real photos).[169] This instrument was probably yet another form of flip-book, which most likely came from France.

7 The Showmen

By the end of 1897 there could hardly have been a town in England that had not witnessed a display of 'animated photographs', yet of the numerous exhibitors who must have been involved in their presentation, only the names of a few are known to us. Apart from the more celebrated, who had generally made their names in other fields, little can be traced of their careers; neither is it always possible to determine the make of apparatus which they used. Some adopted names of their own choosing for the apparatus exhibited, or used a derivation of their stage name. Thus for example we have a Dr. Birteno exhibiting an apparatus by the name of Birtenograph.[1] Another exhibitor, Irving Bosco, billed his machine as the 'Excelsior Cinematographe',[2] yet I have been unable to trace a machine that was actually manufactured under that name. In some cases no name at all is given to the apparatus, although in some instances, this can be ascertained from a statement put out by the manufacturer himself. Other exhibitors happily retained the name originally assigned to it by the maker and so no problem of identification arises, but such instances are relatively few.

In those days, the exhibitor performed quite a different role from that of his counterpart today. He was first and foremost a showman and would often introduce the pictures personally from the front of the screen. He might also keep up a running commentary throughout the performance. Often he would be a well-known entertainer himself, as were Trewey, Devant and Hertz. The more affluent might employ a man to work the projector or at least to assist at the performance, but many showmen were themselves proficient in projecting and often acted in this capacity as well. Films at that time were bought outright, for renters were then unknown, so it is not surprising to find some exhibitors who also made their own films, just as some manufacturers of cinematographic equipment did. Indeed, it was not uncommon for a manufacturer also to be engaged in exhibiting, the most notable example being R. W. Paul. An exhibitor by the name of Edmund A. Robins, utilised the experience he had gained from showing films in the provinces, to write a number of articles on various topics likely to be of help to fellow exhibitors.[3] In addition to giving hints on exhibiting cinematographs[4] and the mending of films,[5] he also wrote on developing and printing.[6] Apparently, a showman in those days was expected to be a Jack-of-all-trades.

Among the exhibitors to be discussed in this chapter are some who had begun showing films in 1896, and consequently have been mentioned already in the previous volume of this history. One of the earliest of these was the conjurer David Devant, who had used one of Paul's first machines. During 1897, whilst still continuing his association with Maskelyne at the Egyptian Hall, he also gave independent performances of animated pictures, as indeed he had done the year before. However, these are not so frequently reported as formerly; one such performance is recorded in June, when he exhibited at a charity bazaar, held in the Botanical Gardens in Regent's Park, which was opened by Princess Louise on Monday afternoon of the 21st. The bazaar was held in aid of the Victoria Hospital for Children, and Devant's show was singled out for special mention along with Jewell's Marionettes.[7]

Devant's personal shows were naturally more in demand during the winter months and his advertisements appeared regularly in *The Era* throughout January and February.[8] He claims to have provided 'over 800 enormously successful exhibitions since

March 19th, 1896, having three machines by R. W. Paul and a repertoire of 136 of the finest and latest subjects, including Motor Car Race, Czar in Paris, Cavalry Charge, &c., and scenes in brilliant colours'.[9] These last were of course coloured by hand. Many of his films were acquired in France and he seems to have had a working relationship with Georges Méliès, even appearing in one of his films — David Devant, Prestidigitateur.

Meanwhile, Devant was still in partnership with Maskelyne at the Egyptian Hall, Piccadilly, where regular film shows were given every afternoon and evening, except for a short interuption in June, when the hall was closed from the 14th to 22nd inclusive, to allow Maskelyne to supervise the camera platform which was being erected on a site in St Paul's Church yard, prior to the filming of the Diamond Jubilee procession.[10] Indeed, films had become a traditional part of the programme at 'England's Home of Mystery' and one such performance is reported in The Era for 2 January:

> . . . Mr Nevil Maskelyne acts as commentator upon the series of animated photographs which is next displayed. The series includes some of the best of those which have been exhibited elsewhere, and in addition, views of Mr Maskelyne engaged in plate-spinning and of Mr Devant doing a wonderful trick in which one rabbit is suddenly turned into two. The odd part of the latter photograph (sic) is that, even with all the advantages of the process, it is impossible to see how the feat is accomplished — a great tribute to Mr Devant's dexterity. The explanations with which Mr Maskelyne accompanies the animated photographs are instructive, interesting, and very musically delivered.[11]

The films featuring Maskelyne and Devant had been made by Paul the previous year, and have already been described in our previous volume. In August, The Era again visited Maskelyne & Cooke's (as the show at the Egyptian Hall continued to be called although Cooke had long since departed) and we select that part of the review which again describes the 'animated photographs':

> . . . Changes have been made in "spools" of animated photographs, and some of the new ones are extremely interesting. There is a scene from the Franco-German war, "The Last Shot", with realistic reports of the guns which the despairing soldiers are seen to fire from the windows of the shattered house. A Spanish bull-fight, with a remarkably fine bull, is also depicted; and, as Mr Maskelyne, who acts as explainer, remarks, "makes us sorry for the animals, and for those who can enjoy such a cruel spectacle." The Mardi Gras Procession at Paris is admirably reproduced; and Mr Devant is shown doing some of his tricks of legerdemain. The musical accompaniments of the Organo Piano are judiciously supplied by Mr Cramer.[12]

This particular musical accompaniment was billed as 'Mr Maskelyne's Mechanical and Automatic Orchestra', and was said to be 'the most wonderful combination of musical instruments in the world.'[13]

During the early part of 1897, Carl Hertz, the American magician, was still away in the antipodes. After completing his tour of Australia, he had moved on to New Zealand where he opened at Auckland on 20 February. There then followed a short season at Wellington during March.[14] One of his performances in Dunedin attracted particular attention owing to a fire which occurred one Saturday night at the Princess's Theatre. The Era gave the following account of the mishap, which might very well have turned into tragedy:

162

Mr Carl Hertz distinguished himself by his readiness and courage at the Princess's Theatre, Dunedin, on the night of Saturday, April 17th. During the exhibition of the Cinématographe the audience was suddenly startled by a bright flame making its appearance in the space between the dress-circle entrance and the barrier at the back of the seats, and this was followed by the screen which was placed round the lantern at the entrance to the centre aisle in the circle becoming ignited. A few of the occupants of the stalls made for the stage, but, generally speaking, men and women alike displayed admirable coolness. Mr Hertz himself appeared on the stage and assured those downstairs that there was no danger, and members of the audience repeated his assurance and advised that all should keep their seats. This had the desired effect, and a minute or so later, when, the fire having been extinguished, Mr Hertz re-appeared on the stage he was greeted with a loud clapping of hands. He expressed his regret for what had happened, especially as it had rendered it impossible for him to exhibit the Cinématographe that night, and informed the audience that all the danger was over.[15]

Like Devant, Hertz too was probably still equipped with apparatus of Paul's manufacture despite the use of the name Cinématographe in the above account, but it will be fair to add that, at the time of the fire, Paul had not yet introduced his new Fireproof Animatographe.

Ever since the Paris fire disaster, the English press had been very sensitive regarding fires at cinematograph performances and no opportunity was lost in reporting even the most trivial incidents. Exaggerated as some of these reports undoubtedly were, they nevertheless provide us with information not readily available elsewhere. A case in point is the report of the fire at the Princess's Theatre just quoted. As another example, we may mention the fire which occurred on Saturday evening, 2 October, at Tong Park Wesleyan Chapel, Baildon, near Bradford. This received very wide coverage in the newspapers and photographic journals and in some of the reports, the nature of the accident was grossly exaggerated and most alarmingly presented, whereas in fact, very little damage resulted.[16] The machine involved was being operated by Messrs Walter Bentley and Rigg, the latter gentleman being, no doubt, John Henry Rigg of Leeds, the inventor of the apparatus being used.[17] The fire started when the film in the projector got stuck and became ignited. Part of the flaming matter then dropped into the bag containing the films that had been already projected and instantly set them on fire.[18] There are other examples of similar mishaps occurring during 1897[19] and the newspapers and fire brigade reports may provide information on several exhibitors long since forgotten. This is a field which calls for further research, but for the present we will return to the main theme of our discussion.

Felicien Trewey, the other veteran exhibitor, need not concern us here, since we have already related the story of his last few months in England. We pass instead to an exhibitor of a different kind, whose career appears to have been solely confined to the exhibiting of films.

Lewis Sealy, also active during the previous year when he was operating the Kineopticon of Birt Acres, gave numerous performances during 1897, but it is not certain whether he still retained the Acres machine. Some of the films shown at his performances were made by Birt Acres, but he included also films from other sources. He began the year with an engagement at the Metropolitan in Edgware Road.[20] This was followed in April with a run at the Hammersmith Varieties,[21] and in May he appeared at the Standard.[22] During August and September he was at Mellison's Grand

Skating Rink, Brighton, where he presented a programme of Jubilee films.[23] Sealy had exhibited the Kineopticon under the name Royal Cinematoscope, but on 2 January the apparatus was advertised in *The Era* as the Birt Acres Royal Cinematographe.[24] The advertisers were the Dramatic & Musical Syndicate, of 19 Buckingham Street, Strand, who presumably were acting as agents, but how successfully is a mute point. Although advertising each week during January and February, thereafter nothing more is heard of them, at least in *The Era*. The projector Sealy used for his engagement at the Metropolitan music hall in January, was billed as Sealy's Cinematoscope, a name Sealy seems to have stuck to for the remainder of the year. Yet it is not at all certain to what make of projector this name actually applied, but whatever the make, the performance at the Metropolitan was given a favourable review in *The Era*:

> . . . Amongst the most notable items in this week's bill is Mr Lewis Sealy's Cinematoscope, which has been re-engaged. Some new pictures are now shown, and these include the approach of a racing train at Gatwick, and the paddock at this sporting centre; the arrival of the Lord Mayor at the Law Courts, the Prince and Princess of Wales's state reception, and the Royal wedding party photographed at Marlborough House, the King's-road and the West Pier, Brighton, on a Bank holiday, Landing at Low Tide, and Church Parade of Troops, Surrey Garden, and an "Unfriendly Call." Each of these pictures is received with unmistakable approval.[25]

Sealy's engagement at the Hammersmith Varieties, was reported at even greater length by the same paper, and it is worth quoting here as a number of films are mentioned in some detail thus providing information which perhaps is not available elsewhere:

HAMMERSMITH VARIETIES

Always desirous of giving their patrons the best of everything in the market, Messrs Acton Phillips have just lately added to their programme a series of exhibitions by Mr Lewis Sealy of the wonders of the Cinématographe — or, as this particular machine is called, the Cinématoscope. The whirligig of time brings about many changes; and few would have thought that the popular "wheel of Life" of our childhood's days would have developed into the wonderful invention that presents to our admiring gaze such faithful scenes of events and places that one may sit comfortably in a cosy stall and enjoy a trip round the world and all the accompanying incidents without any of the inconveniences of travel. Mr Sealy has a fine collection of pictures, and from his store he showed on Monday [29 March] among others a Pierrot and Pierette engaging in a game of cards, the lady getting "werry nasthty" because she loses, flinging the pack in her companion's face, and then kissing and "making it up." In "A Scramble Under Brighton Pier" we see a crowd of urchins contesting for coppers thrown from above, whilst the waves roll in in realistic style. "The Arrival of a Train at Gatwick," a picture full of animation, is the prelude to "The Paddock," with a crowd of notabilities, and horses being led round for inspection. A set of three photos enables us to see the course at Epsom being cleared for the Derby, the preliminary canter, and the race for the Blue Riband of the Turf. A demonstration of loyalty is evoked by a reproduction of the arrival at Marlborough House of the Prince and Princess of Wales with the Princesses Victoria and Maud. This is a capital picture, the features of the illustrious quartet being easily recognisable. Perhaps, though, the best of the series is a scene from *The Broken Melody*. We see Mr Van Biene as Paul, with heart well-nigh broken, seeking consolation from his beloved 'cello. The door slowly opens, and his wife, whom he

164

supposes his faithless, enters. The musician, absorbed in his playing, sees her not. Vera
Approaches, and as Paul finishes his solo, a gentle touch on the arm causes him to turn, and in
another moment husband and wife are locked in each other's arms. This is a really excellent
reproduction of an affecting scene, and brought down some of the loudest applause of the
series.[26]

All the films mentioned in the two reviews just quoted, may have been taken by Birt
Acres. Certainly some are recognisable as being his.[27] In the previous volume of this
history mention was made of the working relationship that existed between Lewis Sealy
and Birt Acres, and apparently this arrangement still existed at this time.

After his London appearances at the Metropolitan and Standard, Lewis Sealy
moved down to Brighton for a short season at Mellison's Grand Skating Rink, in West
Street. Performances took place each day at 12.30, 3, 4.30, 7.30 and 9 o'clock. Price of
admission was 6d and 1/- [2½p and 5p], with reserved seats in the Circle at 2/- [10p].
The films included the Diamond Jubilee procession and Méliès's Greco-Turkish War
series, a programme which was shown throughout most of August and September.[28]
These performances did not form part of a variety or music hall programme, but were
presented as the sole attraction, which was something of a novelty at that time.

Phil & Bernard too, began showing films in 1896, but no clue as to the identity of the
apparatus then used has been found. At the Alhambra Theatre, Leicester Square,
during September 1897, they were operating a Wrench Cinematograph,[29] but advertisements in The Era from January to April refer to an apparatus called the O.S.
Cinematographe.[30] The initials O.S. may stand for the name of the manufacturer,
perhaps Ottway & Son, in which case, the machine used by Phil & Bernard was the
Animatoscope.

During 1897, Phil & Bernard, of 98 Portsdown Road, Maida Vale, London, W.,
fulfilled engagements at various theatres in London and the provinces. Performances
are recorded at the Palace Theatre, Manchester,[31] Grand Theatre, Streatham,[32]
Foresters', Bethnal Green,[33] the Washington, Battersea,[34] and the Alhambra, Leicester Square.[35] No doubt there were many others. The show at the Foresters' during
February, called forth the following comment in The Era:

... No entertainment that affects to be up to date would be complete without animated
pictures; and the latest development of the wonders of photography exhibited by the O.S.
Cinematograph (sic) elicited one of the heartiest manifestations of the evening.[36]

The engagement at the Washington Theatre of Varieties, York Road, Battersea, was
for six nights only,[37] but longer runs were established at other theatres; for instance, the
engagement at the Palace, Manchester lasted ten weeks.[38] However, an announcement
published in The Era on 10 April revealed that Phil & Bernard were about to abandon
their role as film exhibitors, and offered for sale a quantity of apparatus:

... selling to give room for another novelty of ours. The apparatus known as Phil and
Bernard's O.S. Cinematographe consisting of five cinematograph machines, with pedestals,
condensers, lenses, burners, tubing, regulators, indicators, portable screens for back and front
work, with batten and pulley adjustment, electric arc lamps, resistances, plugs, cables, and

about sixty latest subjects, films, English and foreign, will sell complete. Single sets or in part, and can give demonstrations in our private hall.

All engagements which we booked ahead will be carried out.[39]

Commitments already entered into evidently included a re-engagement at the Foresters'[40] and the booking at the Alhambra.[41] The main feature of each was a series of films of the Jubilee.[42] The Alhambra show was given with a Wrench machine, and if Phil and Bernard had been successful in selling the equipment advertised, then most probably this machine was on hire. It therefore seems likely, if this were the case, that a Wrench Cinematograph was used also at the Foresters'. The show at the latter was reviewed in *The Era* on the 21st of August:

> . . . The current bill, given under the direction of Mr Wilton Friend, who knows probably more about the rise and growth of music halls in the East-end than any man breathing, is brought up to date by a timely exhibition of Phil and Bernard's Cinématographe (from the Alhambra). The procession of June 22nd is revivified in many of its most brilliant aspects, the reception given to her most gracious Majesty, on that day of days being re-echoed by the hardy Forestians, who are, to judge by the heartiness of their cheering, among the most loyal of her subjects. Other pictures, exhibited on the screen on the night of our visit included "A Joke on the gardener," "The Serpentine Dance," and "Alexander Park Racecourse and Paddock."[43]

Films at that time carried no titles and it was the custom for some person to announce each film to the audience. At the Forester's this task was undertaken by the manager of the theatre, Wilton Friend, a service which did not go unnoticed by the *Era* in its review the following month:

> . . . The Cinematographe forms a very welcome and interesting item in the current bill-of-fare. The thousands of East-enders who did not see the world-famous Jubilee procession last June have an opportunity of viewing a faithful representation of the impressive spectacle at the Foresters'. In addition there is a variety of other pictures which afford much delight. A snow-balling scene in a village street is highly amusing, and then we are whisked away, as it were, to South America, to witness the manner in which they capture the wild horses who range the prairies. A dexterous throw of the lassoo, and a noble steed loses his freedom forever. Very soon after we find ourselves "assisting" at a bull-fight in Spain, and shuddering at the narrow escapes of the picadors from the fierce charges of the infuriated animal. It should be added that Mr Wilton Friend, the manager, announced the subject of each picture.[44]

Another 1896 exhibitor, was the eminent American illusionist, ventriloquist and humorist — Hercat. At the beginning of 1897, he exhibited at the Regent Theatre, Salford, where his cinematograph took the place of a transformation scene in the pantomime of Blue Beard.[45] In June he was engaged by Lord De La Warr at Bexhill-on-Sea, and according to a report in *The Era*, 'succeeded in attracting to the Kursaal some of the largest audiences ever assembled at that ultra fashionable place of amusement.'[46] On the evening of Jubilee day, 21 June, he was specially engaged to entertain the boys at Rugby School.[47] and on the 19 July he appeared at the Pier Pavilion, St. Leonard's-on-Sea, which was his third engagement at this establishment in twelve months.[48] It has not been established what make of apparatus Hercat used for his performances. Most probably it was Paul's, since he is known to have once been an exhibitor of the Theatrograph.

166

Not much is reported on C. Goodwin Norton, or Vincent Paul for the year under discussion, although both began their association with films in 1896. The latter was evidently much in demand in the north of England for in January it was reported that he had six cinematographs in Liverpool in one week.[49] In the same month Norton, of 38 Marchmont Street, London, was advertising the Vitagraph,[50] which may mean that he was exhibiting the French machine made by Clement & Gilmer, although a photograph published in *Chat* for 6 November 1896 shows him operating what appears to be the Animatoscope manufactured by J. Ottway & Son.[51]

Charles Goodwin Norton was born on 8 April 1856 in Shere, near Guildford, Surrey, and died in Osterley, Middlesex, on 22 March 1940. Like so many film exhibitors of the period, he had taken up cinematography as an adjunct to his optical magic lantern shows, and his film performances follow the pattern of the typical lanternist, with shows of slides and films, given in town and country halls, seaside pavilions, and at private functions and charities.[52] He later tried his hand at film production, but, so far, I have found no evidence to show that he was engaged in film-making activities as early as 1897.

In 1896, Webster & Girling were exhibiting an apparatus which they called the Anarithmoscope. *The Morning Advertiser* reported that 'the Anarithmoscope shows a marked improvement in clearness and steadiness over its rivals. A display of skirt dancing (coloured) was practically perfect.'[53] Quite likely the name given to the apparatus by the exhibitors, was of their own devising and not that of the makers. Webster & Girling worked from an address at 44 Upper Baker Street, London, and their advertisements are to be found in *The Era* during January and February of 1897,[54] although I have found no accounts of their actual performances for that year. No doubt such information would be forthcoming if a search were made of the local and provincial press.

I am unable to discover the true identity of a machine exhibited at the Hammersmith Varieties under the name of Premont & Fonteyn's Biographoscope. The programme consisted of a series of Jubilee films, and according to *The Era*, the performance was excellent.[55] We are told that 'the appearance of Her Majesty's carriage on the field of view is the signal for an outbreak of cheering, and the pictures generally are much appreciated.'[56]

The Excelsior Cinematograph, exhibited by Irving Bosco, is another example of an unidentified apparatus. An advertisement informs us that it 'receives a brilliant reception in the palace scene of Maggie Morton's "Blue Beard" pantomime.'[57] At least one other theatre that year included films in its Christmas pantomime, this was the Royal Opera House, Leicester, where Paul's 'Animatograph' was shown during the performance of Robinson Crusoe.[58]

A Dr Birteno called his apparatus the Birtenograph.[59] He began the year with a three week engagement at the Tivoli Theatre, Leicester.[60] The films shown included 'a motor car race, operatives leaving a Lancashire mill, the sea washing over the rocks at Blackpool, and a military church parade.[61] He also fulfilled engagements at Roscommon, Liverpool, where films of the Jubilee procession and *The Bride Retiring* were received with enthusiasm.[62]

The use of Italian-sounding names by exhibitors of films, was purposely affected no doubt, in deference to theatrical tradition, as so many showmen in the past had come originally from Italy, or so it was believed. For the week commencing 12 July, we have a Signor Polverini presenting a series of films at the London Pavilion. The principal items on the programme were those representing portions of the recent Jubilee procession, but among the other films shown was one which the correspondent of *The Era* described as reproducing a 'Pepper's Ghost' illusion, in which an individual in medieval attire is annoyed by various suddenly-appearing spectres.[63] Obviously this is a reference to the Méliès film *The Haunted Castle (Le Chateau Hanté)* at that time available in England from Philipp Wolff.[64] On Friday, 16 July, Signor Polverini presented, in addition to the Jubilee films, one of Henley Regatta showing the Eton College eight beating Leander. But what was so remarkable about this performance was the fact that the race had only taken place that day.[65] We have reason to believe that the credit for this feat belongs not to Signor Polverini, but to Haydon & Urry, who are known to have filmed the event,[66] and also to have supplied the London Pavilion with their Eragraph projector.[67] Commendable at this achievement surely is, it was not the only instance of a topical event being filmed and screened on the same day, as we shall see when discussing the filming of the Jubilee in chapter 8. I have not determined the exact duration of Polverini's engagement at the London Pavilion, but it was for at least six weeks, and throughout this period the films of the Jubilee continued to provoke an enthusiastic response from the audience.[68] This same theatre today, is still showing films, and the neon signs which for so long have disfigured the front of this handsome Piccadilly theatre have recently been removed and the facade restored to its former splendour.

Exhibitors of films were a mixed bunch in those days, and the most unlikely persons were engaged in their presentation. Le Clair for instance, combined his troupe of trained fox terrier dogs with a cinematograph performance. During the first week in July his double act was to be seen at the Empire, Pontypridd in Wales,[69] and later in the year at the Victoria Theatre, Morley, Yorkshire,[70] and Roscommon, Liverpool,[71] by which time he had acquired R. W. Paul's improved cinematograph.[72] Users of Paul's earlier Theatrograph were J. H. Gee of 14 Regent Road, Hanley, Staffordshire; Frank Haywood, at High Street, Falmouth; and E. H. Page at the Lyceum, Blackburn.[73] At the same time Percival Craig's Cinematograph was advertised at the Colosseum Theatre, Rawtenstall, Lancashire,[74] but it is not known what apparatus he used. E. J. Dale, a well-known illusionist of the day, presented a programme of Jubilee films in August, at the Imperial Victorian Exhibition, held at the Crystal Palace, Sydenham.[75] His apparatus was referred to as the Animatoscope, the name by which Ottway's projector was known. In the same month, Matt Raymond was exhibiting the Cinématographe-Lumière,[76] one of the few recorded instances of its use by a showman since its availability on the English market. It was used too, in an advertising campaign mounted by Lever Brothers and Nestlé, and the novelty of the enterprise was remarked upon in *The Era:*

A novel and interesting form of advertising has been adopted by Lever Brothers, of Port Sunlight, and the proprietors of Nestlé's Milk. These two firms gave a high-class entertainment on Monday [1 November], at the Assembly Rooms of the Agricultural Hall, Norwich, consisting of animated pictures thrown upon a screen by the Lumière Cinématographe. In the series the Sunlight Soap washing competition alternates with a bull-fight in Andalusia, the driving cows into Nestlé's milk factory, and the Diamond Jubilee Procession. The entertainment was under the direction of Mr A. Spencer Clarke.[77]

On 8 December a similar programme was presented at a meeting of the Croydon

Camera Club held before a large audience at the Public Hall.[78] The film performance lasted about an hour and according to a report published in *The British Journal of Photography*, 'was well appreciated by an audience which has now had considerable experience of this photographic development.'[79] The apparatus and films used in the performance were Lumière's, and amongst the scenes which met with particular favour by the audience were *The Bull Fight*, *The Visit of President Fauré to the Czar*, and *The Fire Alarm*. But the film which really seems to have caught the audience's fancy was a 'panoramic' view:

> . . . Much interest was also shown in a scene taken from a railway carriage in motion, the view being of the flying landscape as seen through the carriage window. The effect produced was very remarkable, and when a turnpike road, which ran nearly parallel to the line of rails, came in sight, and on it was beheld a new woman astride a cycle, trying hard to race the train, the audience became uproariously delighted. It should be stated that the above display of moving photographs was given by special arrangements with the proprietors of Nestlé's Milk and Sunlight Soap, who are to be congratulated upon so successfully combining their business with other people's pleasure.[80]

We shall have more to say on the Lever and Nestlé promotions in the next chapter.

An Edison machine was exhibited by the Barron Brothers, who had an address at Tower House, St John's Road, Holloway. Although their machine was referred to in *The Era* as Edison's Kinematographe,[81] its proper name was Edison's Projecting Kinetoscope, or Projectorscope. From 4 January, the Barron Brothers were at the Bedford Music Hall, Camden Town,[82] where they fulfilled engagements totaling three weeks.[83] Performances were given each evening and eighteen subjects were shown nightly, with a change of programme each week.[84] The programme for the first week at the Bedford was briefly reported in *The Era*:

> . . . The programme concluded with an exhibition of the Kinematograph, amongst the subjects illustrated being our lads in red, bicyclists in Hyde-Park, an American liner leaving the Mersey, grand procession of the Czar through Paris, Royal Wedding, the Gay Parisienne, Regatta Day, Finsbury Park Station with train and passengers, fun on the Boulevards, and Loie Fuller, the transformation dancer.[85]

In an advertisement published on 6 March, the brothers claimed to have already spent six months exhibiting at London halls,[86] which if true, means they had been active in the trade since September 1896. However, I have not come across any reference to them before January of 1897. After their London engagements, they moved to Sandgate where they were booked at the Alhambra,[87] and on the 1st of March they began a two-week engagement at the Gaiety, Brighton.[88] Their projector, we are told, had been supplied by Interchangeable Ltd, of 57 St John's Road, Holloway,[89] and whom we know were once suppliers of Edison machines,[90] although later they handled other makes.[91]

Of particular interest is an exhibitor by the name of Hargreaves, who exploited an apparatus called the Phonotoscope, advertised as 'a machine with a mouth to it.'[92] This was an attempt to link the cinematograph with the phonograph. A similar idea had been attempted in 1896 by John Henry Rigg of Leeds.[93] Of course, the principle of linking sound with film can be traced back to Edison's Kinetophone — a Kinetoscope/Phonograph combination — which may have been exhibited in England as one is to be found in the Science Museum, London.[94] How successful was Hargreaves' Phonotoscope is open to question as very little information about it has been found. It seems to have met with a fair measure of success, for it was engaged for six nights at the Lyceum, Blackburn and stayed for twelve.[95] The same thing happened at Roscommon, Liverpool.[96] It was also booked at three other halls in that city.[97]

Even more of an oddity than the Phonotoscope, was William Friese-Greene's design for a portable film show which could be carried about on the person — a kind of walking cinema in fact. It was intended principally for advertising purposes and took two distinct forms. In the first, a frame or support is carried on the man's shoulders, like that commonly employed to support an advertising board above the man's head. Attached to the frame is a translucent screen and a portable film projector capable of being worked by a pulley connected to a conveniently situated hand-operated crank wheel. In the second form of the apparatus, the translucent screen is circular and constitutes a man's hat. A continuous band of film moves on a vertical axis within the hat and in front of which a cylinder moves in the reverse direction. This cylinder is pierced with a series of equidistant slots through which the pictures are to be viewed. For a more detailed description of this absurd apparatus, the reader is referred to the patent specification, number 29,363, of 11 December 1897.

A name which constantly crops up throughout this history, is that of Cecil M. Hepworth. He was an indefatigable commentator on matters dealing with cinematography and it is not surprising that he was the author of the first book on the subject to be published in England. In it he set out to explain the rudiments of the subject, beginning with a brief historical summary (mostly unreliable) followed by an account of the different aspects of the medium from film-making to exhibition. Appropriately titled *Animated Photography: the ABC of the Cinematograph*, the book was published in 1897 by Hazell, Watson & Viney Ltd, and was no 14 of a series of handbooks in the *Amateur Photographer's Library* (88). It was a small crown octavo volume comprising 108 pages, plus twenty pages of advertisements and illustrated with line drawings. In 1900 a second edition appeared in the same format, but with an additional chapter bringing the matter up to date. In all other respects, the text remained the same, except for the advertisement pages at the beginning and end of the volume, which were changed. In the earlier edition, one advertisement is of particular interest as it advertises 'Films on Hire'. The firm responsible was Noakes & Norman of Greenwich, which makes them one of the earliest, if not the first, film renters in the country, although it should be owned that the conditions of hire applied only to purchasers of their Invicta Cinematograph. Other advertisers in this first edition included Newman & Guardia Ltd, Maguire & Baucus Ltd, The Northern Photographic Works Ltd, R. W. Paul, J. H. Dallmeyer Ltd, Ross Ltd, Watson & Sons, Philipp Wolff (who includes a 3-page list of films for sale), Fuerst Bros, W. Wray, The Velograph Syndicate Ltd, Anglo-American Photo Import Office, Voigtlander & Sohn, and E. G. Wood.

In addition to his role as author and correspondent for the photographic press, Hepworth early in 1897, set himself up as a selling agent for certain photographic products,[98] in partnership with his cousin Monty Wicks.[99] The business was carried on

170

ANIMATED

PHOTOGRAPHY

THE A B C OF THE

CINEMATOGRAPH

A SIMPLE AND THOROUGH GUIDE TO
THE PROJECTION OF LIVING PHOTOGRAPHS, WITH
NOTES ON THE PRODUCTION OF
CINEMATOGRAPH NEGATIVES

BY

CECIL M. HEPWORTH

[THE AMATEUR PHOTOGRAPHER'S LIBRARY, NO. 14.]

London
HAZELL, WATSON, & VINEY, LD.
1, CREED LANE, LUDGATE HILL, E.C.
1897

88   Animated Photography: The ABC of the Cinematograph. By Cecil M. Hepworth (Title-page) This was
the first book on the subject to be published in England (*Science Library, University of Nottingham*)

at 22 Cecil Court, a narrow by-way connecting Charing Cross Road and St Martin's
Lane, which location was fast becoming a favourite one with the film trade and was
soon commonly referred to as 'flicker alley'.[100] It was whilst at no 22 that Hepworth
patented a special projection apparatus capable of operating continuously without the
presence of an attendant and intended principally for advertising purposes.[101]

It consisted of a cabinet, not unlike the Edison Kinetoscope, in which were a series of
pulleys at top and bottom and so arranged as to form a convenient spool-bank for
holding an endless band of film. On top of this was the projecting apparatus adapted
from one of the standard machines of the period. The film was led upwards from the
spool-bank so as to pass between condenser and projecting-lens. The projector itself
was connected by gearing and a shaft to the driving mechanism contained in the
cabinet, and the whole was electrically driven and provided with a timing device which
operated a mechanism for switching the machine on and off. A safety device was also

included so that the electric circuit was automatically broken as soon as any undue tension was applied to the film and so bringing the machine to a halt. As far as is known, nothing came of this invention and, it seems, was soon forgotten, eventually even by Hepworth himself, who failed to mention it in his autobiography published in 1951.

In 1895, Hepworth had patented a hand-feed carbon arc lamp which was successfully exploited for several years by Ross Ltd,[102] and in 1898, he was to patent a film developing machine.[103] But it is as a film producer that Hepworth was eventually to make his mark. This was still some little time in the future and his activities during the period under discussion were chiefly devoted to his writing, although he informs us in his autobiography that he was also involved as an exhibitor, giving lantern and film shows throughout the country with a projector obtained from Jacob Bonn of Holborn, having first greatly modified the machine to suit his own particular requirements. The same source also informs us that at one time he was associated with Messrs Lever and Nestlé in their scheme to exploit the possibilities of the film for advertising purposes. The man in charge of the operation was Spencer Clarke, with whom Hepworth remembers travelling about the country quite a lot, although he is unable to recall exactly what his own part entailed in the scheme. He does remember however, that no less than twelve complete Lumière projection outfits were purchased, which would indicate that the undertaking was on quite a substantial scale.

Cecil Milton Hepworth (89) was born in London in 1874 and died in 1953. His father T. C. Hepworth was a lecturer at the Royal Polytechnic Institution in Regent Street, and was the author of a standard work on the optical magic lantern entitled *The Book of the Lantern*, which went into six editions.[104] He also published *The ABC of Photography*, being himself an able photographer as well as an expert lantern lecturer and exhibitor, as was also his son Cecil. But unlike his father, Cecil M. Hepworth combined his lantern shows with specially selected films and presented a well thought out programme that was quite unique for those times. Commenting upon the success of the enterprise, *The Amateur Photographer* had this to say:

> Mr. Cecil M. Hepworth, who, as our readers may be aware, has been associated with cinematograph work for some time, has now arranged a living photograph and lantern entertainment, which he has given with considerable success at various places lately. The entertainment is not merely a heterogeneous collection of views jumbled together without rhyme or reason, as is too often the case with living animated photograph shows. Mr. Hepworth has struck out a somewhat new line in the arrangement of his pictures, animated and otherwise, to make a continuous and coherent entertainment. Those who are desirous of getting up a popular and high-class show during the winter months would do well to write to Mr. Hepworth, 22 Cecil Court, Charing Cross Road, W.C.[105]

A Scottish exhibitor, who made a considerable impact south of the border, was William Walker, of Walker & Co, 19 Bridge Street, Aberdeen. He first came into prominence when his firm was granted permission to film Queen Victoria. This was not his first encounter with royalty however, for he had previously given exhibitions at Balmoral Castle with the optical magic lantern.[106] Thus he was not entirely unknown to the Queen when she gave him permission to take the film. Here is an account of the event as related in *The British Journal of Photography*:

> Messrs. Walker & Co., Aberdeen, had the honour to receive permission to take a cinematograph picture of Her Majesty's departure from Ballater for Balmoral on Saturday morning,

89   Cecil M. Hepworth (1874–1953) (*Barnes Museum of Cinematography*)

May 22. On several occasions Messrs. Walker have had the distinction of giving limelight exhibitions at Balmoral, and to this they can now add the honour of having secured, by means of the cinematograph, a picture of what is always an interesting incident in the Queen's visit to Deeside, namely, the departure from Ballater Station. The instructions given to the firm were that they might take a cinematograph picture just immediately after Her Majesty's carriage started from the station, and the photograph will therefore be appropriately entitled *The Start for Balmoral*. Messrs. Walker, in order to ensure success in their efforts, had two cameras in position in the station yard. The picture taken consisted of a film about seventy-five feet in length, which was passed across the aperture of the camera in about fifty seconds. The total number of exposures, or photographs, taken in the fifty seconds would amount to about 1200. The picture, from a scenic point of view, should prove a very successful one. The Queen's carriage drove past at no great distance from the camera, and it will therefore occupy a prominent place in the cinematograph. A number of other carriages, however, were moving about in the vicinity at the time, so that the picture will have an animated and lively appearance.[107]

Some months later, on 25 October 1897, Walker & Co had the further distinction of presenting a programme of films at Balmoral Castle. Included in the programme was *The Start for Balmoral*, which had been taken the previous May. *The Era* gives the following account of the performance:

The Cinématographe made its appearance at Balmoral on Monday night, when Her Majesty and the Court witnessed what we are informed was a highly successful entertainment given by Mr William Walker, of Aberdeen. The pictures shown were of a very diversified kind, beginning with the stately pageant of the Jubilee, and including such humorous items as clowns, a pantomime sketch, snowballing, and a bicycle spill. Fortunately, the director of the entertainment was able to show some pictures of the heroes of the hour — the Gordon Highlanders — which especially gratified Her Majesty.[108]

The complete programme consisted of the following films:

Her Majesty's Diamond Jubilee — Celebrations in London: the Arrival at Buckingham Palace; Life Guards and Mounted Band of Dragoons; Royal Horse Artillery; Naval Brigade; Her Majesty's Carriage; Colonial Troops. Gordon Highlanders, Castlehill Barracks, Aberdeen — Bayonet Exercise and Volley Firing. Gordon Highlanders leaving Maryhill Barracks, Glasgow. Metropolitan Fire Brigade Scene — Off to the Fire. A Morning Dip — Cavalry crossing a River. At the Zoo — Feeding an Elephant. Children's Fresh Air Fund — 2000 Aberdeen Poor Children marching to Station. The Haunted Castle (humorous). Diamond Jubilee Celebrations — Aberdeen. Union-street, Aberdeen — A Busy Scene. Her Majesty the Queen's Arrival at Ballater — The Royal Guard of Honour, the Royal Scots and Deeside Highlanders. At the Braemar Gathering — March Past of the Clans; a Highland Reel. Train — Arrival at Station. Scene with the Gardener in a Pleasure Park. Near Union Bridge, Aberdeen. Snowballing and Bicycle Spill. At the Pantomime. Clowns — the Long and the Short of it. The Conjurer. Artist sketching Portrait of Her Majesty the Queen.[109]

The projector used by Walker for the Balmoral performance was the Wrench Cinematograph,[110] and those films which had not been taken by Walker & Co, had been supplied by Maguire & Baucus Ltd.[111]

174

90 William Walker, the Scottish pioneer of Cinematography (*Barnes Museum of Cinematography*)

At the age of 13, William Walker (90) was apprenticed to the bookselling business, and after gaining considerable experience in Aberdeen and London, he opened his own shop at 36 Bridge Street, Aberdeen. In 1885, he transferred his business to No 19, specialising in educational books. He later added a lantern department and became well-known for fine triple-lantern exhibitions in the north of Scotland.[112] He then turned his attention to cinematography, both as an exhibitor and film-maker, specialising in local subjects. The exhibition side of the business seems to have been particularly successful and by November 1897, claimed to have given upwards of 300 exhibitions.[113] It was reported in *The Optical Magic Lantern Journal*, that their shows are drawing large audiences in each town they visit.[114] I do not know whether any English towns were visited, or to what extent, if any, business was transacted south of the border. It hardly seems likely that such a go-ahead firm as this would have confined its activities strictly to Scotland.

Of course, not every exhibitor of films was a showman in the accepted sense of the word. Many were merely operators, seldom if ever seen by the audiences they served, for it was then normal practice to adopt back-projection, with the machine and operator situated behind the screen. This not only helped to minimise the noise of the machine, but also enabled a less powerful illuminant to be used in the lantern, since the projector could be placed reasonably close to the screen without intruding on auditorium space which would otherwise be the case were it to be placed on the other side. This mode of projection was more or less essential for performances held in music-halls, but was not always practicable when films were shown in village halls and the like where the stage area was small or non-existent; then ordinary projection from the front of the screen was resorted to. Some film exhibitors, especially of the itinerant type, often interspersed their film shows with a display of lantern slides. The two forms of entertainment were still considered to be complementary, especially as many film exhibitors had formerly been involved with lantern shows.

As we have already noted, many of the equipment manufacturers and dealers too, were involved in the exhibition side of the industry and among those who provided this service were Birt Acres, Jacob Bonn, Chard & Co, Edisonia Ltd, Fred Harvard, Haydon & Urry Ltd, Brandon Medland, Noakes & Norman, R. W. Paul, A. Rosenberg & Co, Twentieth Century Cinematographe Co, and Philipp Wolff.

It was during 1897 that the cinematograph probably made its first appearance at the fairgrounds, and it is generally believed that it was Randall Williams who was the first fairground showman to exhibit films in a portable booth. Williams was formerly a well-known fairground exhibitor of a ghost show illusion, but at the World's Fair held in the Royal Agricultural Hall, Islington, at the end of December 1896, he had replaced this with a film show.[115] The Agricultural Hall cannot be classed as a fairground in the traditional sense, but nevertheless, the event marks the beginning of the exploitation of the cinematograph by fairground people.

Randall Williams exhibited films at several fairs during 1897, but he was not alone in this, and several other showmen are known to have been similarily engaged at the same time, if not before. We can cite as examples, Edwin Lawrence, a former proprietor of a marionette show; Colonel Clarke, exhibitor of a ghost show; and Walls & Hammersley, also formerly ghost show exhibitors. An interesting relic of these days is a handbill now in the possession of Peter Williams (great-grandson of Randall Williams). Although the bill is undated and no reference is made to a particular venue, the fact that animated photographs of the Queen's Diamond Jubilee are mentioned, would seem to connect it with this period. Williams' show is advertised on the handbill as the 'Great Electroscope and Mammoth Philosophical Exhibition', and a statement says that the whole 'is worked by electricity, generated on the premises by our own magnificent engine.'[116]

Much research needs to be done on the fairground film shows, but the following list gives some of the fairs at which films were exhibited during 1897, together with the names of the showmen responsible: Blockley Wakes, North Manchester: Clarke's animated pictures; Williams' Bogiescope [?], Hughes' up-to-date peepshows [?]; Lawrence's cinématographe.[117] Great Cheetham Hill Wakes, Manchester (Jewish district): Clarke's animated picture theatre.[118] Denton Wakes: Lawrence's cinématographe.[119] Ashton-under-Lyne: Chappell's Cinématographe and Phantographe.[120] Manchester District Fair: Clarke's animated pictures.[121] Yorkshire Feasts: Oscar's cinématographe.[122] Bingley, Yorkshire: Williams's cinématographe theatre.[123] Clackheaton, Yorkshire: Hodgson's variety theatre and living pictures.[124] Gorton: Wall's ghost delusion, living pictures, and variety theatre.[125] Old Openshaw Wakes: Chappell & Radford's cinématographe.[126] Hyde New Wakes: Lawrence's cinématographe.[127] Great Horton (Bradford) Feast: Randall Williams with his living photography.[128] Holbeck Feast, South Leeds, Yorkshire: Bartlett's menagerie, circus and cinématographe combination; Randall Williams's living pictures.[129] Batley: Joe Hodgson's variety and cinematograph exhibition.[130] Salford: Clarke's cinématographe.[131] Douglas, Isle of Man: Professor Wood's dioramic and cinematographic lectures.[132] Stockport Fair: Wall's ghost illusion and living pictures.[133] Ilkley Feast: Walton, with his photo booth (converted at night into a cinematograph exhibition).[134] Morley, Yorkshire: Proctor & Bartlett's big combine, including circus, menagerie, and cinematograph; Randall Williams' living pictures.[135] Aldridge: James Chittock's trained dogs and monkeys and cinematograph.[136] The Birmingham Onion Fair: Wadbrook's ghost and electrical cinématographe; Chittock's dog and monkey circus and cinématographe.[137] Nottingham Goose Fair: Randall Williams; H. Hammersley — animated "photos".[138] Hull Fair: Randall Williams; Bartlett's lions and cinématographe.[139] Wigan Fair: Clarke's cinématographe.[140]

There is little doubt that the adoption of 'animated photographs' by fairground showmen greatly enlarged the potential audience for this form of entertainment and thus helped to consolidate the industry during its first formative years. It enabled large sections of the rural population to witness the new medium who otherwise would not have had the chance to do so. We must remember that the principal home of the cinema was still the music-hall and this drew its clientele mostly from the urban population. The fairground on the other hand, was first and foremost an attraction for country folk. Also, it is worth noting, the months of August and September, when the fairs were generally held, was the time when the music-halls could expect their lowest attendances, so in some measure, the fairs helped to keep the film business active just when it was likely to be at its lowest ebb. It might be said, that the fairground bioscope marks the transitional stage between the music-hall and the cinema theatre.

8 The Jubilee

The content of British films, during 1897, was, on the whole, very similar to that of the previous year, many producers still seemingly content to record movement for its own sake. A succession of simple 'actualities' continued to appear, which led Cecil M. Hepworth to complain of the 'interminable street scenes of which there are so many about'.[1] Film makers in France on the other hand, were progressing beyond this phase and were beginning to explore the other possibilities of the medium. The success with which their films were being met in England, led to some theorising on the subject. Speculation on the direction cinematography was likely to take in the future was a topic discussed by *The Photogram:*

> 'As the novelty of the subject wears away, it will be necessary to replace many of the films which audiences are now willing to tolerate, with new pictures having distinct value, either (a) for great technical or pictorial merit, or (b) for the interest of the subject. A popular Derby day is sure to have an enthusiastic run, even if short, and good views of the coming jubilee will have a longer period of appreciation; but a good deal of the future of kinetography would seem to lie in the hands of those who will make up their own subjects for the pictures.'[2]

However, English producers showed little regard for dramatic films and seemed instead to reserve their enthusiasm for topical events, no doubt believing that in this field they were assured of retaining the interest of the public. The University Boat Race, Henley Regatta and the Derby were all grist to their mill, for films of these events were bound to be well received by British audiences. It was a pattern that had already been established in 1896, but now, in 1897, it was given an added impetus, for this was the year of Queen Victoria's Diamond Jubilee.

The Jubilee procession through the streets of London, on 22 June, was an event upon which practically the whole of the British film industry directed its undivided attention. Preparations were put in hand weeks in advance and there was a general jockeying for positions, each producer intent on securing the best possible vantage point, or the fullest possible coverage of the event (91).

There were wild claims for impossible objectives. In an extravagant statement made at a meeting of the London and Provincial Photographic Association on 22 April, Birt Acres, in characteristic fashion, promised 'to have enough film in his camera, on the occasion of the forthcoming Diamond Jubilee Celebration, to last between two and three hours. He also expected to be able to show the same in natural colours.'[3]

There was also speculation on the chances of securing successful films of the procession, and *The British Journal of Photography* sounded this rather pessimistic note:

> *Apropos* of the Jubilee and the large amounts, it is rumoured, that have been offered for advantageous sites by cinematographers and photographers, it will be interesting to see what results will be obtained. Photographs of processions are always disappointing, as they have, as a rule, to be taken from elevated positions, and the view is generally much obstructed by the lavish display of bunting.[4]

Hitherto, the Derby and the University Boat Race were the two national events most

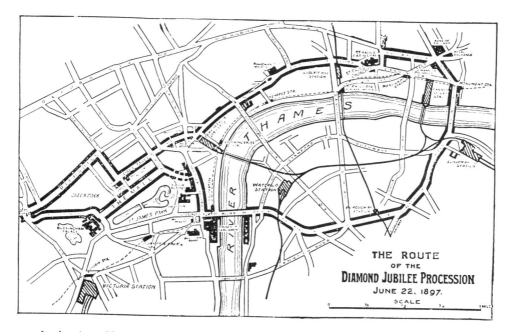

In the above Map the Route of the Procession is indicated by the thick outline; it lay up Constitution Hill, along Piccadilly, St. James's Street, Pall Mall, the Strand, and Fleet Street to St. Paul's; thence by Cheapside, King William Street, London Bridge, the Borough, Westminster Bridge, Parliament Street, Horse Guards' Parade, and the Mall, back to Buckingham Palace.

91 The route of Queen Victoria's Diamond Jubilee procession, 22 June, 1897 (*Barnes Museum of Cinematography*)

likely to receive the widest coverage by British film makers. One or other of these events, according to *The Amateur Photographer*, was 'regarded by cinematographers as a kind of "test object" for the quality of their machines and their own adroitness in operating them.' The journal then goes on to inform us that 'the coming Jubilee has thrown all other "test objects" for the capabilities of a kinetic camera into utter insignificance, and to the Jubilee, and the Jubilee alone, all the lively ones are turning their animated attention.'[5]

No aspect of the coming Jubilee seems to have been left unmentioned. 'Many wonderful Jubilee statistics have been published,' notes *The Amateur Photographer*, 'but if the facts of Jubilee cinematography could be elicited and tabulated, they would surely merit a prominent place among them.'[6] It is with no surprise therefore to find the weather among the subjects discussed:

'The vast army of photographers – animated and otherwise – who are preparing extensively for the celebrations of the Diamond Jubilee, seem to forget, or do not care to remember, to what a great extent they are dependent upon the state of the weather on the great day.'[7]

When the great day arrived, strategic points along the route were manned by eager cameramen, poised with their primitive machines, ready to start cranking immediately Her Majesty's carriage and its retinue of sixteen or so vehicles came into range. More than two dozen cine-cameras were thus positioned ready to record the Queen's

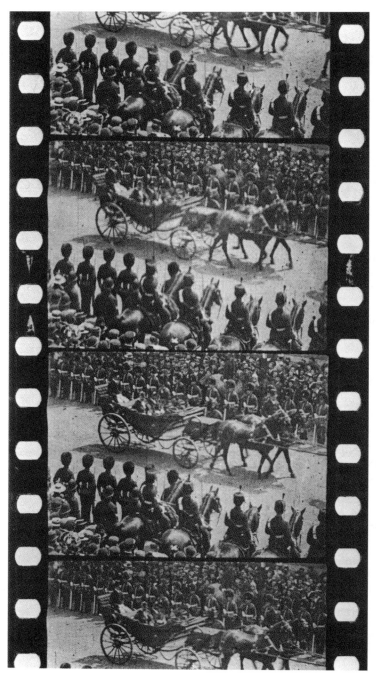

92 Queen Victoria' Diamond Jubilee Procession (R. W. Paul, 1897) Taken at the corner of York Road, Westminster (*Barnes Museum of Cinematography*)

180

progression. Now and again there must have been an anxious gaze skywards and the fervent hope that the sun would not disappear at the crucial moment, behind the clouds that were all too prevalent in the morning sky. Chances of securing successful pictures without sunlight were minimal, and it was upon the weather that these pioneer cinematographers pinned their hopes, for they were otherwise secure in the knowledge that their own ability could achieve the rest.

For a contemporary account of these preparations, we turn to a passage in *The Photogram:*

'At the time of writing every kinetographer is busy with arrangements for making views of the Diamond Jubilee procession, and some of them have already (a fortnight in advance) booked large orders for the resulting positives. Some of the firms make quite a mystery of their intentions, but we know what some of them are doing. The most extensive arrangements of which we have heard are those of J. W. Rowe & Co., who will have six operators at work at different points, including one facing the service on the steps of St. Paul's. J. Neville Maskelyne will photograph the service from his own great grand-stand. The Velograph Syndicate has made arrangements for two or three operators at good points; Dr. J. H. Smith & Co (of Zurich) will have two fine positions in the yard of Charing Cross-station, facing the procession as it comes from Duncannon-street into the Strand; and the Moto-Photo Supply Co. will have one of the best positions on the whole route for commanding the procession itself, at the corner of Parliament-street and Great George-street, overlooking the northern slope from Westminster-bridge. The Lumières (Fuerst Bros.) will have more than one experienced operator on the route, and we understand that both Birt Acres and W. & D. Downey have received valuable official concessions in the matter of positions.'[8]

The Ludgate Kinematograph Film Company arranged to take the procession from the offices of the *European Mail*, in Ludgate Circus,[9] and their plans were made known well in advance, in the pages of *The Photographic News* of 4 June:

' . . . Three machines of the latest pattern are to be used, and pictures will be taken at the rate of 16 a second for two hours, which will include not only all the views of the procession, but the various incidents of interest that may occur among the crowd. Mr Lang Sims, the technical manager of the company, whose name is familiar in the photographic world, is devoting special attention to the preparation of the most up-to-date machines, and these are being manufactured by Messrs Watson & Sons, opticians to Her Majesty's Government, 313, High Holborn, W.C., so that no pains are being spared to secure a good set of films of the Royal Procession'.[10]

From other sources we learn that R. W. Paul had three cameras in the field, one situated at the corner of York Road, Westminster (92), and the other two on the south and north sides of St Paul's Churchyard.[11] The film taken at York Road showed 'the head of the procession with the gigantic Captain Ames leading his troopers, the colonial procession and Canadian and other troopers, and the royal cavalcade'[12] (93a). Paul himself took shots from a window on the south side of St Paul's Churchyard which depicted 'the Cape Mounted Rifle passing St Paul's, the dragoons, the arrival of the royal cavalcade and princes, the Indian escort, and the Queen's carriage entering the Churchyard'[13] (93b,c). Another shot of the Queen's carriage, from the opposite point of view was taken by a Mr. Hunt, one of Paul's assistants, from the front of the

(a)

(b)

(c)

(d)

93 Queen Victoria's Diamond Jubilee Procession (R. W. Paul, 1897) (a) Head of the Queen's procession taken from the corner of York Road, Westminster. (b) & (c) The Queen's procession and carriage entering St Paul's Churchyard, photographed by R. W. Paul from a window on the south side of the churchyard. (d) The Queen's carriage from the north side of St Paul's Churchyard, photographed by Paul's assistant, Mr. Hunt. From frame illustrations published in Cassell's Family Magazine (July, 1897) pp 327–30 (*David Francis Collection*)

Maskelyne pavilion, on the north side of the Churchyard[14] (93d). Paul undoubtedly considered his own position the most important of the three, for it so transpired that the film taken from this point showed a clear view of the Queen as her carriage entered the churchyard.[15] It is also likely that Paul designed the special tripod, now in the Science Museum, London,[16] with this position in mind (94). The tripod is fitted with a revolving head, but whether this was actually used for a panning shot or merely to facilitate the positioning of the camera, is not known. Only an examination of the actual film itself can decide this point. However, a description of the tripod written at the time, states:

'The camera could be slewed round horizontally so as to follow a moving object and keep it in the centre of the field of vision by means of a horizontal worm wheel. It could also be tilted in any direction with the aid of a spherical seat on the short tripod which supported it. In brief it was under complete management.'[17]

This certainly makes Paul one of the earliest, if not the first, to devise a means for panning the camera in order to keep an object moving past the camera in the field of view. The importance of this simple step in the evolution of film technique cannot be overemphasised.

94 Paul's Cinematograph Camera No 2, 1896. Used by R. W. Paul for filming Queen Victoria's Jubilee procession in 1897, for which purpose the special stand for revolving the camera was designed (*Science Museum, London*)

Paul's coverage of the Jubilee procession was the subject of a special article published in the July issue of *Cassell's Family Magazine*. It was written by John Munro and entitled 'Living Photographs of the Queen'.[18] It is from this article that the above quotation concerning the tripod is taken. The same source also provides us with a few particulars about the camera itself:

'A tachometer, or speed indicator, tells the number of pictures being taken in a second at any moment, and a revolution counter shows the number taken during the whole time the instrument is at work. There is also a view "finder", which gives a horizontal picture on a screen of ground glass corresponding to that impressed on the film, and shows the photographer what he is to expect. The working speed of the camera, that is to say the number of pictures taken in a second, is controlled by altering the strength of the electric current, and

(a)

(b)

95   Paul's Animatographe Camera, which was used to film the Jubilee procession. (a) R. W. Paul operating the camera. (b) View of the interior. From illustrations published in Cassell's Family Magazine (July, 1897) pp 328 and 329 (*David Francis Collection*)

consequently the power of the motor, by a switch and "rheostat," which is a sort of Sluice-gate for the current.'[19]

We are also informed that the camera was driven by an electric motor of one-eighth horse-power[20] (95).

Recalling the events of 1897 in a lecture to the British Kinematograph Society, delivered on 3 February 1936, Paul had this to say about the filming of the Jubilee:

'An outstanding event of 1897 was the Diamond Jubilee of Queen Victoria, with its magnificent pageantry of royalties and troops from all over the world, and the touching ceremony at the steps of St. Paul's Cathedral. Large sums were paid for suitable camera positions, several of which were secured for my operators. I myself operated a camera perched on a narrow ledge in the Churchyard. Several continental cinematographers came over, and it was related of one that, when the Queen's carriage passed he was under his seat changing film, and of another, hanging on the railway bridge at Ludgate Hill, that he turned his camera until he almost fainted, only to find, on reaching a dark room, that the film had failed to start.'[21]

These tales of the tribulations of Continental cameramen need to be taken with a pinch of salt. I have come across other examples in the literature of the period.[22] We do have however, an instance of a similar misfortune which befell J. N. Maskelyne, lessee of the Egyptian Hall, Piccadilly. Maskelyne had gone to great pains to secure a favourable vantage point from which to film the special ceremony which was to take place on the steps of St Paul's and for this purpose he had rented a first floor window at No 4 St Paul's Churchyard. There was a projection of from one to three feet outside the window on which a staging or platform was to be erected to support his camera. As this work required Maskelyne's entire attention, the performances at the Egyptian Hall were temporarily suspended and the hall closed for nine days.[23] Maskelyne's preparations for filming the great event became the subject of an amusing cartoon in the theatrical paper *Entr'acte*. Here he is shown in conversation with Queen Victoria to whom he is saying: 'I am a conjurer by profession, and if I succeed in making thousands of sovereigns out of one, I am sure your gracious majesty will applaud the feat.' (96).

Unfortunately, the freeholders of the premises in St Paul's Churchyard, Messrs Wasson & Co, objected to the use to which their property had been put, and sued Maskelyne for trespass. Maskelyne alleged in court, that the case had been brought by Wasson out of spite, because he had refused to pay for the additional area which the camera platform provided. Mr. W. A. Rouch, a manufacturer of photographic apparatus, stated on Wasson's behalf, that in his opinion, the projection over the plaintiff's premises was the most perfect site for taking photographs of the Jubilee procession and estimated its value at £20. Despite Rouch's favourable opinion of the site, Maskelyne informed the court that no photographs had in fact been taken, 'because the site was bad, and only the backs of the persons forming the procession could be taken.' The jury returned a verdict for the plaintiff, and awarded him one farthing damages, but as the defendant had paid 40 shillings into court, the judge at the Lord Mayor's Court, at which the case was tried, gave judgement for the defendant with costs.[24]

R. J. Appleton & Co filmed the procession as it passed St George's Church in the Borough,[25] and Alfred Wrench, of J. Wrench & Son, had 'a fine position at the corner of King William Street', the camera used being the one patented by him and extensively

MR. MASKELYNE'S SCHEME IN ST. PAUL'S CHURCHYARD.

MR. MASKELYNE, TO HER MAJESTY: — "I AM A CONJURER BY PROFESSION, AND IF I SUCCEED IN MAKING THOUSANDS OF SOVEREIGNS OUT OF ONE, I AM SURE YOUR GRACIOUS MAJESTY WILL APPLAUD THE FEAT."

96 J. N. Maskelyne's intention to film Queen Victoria's Jubilee, inspired this cartoon in the theatrical paper Entr'acte (*British Library*)

used throughout Great Britain.[26] Harold A. Saunders, with a Motorgraph Camera, had taken up his postion on behalf of W. Waton & Sons, by whom he was employed, but his actual point on the route is not recorded.[27] Neither is that of G. Albert Smith, whom we know was also present and took a number of films.[28] Philipp Wolff, or his representative, was in attendance too, but his position likewise is unknown.[29] Chard & Co seem to have had several sites judging from the content of the five films they subsequently issued, viz.: *The Queen at Temple Bar; Procession Entering the City; Queen Entering the Borough; Procession Crossing London Bridge;* and *Colonial Premiers in St James's Street.*[30]

Somewhere along the route was the large Mutograph camera, possibly operated by W. K. L. Dickson himself, for the American Mutoscope company.[31] The London Stereoscopic Company appear to have had more than one cinematographer present, for they later announced that they had 'a selection of films taken from unique positions'.[32] We know that they had several still photographers covering the procession, and from the views that were subsequently published,[33] it is possible to learn the actual vantage points from which they were taken. These show the procession passing down King William Street; passing the eastern end of Cheapside; and crossing London Bridge into Southwark. Since the Company's cinematographers are likely to have shared the same positions, we can expect the films to show similar viewpoints. The stills may therefore prove useful to film archivists in helping to identify the films themselves should they still exist. The London Stereoscopic Company had premises at 54 Cheapside, so it is highly likely that some of the procession was also recorded from that vantage point.

The Velograph Syndicate were suitably positioned at the grandstand outside Charing Cross Railway Station;[34] and Professor Joly's Cinématographe caught the procession from a commanding position at the corner of Piccadilly and St James's Street,[35] whilst Birt Acres is said to have had a favoured position within the precincts of Buckingham Palace.[36]

It was an amazing array of pioneer cinematographers, representing almost every major and minor film producer in Great Britain. This was the first time that any event had been so extensively covered by the motion picture camera and presages the work of the newsreel cameramen of the 20s and 30s, or even that of present day television. The sheer scope of the undertaking is best realised by glancing at a list of the film-makers supposed to have taken part in the enterprise:

R. J. Appleton & Co
British Cinematographe Co, Ltd (Prof Joly's Cinématographe)
Chard & Co
W. & D. Downey
Fuerst Bros (Lumière); more than two operators.
Haydon & Urry Ltd
London Stereoscopic Co; two or three operators.
Ludgate Kinematograph Film Co; three cameras.
Moto-Photo Supply Co (Prestwich)
Mutoscope & Biograph Syndicate Ltd (American Biograph)
Northern Photographic Works Ltd (Birt Acres)
Robt. W. Paul; three operators
J. W. Rowe & Co; six operators
Dr J. H. Smith & Co (Zurich); two operators
Velograph Syndicate; two or three operators

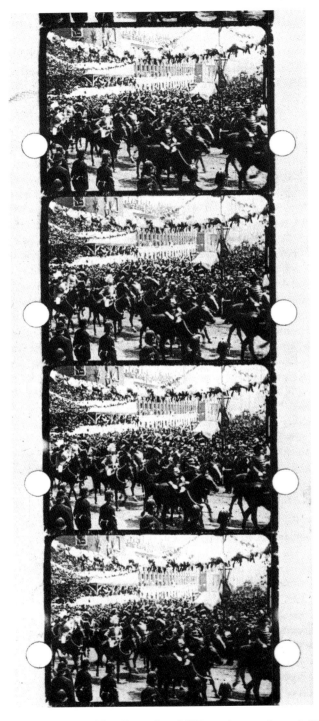

97   Queen Victoria's Diamond Jubilee Procession (1897, producer unknown) Film taken with the Cinématographe-Lumière. (*Kodak Museum, Harrow*)

W. Watson & Sons
Philipp wolff
J. Wrench & Son

No doubt there were others too, for whom no records have yet been found. Representatives from abroad were surely present in larger numbers than the list suggests. It could very well be that the true numbers present far exceeds the already extensive list of names printed above.

As far as the weather was concerned, things did not turn out too badly, although 'none of those who took up a position previous to Pall Mall were favoured with a glimpse of sunlight until after Her Majesty's carriage had passed'.[37] But from the number of films subsequently placed on the market, it would seem that the majority of cameramen, at other points along the route, managed to secure successful pictures. For example, Robt. W. Paul[38] and Philipp Wolff[39] were both able to offer twelve films each, and Fuerst Brothers, seven,[40] the latter being photographed by Jules Fuerst with the Cinématographe-Lumière[41] (97). 'A grand series of six films' was also offered by Haydon & Urry Ltd,[42] and Alfred Wrench too, obtained 'an excellent series of films'.[43] The total length of the original film exposed by Wrench was about 800ft, which was subsequently sold as separate sequences of 75ft each and one of 100ft.[44] A writer for *The Optician* who had seen the films, pronounced them 'exceedingly clear and well defined'.[45]

Harold A. Saunders had exposed two spools of film, each about 500ft, which were put on the market by W. Watson & Son in lengths of about 75ft.[46] The results obtained by the Velograph Syndicate (98) are described by G. R. Baker in his regular article for *The British Journal of Photography:*

> 'A number of cinematograph cameras were in use on the memorable June 22, some to take the films of the ordinary length, say, of seventy-five feet, while others were provided with spools and phenomenally long film, running if I am correctly informed, to more than 1000 feet; but of the results of one apparatus, at least, I can speak with certainty, for, within forty-eight hours of the procession, I was favoured with prints and transparencies of a portion of an exposed film 180 feet long, and the results which lie before me must be gratifying to Mr. A. Langfier, the Managing Director of the Velograph Syndicate, who was responsible for the work, and succeeded so well at the Grand Stand outside Charing Cross Railway Station.'[47]

Of course every effort was made, to get the results on to the market as quickly as possible, but the keenest competition was naturally between those film producers who were also engaged in the exhibition side of the business. For them it was a mad rush to screen the films within the shortest possible time after the event. Even in 1896, Robt. W. Paul had succeeded in showing the film of the Derby within twenty-four hours of the race, and one would have expected him to have exceeded this record in the case of the Jubilee films. But in fact, it was not until Friday evening (the procession having taken place the previous Tuesday) that his Jubilee films were shown at the Alhambra Theatre, Leicester Square.[48]

Pride of place as regards swiftness of delivery, must surely go to the Bradford *Daily Argus* and R.. J. Appleton & Co, who succeeded in publicly showing a picture of the procession on a screen in Bradford on the evening of Jubilee day. 'A van, specially fitted for developing, printing, etc., was attached to one of the trains for Bradford, and by midnight of the 22nd the view of the whole procession was projected on to a screen facing Foster-square, which was thronged by thousands of people.'[49]

189

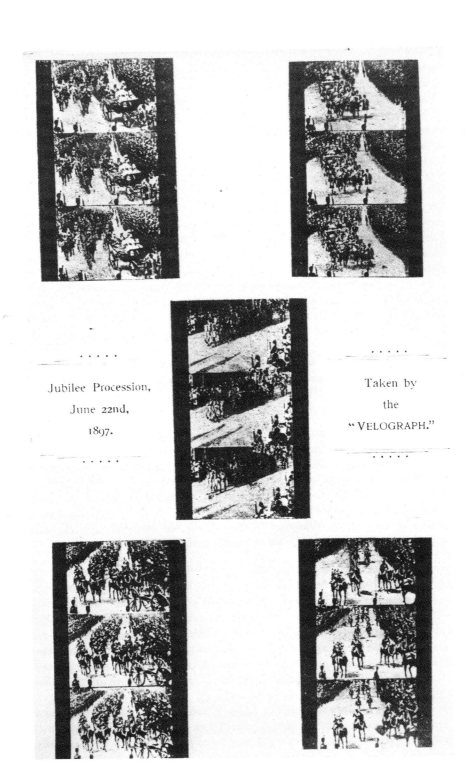

Jubilee Procession,
June 22nd,
1897.

Taken by
the
"VELOGRAPH."

98 Jubilee films advertised by the Velograph Syndicate in The Magic Lantern Journal Annual 1897–8 (*Barnes Museum of Cinematography*)

R. J. Appleton & Co, and their sponsor, the *Argus* newspaper, were fortunate too during the actual filming of the event, and as *The Photogram* remarked, 'both good management and good luck seem to have befriended them, for the eclipsing parasol of Her Majesty the Queen was raised just as she passed their stand and a happy smile (duly recorded) passed over the royal countenance.'[50]

At a performance given before Wakefield Photographic Society on 2 September, Appleton & Co showed five films of the procession and according to the published report, The Prince of Wales, The Duke of Cambridge, and Lord Wolseley were all prominent and were easily recognised by the audience.[51]

Paul's Jubilee films had been booked by Alfred Moul, manager of the Alhambra Theatre, for a period of eight weeks, at a fee of £30 per week,[52] but after only three performances the films were withdrawn owing to a dispute over the terms of the contract. Paul took the matter to court and the case was heard on 23 February 1898. The outcome of the action will be described later, but in the meantime we will follow the course of events which followed from this dispute.

The films were shown for the first time on Friday evening, 25 June,[53] and again at a matinée performance on the following day.[54] According to the court proceedings, it was immediately afterwards that the row started. However, things were not apparently brought to a head, for the films were given a third performance on the following Monday. By this time however, the dispute must have reached a stage where there was no likelihood of a settlement and the Monday performance proved to be the last. From the account published in *The Era*, the performances had every prospect of being a great success:

'Mr. Alfred Moul, at last Saturday's matinée at the Alhambra, announced a new series of pictures by Mr. Paul, taken on the day of the Jubilee at two points on the route. The development of the series, by means of the Animatographe, gives a very good idea of the memorable scene at St. Paul's the procession is seen entering the churchyard, the Queen herself turning her head to look at the cathedral as the carriage passes. The face of Her Majesty is clearly visible under the sun shade. The other pictures show the head of the Colonial procession passing from Westminster-bridge. When the pictures were shown on Monday the house was packed, among the audience being Prince Rudolph of Austria, and a detachment of Borneo native police, and some of the Indian visitors. After the last picture had flashed off the scene the whole house rose and sang a verse of "God Save the Queen." The band very cleverly struck the key and joined in. This was followed by ringing cheers, the Borneo men meanwhile standing at the salute.'[55]

The management of the Alhambra no doubt regretted the loss of what promised to be a highly successful run, but with so many other Jubilee films available on the market, it is not likely that it was unduly put out by Paul's departure. Indeed, within nine days his place had been filled by J. W. Wrench & Son, whose Jubilee films were presented by means of their own Cinematograph, Paul's Theatrograph projector (or Animatographe as it was called at the Alhambra) naturally being no longer available to the management. The Wrench performances seem to have met with a fair measure of success, as the following comment in *The Era* indicates:

'At the Alhambra, on Thursday night [8 July] the audience were treated to a second edition of the Jubilee procession by the aid of the Cinematographe (sic). The most striking and interesting features were effectively reproduced, and the exhibition was voted a great success.'[56]

The comment in *The Optician* was equally favourable:

'The sensation of the week at the Alhambra Music Hall is an exhibition of living pictures of the Royal Jubilee Procession, taken and reproduced by Wrench's patent cinematograph. The series is an exceptionally fine one, and the marvellous verisimilitude of the pictorial pageant wins — as it amply merits — great applause.'[57]

The Wrench Cinematograph was of course a very trustworthy machine and the Jubilee films were described by *The Optical Magic Lantern Journal*, as 'an excellent series.'[58] Their total length, according to the same source, was about one thousand feet, but another source states that the actual films shown at the Alhambra lasted for about five minutes.[59] We are also informed that 'the directors of the Alhambra Theatre, ever anxious to have everything of the best, have secured the exclusive right for two months of exhibiting these pictures within a prescribed radius.'[60] This statement however, proved incorrect, for Wrench informed the editor of *The Optical Magic Lantern Journal*, in which the report appeared, that the terms were for 'an indefinite period' and not 'for two months' as stated, adding that 'Messrs. Wrench can, of course, supply cinematographic pictures of the Jubilee procession, it being only one particular series which is in the meantime reserved.'[61]

Paul must have felt that he had been treated abominably by the management of the Alhambra, especially after so long an association with that theatre. His Animatographe had been a regular feature of the programmes there since 25 March 1896, and one can understand his determination not to let the matter rest but to seek redress in a court of law. Fortunately, he still had valuable connections with other music halls in London. The same programme that was shown at the Alhambra for the last time on Monday, 28 June, was also presented at the Tivoli Theatre in the Strand on the same evening. A brief comment on the performance, published in *The Era*, states:

'Mr. R. W. Paul fills out a much-appreciated interval with his Jubilee pictures, exhibited by means of the Theatrograph. The arrival of the Queen's Carriage and the Royal Princes in St. Paul's-churchyard elicit loud cheers, and the victory of Galtee More in the Derby of 1897 is also hailed with lively satisfaction.'[62]

Similar shows were presented at the Oxford[63] and Paragon music halls, the latter receiving the following notice in *The Era:*

'. . . and then, to crown all, there is Mr. R. W. Paul's Theatrograph, with an exhibition of pictures of the Diamond Jubilee procession taken in St. Paul's Churchyard and Westminster. As an accompaniment to the picturesqueness of these animated views of the great event of the year Mr. Worswick's band play a selection of national airs, and when Her Majesty is seen at the foot of the steps of the great City cathedral a very hearty cheer goes up. So great, indeed, is the enthusiasm that Mr. Paul obligingly repeats the "picture", The Jubilee views are supplemented by other subjects, such as the Prince of Wales' Derby last year, followed by a realistic representation of this year's race. Loud laughter is evoked when that very popular event of the Music Hall Sports, the comic costume scramble is seen.'[64]

Paul's Jubilee films were also being shown at many other theatres throughout the country, including for example, the Palace, Bristol; Empire, Cardiff; and Palace Theatre, Douglas, Isle of Man.[65]

192

The case of Paul v. Alhambra Company, Limited, was tried at the Queen's Bench Division before the Lord Chief Justice and a special jury. In this case, the plaintiff (R. W. Paul) claimed to recover from the defendent company damages for wrongful dismissal from their employment, and for breach of contract to employ him. The defendant denied liability. The Alhambra maintained that under the agreement, Paul's performance should be exclusive for London and that he should not perform within ten miles of the defendant's theatre. These terms the plaintiff repudiated, stating that although it was understood that he should not play at competing places like the Empire, the question of where he should exhibit in the Metropolitan district was left to his discretion, as under his original contract. The jury took three-quarters of an hour to reach their decision and returned a verdict in favour of the plaintiff for £150 and judgement accordingly.[66]

Among the most successful films of the Jubilee were those shown at the Empire Theatre, Leicester Square, by Prof Jolly's Cinématographe (Joly's Patent), a lengthy review of which appeared in *The Era* on 24 July:

'Those loyal subjects of Her Majesty who did not witness the glorious pageant of the Queen's progress through the streets of London to the thanksgiving service at St Paul's, on June 22nd, should not miss the opportunity of seeing the wonderful series of pictures at the Empire, giving a complete representation of the Jubilee procession. We owe much to the recent development of scientific photography; and by the invention of the cinématographe a means has been discovered for the preservation of what is to all intents and purposes living representations of memorable events. Our descendents will be able to learn how the completion of the sixtieth year of Queen Victoria's reign was celebrated in the capital of the country. The views of the procession are taken from a commanding position at the corner of Piccadilly and St. James's-street, and bearing in mind the difficulties necessarily attendant upon such an undertaking, the pictures are for the most part surprisingly clear and distinct. There is in the theatre a repetition in some degree of what actually happened along the line of route on Jubilee Day. The fine body of Colonial soldiers are instantly recognised and enthusiastically cheered as they gallantly swing by. There is also a cordial greeting for the Guards, the Artillery, the Lancers, the men of the Naval Brigade, and the picturesque Indian contingent. The burly drum-major of the London Scottish band comes in for special recognition, for he is a notable and conspicuous figure in the procession. After carriage after carriage rolls by one becomes almost dazzled by the ever-moving spectacle. Some amusement too may be found in watching the eager crowd in the foreground, and the strenuous endeavours of some of its members who are short of stature to obtain a good view of the passing show. No fewer than 22,000 pictures were taken for the purpose of being utilised in this representation of one of the most memorable events of the century, and it is with a burst of loyal enthusiasm that the audience recognises the Royal carriage and its occupants. Happily the vehicle stopped for a few seconds at this point, and Her Majesty is seen to bow graciously in acknowledgment of the hearty English welcome she receives from the crowd. Professor Jolly's cinématographe ought to prove a strong attraction at the Empire for some time to come.'[67]

This review was published more than a month after the event took place, yet the films of the Jubilee still managed to attract members of the public in sufficient numbers for them to remain the principal attraction on the bill. Moreover, their continuing popularity called forth a further comment, in the same paper, on 7 August:

'Wonderful indeed, are the achievements of modern science; and not the least astonishing of

THE NATIONAL
PALACE THEATRE
of Varieties, Croydon.

Lessees:—THE NATIONAL PALACE OF VARIETIES, CROYDON (LTD.).
Directors:—MESSRS. HERBERT CAMPBELL, DAN LENO,
HARRY RANDALL, FRED WILLIAMS, HENRY JOYNER, and
G. E. S. VENNER.
General Manager: Mr. J. SPARROW. Resident Manager: Mr. P. A. LENNON.
Secretary: Mr. G. E. S. VENNER.

PROGRAMME

FOR

MONDAY, AUGUST 9th, 1897,
AND EVERY EVENING DURING THE WEEK.

1   OVERTURE
(Band).

2   The SISTERS DE CASTRO AND
MAUD STONEHAM.
In Novel Musical Sketch, entitled—
"HIS LORDSHIP."

3   Miss EMMA CHAMBERS
(The Popular Comedienne and Burlesque Actress).

4   The McCONNELL FAMILY.
In Operatic Trios, &c.

5   Miss LILY WELFORD (Serio & Speciality Dancer)

6   Special and Most Expensive Engagement of
THE VELOGRAPH
Series of ANIMATED PHOTOGRAPHS. A Selection from the following
Views will be shown Every Evening:—
THE DIAMOND JUBILEE
(The Procession in its entirety). Her Majesty the Queen and Royal Family at
the State Garden Party, Buckingham Palace—The Royal Regatta,
Henley 1897—The Derby, 1897—The Ascot Gold Cup, 1897—The Flying
Scotchman—The Seaside—Military Drill—London Life—and others.

7   The FIGAROS
(Continental Operatic Duettists and Dancers).

8   Lieut. WALTER COLE
(The Great Ventriloquist, with his "Merry Folks.")

9   Mr. GEORGE BEAUCHAMP
(The Great Comic Vocalist).

10   Professor ROBERT GILBERT'S
TROUPE OF ACROBATIC DOGS.
Introducing Novel and Original Tricks.

11   REZENE AND ROBINI
(Burlesque Trapeze Artistes).

"GOD SAVE THE QUEEN."

Musical Director: Mr. LEON A. BASSETT.
Stage Manager: Mr. J. CROWLEY.

THIS PROGRAMME IS SUBJECT TO ALTERATION.

The Numbers Shown from the sides of the Stage will correspond
with those on the Programme.

Pianoforte supplied by G. and A. WEBB.
Doors open at 7.30.   Commence at 7.45.
Saturdays, Early Doors at 6.45.   Commence 7.30.   Extra Talent.

99   Programme of Jubilee films presented by the Velograph Syndicate at the Palace Theatre, Croydon, 9
August, 1897 (*Science Museum, London*)

these is desplayed in Professor Jolly's improved Cinématographe. You sit in your stall at the Empire, and the entire Jubilee procession, including, we are told, 22,000 pictures, passes before your admiring eyes. Those who did not see the procession can console themselves with a counterfeit presentment which reproduces every movement and every form; those who did will be pleasantly reminded of the great day. By-the by, we may observe that the almost deserted condition of the tiers of seats near the Horse Guards bear witness to the truth of the tales about certain speculators' losses on Jubilee Day.'[68]

The crowning success occured on 23 November when the manager of the Empire supervised a command performance of Joly's Cinématographe at Windsor Castle. A full programme of films was presented, which included the Diamond Jubilee Procession and an appropriate orchestral accompaniment.[69]

A similar success had attended the Jubilee films taken by the American Biograph, when a performance was given for the Prince of Wales at St James's Palace on 20 July.[70] The films were also shown at the Palace Theatre of Varieties, Cambridge Circus with a specially composed music score, which received due praise in *The Era*:

'Amongst the views exhibited in the American Biograph at the Palace are representations of the Diamond Jubilee Procession and others taken during a sail round the fleet at the recent naval review. These, with photographs from the military parade at Aldershot, are well worth a visit to this handsome and well-managed music hall. Special praise is due to the music composed by Mr Alfred Plumpton to accompany the exhibition of the Biograph pictures.'[71]

A performance was given at Balmoral Castle for Queen Victoria on 25 October, by William Walker, of Aberdeen.[72] The programme, which was projected by a Wrench Cinematograph,[73] included six films of the Jubilee procession obtained from Maguire & Baucus Ltd.[74] These were probably the Lumière films photographed by Jules Fuerst.

Phil & Bernard were advertising a film of the Jubilee procession lasting a quarter of an hour without a break, and claimed to be able to project a 18ft picture, operating from the back of the stage.[75] The Jubilee films were probably obtained from J. Wrench & Son, and performances were given at the Alhambra, Leicester Square,[76] and the Foresters Music Hall, Bethnal Green.[77]

At the London Pavilion, Piccadilly Circus, Signor Polverini was exhibiting a series of Jubilee films,[78] which we have reason to believe, were supplied by Haydon & Urry Ltd, who also, it is understood, were the suppliers of the projector used during the performances. This Islington firm had recently been equipped with extensive facilities for producing their own films[79] and the Jubilee series were probably among the first of their successes. Six episodes of the procession were offered for sale at £4 each, and each film was 75ft in length.[80]

For the week commencing 9 August, the Velograph Jubilee films were the main attraction at the National Palace Theatre of Varieties, Croydon, where they were supported by other films from the same producers. A printed programme of the performances is in the Charles Urban Collection at the Science Museum, London (99).

I think it would be true to say that more films of the Jubilee were sold in England during 1897 than of any other subject. Almost every dealer listed some aspect of the event and almost every showman at one time or another included the subject in his programme. It would be pointless therefore, and well nigh impossible, to attempt to list

CORN EXCHANGE,

CHELMSFORD.

Friday and Saturday, Oct. 1 & 2,

A HIGH-CLASS EXHIBITION OF THE VERY FINEST

ANIMATED
PHOTOGRAPHS

Will be given in the above Hall under the Joint Management of the Proprietors of

NESTLE'S MILK AND SUNLIGHT SOAP.

IN ADDITION TO A NUMBER OF OTHER CAREFULLY SELECTED PICTURES, THE

Queen's .
Diamond
Jubilee .
Procession

Will positively be reproduced . .

by means of nearly 1,000 feet of Animated Photographic Film. The whole will form absolutely the Largest and Finest Series of

LIVING ✳
MOVING ✳
PICTURES

Ever presented in England.

FOR LIST OF SUBJECTS,
SEE SMALL
BILLS AND PROGRAMMES.

≫ ADMISSION SIXPENCE. ≪

A Few Reserved Seats, ONE SHILLING.   Doors Open at 7.30.   Commence at 8.

All Persons presenting a Nestle's Milk or Sunlight Soap Wrapper will be admitted at HALF-PRICE TO ALL SEATS.

All Communications respecting the above to be made to H. SPENCER CLARKE, 59 and 60 CHANCERY LANE, LONDON, W.C.

Printed by FEILDEN, McAllan & CO., 52 Gray's Inn Road, W.C.

100   Poster advertising a film show at the Corn Exchange, Chelmsford, Essex. This was one of many performances given throughout the country by Messrs Neslé & Lever (*Kodak Museum, Harrow*)

101 A cardboard imitation Jubilee medal (1¼in dia) issued by the Mellin's food company to advertise a series of film shows (*Barnes Museum of Cinematography*)

every occasion when Jubilee films were shown, or to attempt to list the dealers from whom they were to be obtained. Instead, we will conclude this survey by looking at a novel form of advertising to which the Jubilee films gave rise. This was an advertising campaign which was launched by Lever Brothers and Nestlé whereby a series of cinematograph performances were given throughout the country featuring 'Queen Victoria's Diamond Jubilee Procession'. All persons presenting a Nestlé Milk or Sunlight Soap wrapper were admitted at half-price to all seats, the normal price of admission being sixpence. The apparatus used for the exhibitions was the Cinématographe-Lumière and the total length of the Jubilee film was nearly 1,000ft. Since this was not long enough by itself to provide a full-time entertainment, the programme was augmented with other films[81] (100). In charge of the enterprise was H. Spencer Clarke, whose offices were at 59 & 60 Chancery Lane, London. One of his assistants at this time was the future British film producer Cecil M. Hepworth. Messrs. Nestlé and Lever were not alone in sponsoring film shows as a form of advertisement, Mellins Foods also seem to have used the Jubilee films for the same purpose, as a small silvered-card token in the Barnes Collection testifies (101).

It would be beyond the scope of a history of this kind, to take note of the numerous performances of the Jubilee films which took place abroad, but it is interesting to note the eagerness shown by the English press in reporting their presentation in India. Of course, the sub-continent was then the most valued possession of the British Empire and Queen Victoria was after all, Empress of India. It is only to be expected then, that the Jubilee films should be shown to her subjects in this part of the world.

By 20 August, films of the Jubilee had reached Bombay, but, from a report published in a local newspaper, the opening performance was not very successful: 'Either the light used or the focus of the instrument need to be adjusted before the exhibition can be pronounced a complete success.'[82] A report from Calcutta was much better and the films were said to have drawn large crowds at the Theatre Royal. On the last day of the performances there, 'the children of the various schools, to the number of about 600, were provided with seats, and it proved a most interesting treat for the children.'[83]

Anyone who has recently seen snippets of the Jubilee films will not deny that they now seem incredibly primitive and appear to have an air of unreality about them which not even a modern commentary or sound track can dispel. True, the images are in motion and the scenes are recognisable, yet they seem strangely devoid of any life, as if it were a shadow-show that was passing before our eyes. We may wonder why such a marvellous pageant fails to stir us. The answer of course is simple, the films have been taken with a total lack of understanding of the cinema medium and the whole atmosphere of the occasion is lost. The little incidental scenes necessary to complete the picture are all missing. We are never shown the faces of the cheering crowd, the children, or the fluttering flags and decorations. We long for a simple camera movement, a close-up; in short, the enlivening rhythms of the cinematic art. It is then that we begin to realise how far the cinema of 1897 had yet to go.

Yet crude as these Jubilee scenes may appear today, in one respect this historic event had a significant influence on camera design, and so eventually, on film technique. The sheer length of the procession necessitated an increase in the film capacity of the camera if the greater part of the pageant was to be recorded. Consequently, exterior film boxes capable of carrying from 500 to 1,000 feet of film were brought into use. One must remember that previously, the capacity of the average camera had been from 40 to 75 feet. In one other matter too, the Jubilee may be said to have played a not insignificant part. This was in freeing the camera from a fixed position on the ground where its normal viewpoint was at eye-level. The procession, enclosed as it was within a mass of tightly packed spectators, required the camera to be placed in an elevated position above the crowd and some of the spectacular shots which resulted are remininscent indeed of the Italian epic films of the next decade.

In any study of the development of film technique, the lesson to be learned I think, is not to neglect the actuality film in favour of the fiction film, for it is in the former that many of the innovations in film technique are to be found. Already by the end of 1897, the camera had been used to startling effect in recording everyday occurences. Thus we have the Lumière cameraman Promio, filming from moving objects (the travelling shot); the Biograph camera taking up a position on the front of a locomotive (the tracking shot); and, of course, the photographers of the Jubilee procession shooting from on high (the elevated shot). Such shots were rarely used, if at all, in the fiction films of the period, except perhaps in certain trick films when a special effect was required.

So far, we have examined the film in its role as entertainment and as a record of everyday life, but before bringing this volume to a close, there is a third aspect of film which needs to be mentioned and that is its function as a research tool in the service of science. By the end of 1897, scientific cinematography had become a reality and had been already applied in the fields of biology, mineralogy and medicine. In biology for example, cinemicrography (as cinematography through the microscope is now called) had been successfully accomplished by Dr R. L. Watkins of New York[84] who was able to record and reproduce the movements of objects so small as blood corpuscles, rotifers, etc.[85] Crystallography too was being studied by this means, both in America and Italy, so that the birth of crystals could be minutely observed.[86] In Germany, time-lapse cinematography had been applied to the growth of plants,[87] whereas in England this method, apparently envisaged as early as 1896[88] was being used by Birt Acres in the study of cloud formations.[89] In April of 1897, Dr John Macintyre demonstrated X-Ray cinematography at a meeting of the Glasgow Philosophical Society, for an account of which we quote a contemporary review:

'... Controlling the motions of a frog's limbs by mechanical means, he illuminated them by a Crookes' tube, actuated by a ten-inch spark coil. He then covered the instrument with lead foil, presumably removing the lens, and substituting for it a lead diaphragm, with small aperture. Then illuminating the tube, and setting the kinematograph, supplied with thirty-five feet of film, in motion, he obtained a series of views of the skeleton, which, placed in the instrument, enabled him to show to a large audience the actual movements of the bones of the limbs.[90]

Frame illustrations from Dr Macintyre's film were subsequently reproduced in *Archives of Skiagraphy*,[91] a quarterly journal devoted to X-rays and which very soon changed its name to *The Archives of the Rontgen Ray*.[92] Such was the interest shown in Dr Macintyre's work that on 5 November his apparatus was shown by Dr Norris Wolfenden to members of the Rontgen Society at a meeting held in St Martin's Town Hall.[93] High speed cinematography (for slow motion effects),[94] stereoscopy,[95] and colour[96] had all been contemplated by the end of 1897, but it would probably be true to say that no practical results in these fields had yet been achieved.

Appendix 1

G. ALBERT SMITH'S CASH BOOK (Entries for the year 1897)

FILM FACTORY

1897	Received	£	S	D	1897		Paid	£	S	D
Jan.					Jan.	1	Level [spirit level]		1	6
							Box transparent paints		5	.
							Brown paper		1	.
							Lens for camera		15	.
							Wood case for Printer		5	6
						4	Timber for Dark Room (Peerless)	3	1	.
						6	Taker, complete (Darling) [Cine-camera supplied by Alfred Darling]	16	.	.
							4 Extra aluminium Reels (do) [Also supplied by Darling]	1	4	.
						7	6 Brass wire developing Frames	2	5	.
							Nails 1/7, 1/3, Screws -/8, -/6, Bolts -/10 (Dark Room)		4	10
							4 sq. ruby & 4 orange glass	2	1	2
							4 Developing Trays (Wood)	2	3	6
						8	2 Iron Ventilating elbows 6/- (Hooper)		6	
						9	Pair Scales & weights (Hall)		12	.
							Carpenter — 44 hrs at 8d	1	9	4
						11	5 negative & 1 positive Film (Blair)	4	10	.
							2 Earthenware barrels		16	.
							Taps for ditto			10
							2 lbs Hydroquinone (Adams)	1	3	.
							Tripod Stand for Camera		12	.
							Forward	37	16	8

1897	Received	£	s	d	1897	Paid	£	s	d
						Forward	37	16	8
					Jan. 6	Axel Holst — salary			
						fr Dec 31	3	.	.
						View Finder		1	3
						Earthenware Sink &			
						Brass Plug	1	7	6
						Do: extra on			
						exchanged plug		1	
						⌈ Mr Holst: Rail to			
							London		7	6
						⟨ Do: Cabs, Porters,			
							etc		4	8
						⌊ Telegram			6
						Developer			
						(Salmon's)		3	.
					13	Axel Holst: salary			
						from Jan 7	3	.	.
					20	Do " Jan 13	3	.	.
					13	Rail Mr Holst —			
						London fetch			
						printer		7	6
					14	Cash (Holst –			
						returning London)		4	6
					15	Wire [telegram] to			
						A. Holst			10
					21	Do			10
					22	Fare Southampton to			
						London, retn.		11	6
						Printer. J. Bonn	3	.	.
						Axel Holst. salary			
						to 27	2	.	.
					26	Southampton to			
						Brighton retn.		10	
					27	Wire to Holst -/9			9
						Forward	55	18	.

1897	Received	£	s	d	1897		Paid	£	s	d
							Forward	55	18	.
						29	Telegrams: Blair retn. 1/2 Holst -/10		2	.
					Feb.	1	Salary: A. Holst, to Feb 3	3	.	.
							Cash Book (Jan 1)		1	6
						3	Wire: Blair			9
						4	Southampton to Brighton retn.		10	.
						9	A. Holst: Salary to Feb 10		2	.	.
						27	A. Holst: salary to Feb 24		2	.	.
					Mar.	11	A. Holst: salary to March 3		2	.	.
						12	Library: 2 Handbooks		1	6
					Jan.	29	12ft india-rubber tubing at -/2½		2	6
						27	Chemicals – S. Drug Co,		11	4
							Print measure			9
							Brackets & screws 1/8. Nails -/3.		1	11
							Corks -/8. Glass-paper -/6. Tin Box -/3		1	5
							Potash		1	2
							Paraffin & Candles -/6 Tip -/2			8
							Holst – Railway 3-/. Do. 7/6. Wire -/8.		11	2
							Acetone 2/6. Clips 1/6 little glasses -/6		4	6
							Forward	69	9	2

1897	Received	£	s	d	1897	Paid	£	s	d
						Forward	69	9	2
Apr. 13	Watsons & Sons: 3 "Football" Films	6	.	.	Jan. 14	Bonn's men – overtime (Printer)		5	.
14	W. Heath & Co. Football Film	3	.	.	Mar. 20	Blair's developer (unmixed chemicals)		1	
15	J. Ottway & Son. Football Film	2	5	.		Glass cutter -/6			
						A. Holst (wages)	3	.	.
					26	Stamped envelopes		1	10
					27	Mr Holst (salary)	3	.	.
						Yellow glazed lining			10
						Whiskers & spirit gum			6
						Parcel post – returns to Blair (twice) -/6 -/6		1	½
					Apr. 2	Postage of films – Ottway & Hughes			9
					3	A. Holst – wages	3	.	.
						Do. (Fare from London)		4	2½
						European Blair Camera Co (films)	5	11	.
					9	Handbook -/6			
					10	A. Holst: wages	3	.	.
						Do. Fare to London		4	2½
						Postage on sample films		1	3
					13	Expenses London: calls on dealers		10	.
						Wood for D.room shelves (Peerless)		1	5
					17	Darling: on acct. of perforator	2	.	.
	Forward	11	5	.		Forward	90	12	2

1897		Received	£	s	d		1897	Paid	£	s	d
		Forward	11	5	.			Forward	90	12	2
May	7	David Devant 1 Football Film		2	10	.	19	Lock & key: Factory door			6
							22	Earthenware Tap – Soda Jar		3	6
								Edison Clamp – mending films [Film splicer]		7	6
								1 Doz. Tin Boxes for Films		3	.
							24	Postage (Watson) -/3 Do (return) -/3			6
							May 1	Two handbooks		1	6
							6	Postage (Watson) -/3 Ottway -/3 Devant -/3			9
								36 Labels -/3. Stamps 1/-		1	3
							8	Newspaper wrappers			9
								2 Handbooks			9
								Stamps for *Hove Echo* -/6, 5/-, -/5, 1/-, -/10		7	9
							10	Sink brushes			7
								Brown Paper for cracks		1	6
								Jack towel & roller		1	.
							11	Postage – 2 Football to Watson [i.e. 2 football films sent to Watson]			3
							18	Fare & expenses – Westminster [Film]		12	6
							20	Tip 1/- (midgets coachman Buses 1/-		2	.
								Hypo (10 lbs)		1	8
								Incandescent gas mantle		1	3
							21	Banfield: Incandescent gas		10	.
		Forward	13	15	.			Forward	93	10	8

897	Received	£	s	d	1897	Paid	£	s	d
	Forward	13	15	.		Forward	93	10	8

		£	s	d			£	s	d
May 27	Watson: printing football on Fitch [i.e. print of football film made on film manufactured by Fitch & Co. and supplied to W. Watson & Sons]	1	.	.	21	2 lbs Glycerine 3/-. 3 lbs Alum -/10½		3	10½
						Expenses taking midget		2	.
					25	Postage stamps		1	.
	Do.: 2 Football on Blair [i.e. two prints of the football film made on film manufactured by the European Blair Camera Co, and supplied to W. Watson & Sons]	4	.	.	26	Parcel samples to Watson			4½
					27	Returning Wrench's sample negative			3
					28	Darling; on acct. of Perforator [Further payment on the perforator made by Alfred Darling]	5	.	.
					June 1	Two apron files		1	9
					3	Peerless – 4 -3×1 yellow deal [Timber]		2	4
					8	Specimen of printing (boat) Wrench [i.e. sent to J. Wrench & Son]			3
					15	Rail – London re-taking Jubilee [i.e. preparations for filming Queen's Jubilee procession] Blair: 12 films 8.8.0. & carr. 1/7 Cr. Perf 5/- [latter items refers to the cost of carriage on Perforator]	8	4	7
								10	.
					19	Chemicals: F.W. Salmon	1	3	9
					22	⎰Fares London (2)			
						⎱Jubilee Day		15	.
						⎰Expenses		5	6
					23	Delivery parcel positives fr Blair			6
						Do. parcel Negatives			6
					Jul. 1	Rail 3/- & tips 1/-			
						Hastings: 2 negs		4	.
						Gas jet for Dark Room		2	.
					2	Stamped envelopes		1	10
	Forward	18	15	.		Forward	110	10	2

1897		Received	£	s	d	1897		Paid	£	s	d
		Forward	18	15	.			Forward	110	10	2
Jul.	31	Watson: Developing, Printing & Films – per Ledger	10	16	7			Material for changing Bag		4	6
Aug	10	J. Williamson: Bonn's old Printer	3	10	.		9	Alum			6
								Pitch for wood trays			6
								2″ Dallmeyer Lens (for Bender)	2	17	6
							15	Postcards -/6. Stamps 1/-		1	6
							17	Towel airer for drying films			6½
							19	Tips re "Miller & Sweep"			6
							21	Ottway Postage 5 films on appro			5
								Towel Airers 1/-, 4/6 Carpenter's Tip (stands) 2/6		8	.
							24	Blair for films to June 24	12	13	.
								⌠ Miller & Sweep	– Two mens 10/-, 10/- Flour, Properties, etc.		.	.
									Refresht. Tip for		4	.
								⌊ starting Mill		2	6
						Jul.	22	⌠ Hammond:	Carpentry-Dark	Room		1	3	8
								⌡ Hammond: Plumbing	& material		2	8	6
									Hammond: Gas –	connecting Meter			2	5
								⌊ Hammond: Plumbing sink			3	.
							30	Rail London re Watson & Blair		7	6
						Aug	9	Rail etc Winchelsea (Ellen Terry)		7	6
		Forward	33	1	7			Forward	132	16	8½

1897		Received	£	s	d	1897		Paid	£	s	d
		Forward	33	1	7			Forward	132	16	8½
Aug	29	[Film] Winder				Aug	9	Darling: Balance on			
		(Williamson)		10	6			Perforator	1	.	.
Sep	1	Watson (per ledger)	25	7	9			Do: Printing			
								machine	5	.	.
							14	Wire – Ellen Terry			7
							23	Dallmeyer: 3″ lens	2	8	.
								Blair: on acct. of			
								films	10	.	.
							24	Gas burner & nipple			
								for lamp		1	6
								Stamps		1	.
							27	Fare, etc London		10	6
							27	Blair – for films			
								to date	16	18	9
							28	Tips to Pierrot			
								team on beach		6	.
							Sep	1	Printing Frame		1	6
								Fitch negative Film			
								(per Watson)		16	6
							3	Gas (to midsummer)		1	.
								Sea Going Car.			
								Fares 1/3. Tips 1/-		2	3
							4	Ditto -/5. Le			
								Page's Fish Glue			
								-/6			11
								Fares – sea going			
								car			5
							6	Darling (Winder –			
								sold Aug 29)		8	6
							8	Incandescent gas			
								mantel		1	3
							11	6 Swimmers (Pole)			
								1.1.0. extra Tips			
								2/6	1	3	6
								Fares to Southwick			
								& back		1	2
		Forward	58	19	10			Forward	172	.	.½

FILM FACTORY

1897		Received	£	s	d	1897		Paid	£	s	d
		Brought forward	58	19	10			Brought forward	172	.	.½
Sep	18	Williamson: Rough ⎫ Sea, Clubs, ⎪ Pierrots, Stained ⎪ [dyed] Westminster, ⎮ Cricket & Football ⎰ (1) Sailing & Car ⎪ (1) Watson's ⎪ Jubilee Naval Bri- ⎭ gade	11	.	.		13	Postage samples Watson -/5. Stamps 1/-		1	5
								Train to Dyke			10
								Wire to Blair for Negs			6
							16	Trams Southwick – futile Paddling		1	.
							17	Trains Do – unsatis- factory do		1	6
							18	Trains do – Satisfactory		1	6
								Williamson – 9 lbs hypo		1	4
								Do Hire Camera out- ⎫ fit 10/-; plates ⎪ 2/3 Carriage, etc, ⎬ Tower Cottage, ⎪ Winchelsea 1/3 ⎭		13	6
								Dark Room Gas lamp 5/-. R. Glass [i.e. Red Glass] -/6		5	6
							20	Mr & Mrs Tom Green (Clothes Line)		10	.
							23	Tom Green 10/- & W. Carlile (Comic Shaving)		10	.
							24	Fares, etc London. Cab to Devant		10	.
								⎧ Miller & Sweep: ⎪ Two men 10/- 10/-	1	.	.
								⎨ Flour & Sweeps ⎩ tools. Starting		2	6
								⎪ Mill 3/-. Refresh- ⎩ ments 2/-		5	.
							28	Tom Green "Comic Face" & on acct.		7	6
							30	Do & Mrs Green (Weary Willie)		10	.
							2	L.Shaw cleaning back of films		1	2
		Forward	69	19	10			Forward	177	3	3½

1897		Received	£	s	d	1897		Paid	£	s	d
		Forward	69	19	10			Forward	177	3	3½
Oct	6	Hughes: Waves 2.5.0., Pierrotts (sic) 2.5.0., Train 2.5.0.	6	15	.	Oct	2	Fare Hastings (Love on Pier)		5	.
	9	David Devant: Miller & Sweep	2	10	.		4	Postage: Samples Hughes, Devant, Wolff		1	1
		Hughes: Westminster 2.2.0. Clothes Line 2.2.0.	4	4	.		6	Blair: Films to date	20	9	11
	18	Owen Brooks: 16-tooth s-wheel [Sprocket-wheel]	10		6			Tom Green: on acct X Rays	3		.
	21	Wolff: Football 2.0.0. Miller 2.0.0.	4	.	.		7	Do: Balance X-Rays	10		.
	29	Watson: Films, etc (per Ledger)	31	18	.			Packing case -/6. Postage -/4			10
	28	David Devant: "X Rays"	2	10	.			Stamps 1/- India rubber rings 1/-		2	.
	29	Wyndham (Poole) X Rays	2	5	.		11	Postage -/6, -/2, -/3, -/3		1	2
								Lens – skeleton's shirt [Costume for X Ray film ?]		1	.
							12	Stamps -/6 Labels -/2 Stamps -/6		1	2
								Fares Hastings 13 & 16 to see Hughes		8	4
							20	Expenses Southwick – P. Express [Portsmouth Express train film]		1	.
							21	Do London "Trafalgar Day"		10	6
							23	Postage: Ottway 6½ Watson -/1½			8
								A. Darling: on acct. sprocket-Printer	5	.	.
							25	Postage: Hughes -/6 Watson -/5½			11½
								Do: Blair			2
								Stamps & cards		2	.
							28	Postage Devant -/3			3
								Brown Paper & tacks 1/6		1	6
		Forward	124	12	4			Forward	205	3	10

1897		Received	£	s	d	1897		Paid	£	s	d
		Forward	124	12	4			Forward	205	3	10
Nov	9	W.C. Hughes: Films per Ledger	33	12	.	Sep	15	2-75 [ft] Negatives – Fitch – Watson	1	10	4
	20	2 Positives supplied Collings July 1	1	8	.			Royalty Watson's Naval Brigade	1	.	.
							30	Large Lime			4½
	25	J. Williamson: Films per Ledger	16	.	.	Nov	4	Blair: Films to date	42	4	.
	27	P. Wolff: 11 Films per Ledger	19	5	.		5	Postage & stamps		2	6
Dec	10	Owen Brooks – Maid in Garden [Hanging out the Clothes]	2	2	.		6	Envelopes -/6 Stamps 2/-		2	6
	11	Williamson: Haunted Castle [This was a Méliès film]	2	13	.		10	Postage – Films Noble			7
							15	Post: Watson -/3 Register Wolff -/5 Stamps (postage)	1		8 .
							19	Freeman: Sink & Plug	1	7	6
							19	Mr T. Green. 2 Negatives "Reversal" [Reference to the reverse action film "Tipsy, Topsy, Turvey"]		7	6
							23	Postage (Devant) -/2½ Wire – Rider 1/2½		1	5
							26	Postage (on appro) 1/- Bands, Labels	[no entry]		
							27	Stamps 1/- Postage -/5½ Stamps -/6½		2	.
						Dec	2	F. W. Salmon: Chemicals	4	2	5
								Blair: Films to date	24	12	3
							9	Postage. Blair. Devant, etc		2	.
								Do. Brooks -/4½ Blair -/4 Stamps 1/6		2	2½
		Forward	199	12	4			Forward	281	3	1

Received

1897		Received	£	s	d
		Forward	199	12	4
Dec	21	Winder (Williamson)		10	6
	22	Owen Brooks ("Sausages") [i.e. film called Making Sausages]	2	2	.
	24	J. Williamson on acct of Films	10	.	.
	24	Watson & Sons: per Ledger	42	14	.
1898 Jan	3	J. Williamson: on acct of Films	15	.	.
	4	Blair: Acct as per Ledger (Perforating etc) contra.	9	1	8
	8	A. Darling – on acct machine [This item is crossed out]	4	.	.
	8	W.C. Hughes: Films per Ledger	12	15	8
	11	David Devant: Miller & Sweep	2	10	.
	15	J. Williamson: Films per Ledger	40	3	.
		Forward £	334	9	2

Paid

1897		Paid	£	s	d
		Forward	281	3	1
Dec	11	Gas to Michaelmas. 5/6 Meter 1/-		6	6
	4	150 Copies Hove Echo [Evidently the issue for 27 Nov. which contains article re Smith's films]		12	.
		500 Note Heads		12	6
		200 List of Films [i.e. cost of printing Smith's first film catalogue]		10	6
	23	Labels -/2, Post -/3, Do -/3, Do -/3			11
	24	Cleaning 12 films		2	.
		Post -/6 Wire: Owen Brooks -/6		1	.
	23	Watson: Fitch positive 15/- Post -/2		15	2
	28	Post: Wolff -/4 Stamps -/8		1	.
1898 Jan	3	Lizzie Shaw – polishing 12 [films]@ 2d		2	.
	4	Blair: Films to date	46	3	7
		Stamps 2/-		2	.
	8	Inc. gas mantle		1	3
		A. Darling: on acct. machine	4	.	.
	10	Postage -/4 Stamps -/6		1	.
	13	Post -/2 Wire Blair -/6			8
	15	J. Williamson: (Oxygen)		1	3
		Do developing chemicals	6	7	3
		Packing case – Watson			3
		Forward £	341	3	11

Appendix 2

Catalogue of Lumière films issued by Maguire & Baucus Ltd. (Published in *The Optician*, vol 14 (23 September 1897) pp 122–27.

GENERAL VIEWS

No.	Name	Code Word
1001	Spinning Plates	Abbey
1002	Workshop of Ciotat	Abduct
1003	Aquarium	Abide
1004	Ostrich at the Zoo, Paris	Abject
1005	Arrival by Cab	Able
1006	Felling a Tree	Abroad
1007	Arrival by Steamer	Abound
1008	Arrival of Train at Station	About
1009	Fishing Smacks Leaving Harbor	Above
1010	Fishing Smack at Sea	Abroad
1011	Sea Bathing	Absent
1012	Negroes Bathing	Absorb
1013	See-saw	Abstract
1014	Farm-yard Scene	Abuse
1015	Children's Ball	Accent
1016	Boxing Match	Accord
1017	Bicyclists	Accost
1018	Gold Fish Globe	Accuse
1019	Loading Barrels on Trolley Car	Acid
1020	Steam Boiler	Acre
1021	Flock of Swans	Action
1022	Concert	Actor
1023	Procession "Sun Car"	Adder
1024	Procession "Roman Warriors and Abyssinians"	Adieu
1025	Baby Competition	Adopt
1026	Fighting Cocks	Admit
1027	Ball Rolling Competition	Admire
1028	Unloading Grain	Adrift
1029	Stage Dance	Adult
1030	Japanese Dance	Advice
1031	Tyrolese Dance	Afar
1032	Departure by Cab	Affect
1033	Departure of Wheelmen	Afloat
1034	Unloading a Ship	Afoot
1035	Duel with Pistols	Afraid
1036	Procession Passing Young Ladies' School	Agree
1037	Landing from Steamer	Agent
1038	Lady Acrobats	Ahead
1039	Departure of a Transatlantic Liner	Aim
1040	Falling Wall I and II	Air
1041	Cat's Breakfast	Alder
1042	Writing on the Wrong Side	Allow
1043	Children's Sports	Almost
1044	Herd of Elephants	Alum
1045	Children Catching Shrimps	Amaze
1046	Embarking a Horse	Baboon
1047	Embarking Fishing Nets	Badge
1048	Embarking for a Promenade	Badger
1049	Child and Dog	Ballad
1050	Children Playing Marbles	Balm
1051	Blacksmiths at Work	Bandit
1052	Gale at Sea	Bard
1053	Japanese Juggler	Barge
1054	The Lion	Banner
1055	Bicycle Lesson	Barn
1056	Japanese Wrestlers	Bait
1057	Launching a Vessel	Base
1058	Hauling in Fishing Nets	Bay
1059	Ploughing	Beet
1060	Washerwoman	Beach
1061	Sheep at Slaughter-house	Bellow
1062	Shoeing a Horse	Bible
1063	Carpenters at Work	Birch
1064	Burning Weeds	Bird
1065	Market Scene	Bison
1066	Negroes Sweeping	Blank
1067	Baby's First Steps	Blast
1068	Fishermen Mending Nets	Blaze
1069	Fishing for Gold Fish	Bleak
1070	Fishing for Sardines	Block
1071	Flock of Pelicans	Blow
1072	Game of Ball	Blossom
1073	Game of Cards	Blur
1074	Game of Backgammon	Blush
1075	Hunting the Sparrow Hawk	Boar
1076	Firemen, Departure of Fire Engine	Broom
1077	Firemen, Getting Ready	Bond
1078	Firemen, Playing on a Fire	Book
1079	Firemen, Life Saving	Boom

COMIC SUBJECTS

FRANCE

ENGLAND

SPAIN

AUSTRIA-HUNGARY

ITALY

1279–King and Queen of Italy
leaving the Palace ....Found
1280–Naples Via Marina ....Frail
1281–Naples Via Roma ....Freak
1282–Harbor and Vesuvius ....Frank
1431–A Street Scene in Naples ....Frame
1432–Santa Lucia ....Freeze
1283–Procession at the Marriage
of the Prince of Naples ....Free
1284–End of Marriage Pro-
cession of the Prince of
Naples ....Fresh
1285–Piazza Colonna, Rome ....Frost
1286–Piazza Termini, Rome ....Fume
1287–Fountain of Trevi ....Fumble
1288–The Station ....Fun
1289–Dance of the Ciocciari ....Furrow
1290–The Forum ....Fuse
1429–Ripetta Bridge ....Fur
1291–Arrival of Gondola ....Future
1430–St. Mark's Place ....Gable
1292–Pigeons on the Place St.
Mark ....Gage
1293–Tramway, Venice ....Gale
1294–Grand Canal with Gon-
dolas ....Garret
1295–Panorama of the Grand
Canal (taken from a boat)........Gash
1296–Panorama of St. Mark's
Place (taken from a
boat) ....Gaunt
1297–Carabiniers..................................Gem
1298–Italian Infantry..........................Giant
1299–Bersaglieri....................................Gift

RUSSIA

1300–The Sovereigns and
Guests going to the
Coronation Ceremonies
(Red Staircase)......................Glass
1301–The Empress Mother and the
Grand Duchess
Eugenie driving........................Gild
1302–Czar and Czarina entering the
Church of Assump-
tion ....Gleam
1303–Count of Montebello and
Gen'l de Boisdeffre
going to the Kremlin.............Glimps
1304–Countess of Montebello ....Glitter

1305–Admiral Sallandronze and
Gen'l Tournier ....Gloat
1306–Asiatic Deputation ....Globe
1307–Rue Tverskaia, Moscow ....Gloom

SWITZERLAND

1308–Bridge over the Rhine.................Gloss
1309–Cascade, Switzerland ....Glove
1310–Procession of Arabs ....Glow
1311–Egyptian Dance............................Goat
1312–Village Fete ....Gone
1313–Returning to the Stables.............Good
1314–Bel-Air Place ....Gore
1315–Procession, Interlaken ....Grave
1316–March of the 8th Battalion ....Gravel
1317–Waterfall of the Rhine
(closely seen) ....Greek
1318–Waterfall of the Rhine
(seen from a distance) ....Grey

UNITED STATES

1319–Broadway, New York ....Grim
1320–Arrival of Train at Battery
Place ....Grist
1321–Brooklyn Bridge.......................Groom
1322–Metropolitan Elevated
R.R. ....Group
1323–Broadway and Wall St..............Grove
1324–Passengers descending
from Brooklyn Bridge.............Guide
1325–Union Square............................Guise
1326–Broadway and Broad St..............Gush
1327–Skating at Central Park ....Hack
1328–Broadway and Union
Square.....................................Habit
1329–Whitehall Street ....Hale
1330–Fulton Street, Brooklyn ....Hallow
1331–Washington Street, Boston..........Hand
1332–Market Street ....Harbor
1333–Commercial Street.....................Harem
1334–Atlantic Avenue.........................Harsh
1335–Fremont Row............................Harvest
1336–Chicago Policemen Parade ....Hatter
1337–Michigan Avenue ....Haven
1338–Ferris Wheel ....Hazard
1339–Niagara Falls (ten differ-
ent views) ....Head
1340–Whirlpool Rapids.....................Health
1341–The White House (Execu-
tive Mansion) ....Heard
1342–Parade of D. C. Artillery.............Heat

1343–Parade of Young Men's
    Blaine Club............................Heavy
1344–Parade of D. C. National
    Guard ....Hedge
1433–McKinley Addressing the
    People ....Hence
1436–Panorama, American cruiser
    San Francisco........................Hemp

MEXICO

1345–The President taking
    leave of his Ministers..............Helm
1346–Transport of the Bell of
    Independence...........................Help
1347–Ruraux Galloping.................Hemlock
1348–The President Promenad-
    ing...Herald
1349–Bayonet Exercise ....Herb
1350–Lassoing a Wild Horse ....Hero
1351–Indian's Meal...............................Hide
1352–Lassoing a Wild Buffaloo ....Hinge
1353–Mexican Dance.............................Hive
1354–Lassoing Buffalo for work ....Holly
1355–Indian Market on the
    Viga Canal.............................Home
1356–Mexican Riding Bucking
    Bronco ....Honor
1357–Bathing Horses ....Hook
1358–Spanish Street Dance ....Hope

EGYPT

1359–Embarking at Alexandria ....Host
1360–Place Mechemet Ali ....Hour
1361–Arrival of Train at
    Ramlek...................................Howell
1362–The Khedive and His
    Escort.....................................Human
1363–Procession of Sacred
    Carpet....................................Hunt
1364–Bedouins with loaded
    Camels ....Ideal
1365–Bridge of Kasr-el-Nil ....Image
1366–Camels leaving Bridge of
    Kasr-el-Nil............................Idol
1367–Mules Leaving Bridge of
    Kasr-el-Nil ....Import
1368–Kasr-el-Nil ....Imprint
1369–A Funeral in Cairo ....Incense
1370–Place de la Citadelle ....Inclose
1371–Place du Gouvernement..........Increase
1372–Place de l'Opera ....Indigo

1373–Place Soliman Pasha ....Induct
1374–Rue Sayeda-Zenab ....Inflate
1375–Rue Ataba-el-Khaira ....Infirm
1376–Rue Sharia-el-Nahazin ....Inmost
1377–Rue Laht-el-Rab ....Intense
1378–Dikes on the Nile ....Irksome
1379–Tourists under Palm Trees.........Ivory
1380–Sakkarah Village (Men
    Riding Mules) ....Item
1381–The Pyramids (General
    View) ....Janut
1382–Descending the Great
    Pyramid.................................Jealous
1383–Departure from Cairo ....Jest
1384–Departure from Benha....................Jilt
1385–Departure from Tauch..............Jungle
1386-1393–Panorama of River
    Nile (8 different views)...........Jump

TURKEY IN ASIA

1394–Train arriving at Jaffa ....Launch
1395–Jaffa Market No.1 ....Laugh
1396–Jaffa Market No.2 ....Law
1397–Jaffa Market No.3 ....Leaf
1398–Unloading a Vessel.....................Lead
1399–Panorama from Train,
    Jaffa to Jerusalem ....Leech
1400–Panorama taken from
    moving Train (Hills) ....Learn
1401–Jaffa Gate (East Side).................Lease
1402–Jaffa Gate (West Side)............Lecture
1403–The Holy Sepulchre....................Leah
1404–The Sorrowful Path ....Lemon
1405–The Sorrowful Path and
    Holy Sepulchre ....Lend
1406–A Street in Jerusalem ....Lever
1407–Caravan of Camels......................Limit
1408–Train Leaving Jerusalem ....Linger
1409–A Square in Bethlehem............Liquid
1410–Canon Square ....Lobby
1411–Souk-Abou-el-Nassahr...............Locust
1412–A Street of Damascus ....Lodge
1413–Souk-el-Fakhra ....Lofty

TURKEY IN EUROPE

1414–March of Turkish Infantry
    ...Loiter
1415–March of Turkish Artillery
    ...Lume

1416–Panorama of the Golden
      Horn ....Loop
1417–Shores of the Bosphorus
      (Panorama) ....Loyal

AUSTRALIA

1418–The Mob ....Mantel
1419–The Governor's Arrival ....Marsh
1420–Balancing Scales ....Most
1421–Bringing out Horses ....Mare
1422–The Race Track ....Medley
1423–Presenting the Winner ....Member

AFRICA

1441–Sword Dance No.1 ....Moral
1442–Sword Dance No.2 ....Mother
1443–Young Girls Dancing ....Motor
1444–Negro Women Dancing ....Motto
1445–Negro National Dance ....Muddle
1446–March of Negro Tribes ....Mute
1447–Young Negro Savages at
      a Meal, No.1 ....Muster
1448–Young Negro Savages at
      a Meal, No.2 ....Nabob
1449–Toilet of Young Negro
      Savage, No.1 ....Nail
1450–Toilet of Young Negro
      Savage, No.2 ....Narrow
1451–Young Negroes in Recrea-
      tion ....Nation
1452–School for Young Negroes ....Navel
1468–Presidential Train ....Observe
1469–President Unveiling Cere-
      monies Paul Baudry
      Monument ....Occur
1470–President after the Cere-
      monies ....Obtain
1471–The Sables Band ....Onward
1472–President Arriving at
      Carnet ....Opera
1473–The Sablaise's Arriving ....Orphan
1474–President Arriving at the
      Sablaise Ball ....Oval
1475–The Sablaise Ball ....Paddle
1476–Arrival of the Elan ....Page
1477–The Arsenal (Panorama) ....Pale
1478–President Arriving at the
      Arsenal ....Palm
1479–Child Addressing the
      President at Military
      Hospital ....Palace

1480–Decorating Saints ....Panic
1481–President's Escort leaving
      Depot.....................................Parch
1482–Panorama of La Rochelle
      Port ....Parlor
1483–The President Arriving ....Parrot
1484–Reception to the Fleet...............Parson
1485–The President Arriving
      at St. Marie ....Patient
1486–Department of the President
      ...Patron
1487–Carriage Arriving at the
      Depot.....................................Peace

JUBILEE FILMS

1489–Crowd following Procession ......Quaint
1490–The Queen's Carriage ....Queen
1491–Foreign Princes and
      Nobility ....Quad
1492–Ambassadors ....Quack
1493–Life Guards and Mounted
      Band of the Dragoons.............Quart
1494–Marine Artillery ....Query
1495–Colonial Cavalry ....Quota
1496–Horse Artillery ....Quick

FRENCH MILITARY
VIEWS

1497–99th Infantry Regiment,
      Assault on the portico
      (gymnastic) ....Rabbit
1498–99th Infantry Regiment,
      Sword Duel...........................Rabble
1499–99th Infantry Regiment,
      French Boxing........................Race
1500–99th Infantry Regiment,
      Club exercise....................Racing
1501–99th Infantry Regiment,
      Horizontal bars ....Rack
1502–99th Infantry Regiment,
      Long jump............................Racket
1503–99th Infantry Regiment,
      Rings and Trapese ....Racking
1504–Artillery, Defiling at a trot ....Racy
1505–Artillery, Galloping and
      forming line ....Radiance
1506–Dragoons, Defiling at a
      gallop.................................Radiate
1507–Dragoons, Leaping obsta-
      cles in two ranks ....Radish

1508–Dragoons, Leaping obstacles in several ranks ....Radius
1509–Dragoons, Leaping obstacles in a body ....Raffle
1510–Dragoons, Combat with lances ....Raft
1511–Dragoons, Lance drill ....Rag
1512–Dragoons, Sabre drill ....Rage
1513–Military, Review, Artillery galloping ....Raging
1514–Military Review, Infantry defiling....................................Raid
1515–Military Review, Train of carriages.........................Raiding
1516–Military Review, Firemen passing................................Raider
1517–Military Review, Presenting decorations I........................Rail
1518–Military Review, Presenting decorations II ....Railroad
1519–Soldiers at meals ....Railway

ENGLISH MILITARY VIEWS

1520–London: Guards leaving St. James's Palace ....Raiment
1521–London: Scotch Guards in Hyde Park ....Rain
1522–London: Guards on foot Rifle drill..............................Raining
1523–London: Guards on foot Bayonet exercise ....Rainbow
1524–London: Guards on foot Muscular drill ....Rainy
1525–London: Guards on foot March to the Front ....Raise

BELGIUM

1526–Brussels: Boulevard Anspach...................................Rally
1527–Brussels: The Stock Exchange ...Rallying
1528–Brussels: Place de Brouchére ...Ramble
1529–Brussels: Grande Place ....Rambling
1530–Brussels: Ste-Gudule ....Ramify
1531–Antwerp: Arriving in a boat.................................Rampart
1532–Antwerp: Panorama of the town taken from a boat ....Ramrod

SWEDEN

1533–Stockholm: Entrance to Castle in Old Stockholm
...Rancour
1534–Stockholm: Arrival of a boat and landing at the Exhibition ....Range
1535–Stockholm: Arrival of the Guard at the Royal Palace I.................................Rank
1536–Stockholm: Arrival of the Guard at the Royal Palace II ....Rankle
1537–Stockholm: Arrival of the King at the Exhibition ....Ransack
1538–Stockholm: Arrival of the Crown Prince at the Exhibition............................Ransom
1539–Stockholm: Royal Procession entering the Exhibition................................Rant
1540–Stockholm: Fight in Old Stockholm...........................Ranting
1541–Stockholm: Entrance of the Exhibition...........................Rap
1542–Stockholm: Arriving at the Exhibition in a boat........Rapper
1543–Avesta: the Chutes ....Rapture
1544–Castellholmen: Panorama............Rare
1545–Norrström: Disembarking
...Rarefy
1546–Norrström: Panorama ....Rarity
1547–Salstjöladen: Panorama, Train leaving Station.............Rascal
1548–Strandiragen: Panorama ....Rasher

MISCELLANEOUS

1549–King of Italy and Prince Victor reviewing ....Rashness
1550–Prince and Princess of Naples ....Rasp
1551–King and Queen of Italy and Escort ....Rasping
1552–Trotting Races ....Ratchet
1553–Donkey Races. I. Preliminary canter........................Rate
1554–Donkey Races. II. The race..Rating
1555–High Jump..............................Ratable
1556–Panorama of Meudon..............Rather

CAVALRY EXERCISE AT SAUMUR
Military Tournament

The Riding Master

Exercises on the Ground

FRANCE

THE FRENCH PRESIDENT'S VISIT TO RUSSIA

Appendix 3

British Films of 1897

This is a continuation of the list which appeared in the previous volume of this history and which covered the years 1895–6. In drawing up the present list, the same procedure and classification is followed, that is to say, it is the earliest known reference to a particular film which is given and the type of film is indicated by the appropriate letter, or letters, thus: [N] = news film; [N-F] = non-fiction; [F] = fiction film; and [S] = science film. At this period, films were not supplied with main-titles, so the titles under which the films are listed below are therefore arbitrary. Also, the exact dating of many of the films is not possible from the evidence available and in some cases therefore, the month cited must be regarded as tentative. Where known, the official catalogue number of the production company is added, together with the original footage. Unless otherwise stated, all films are 35mm in width.

Birt Acres

1 *An Unfriendly Call* (Month and year uncertain) [F]
   Ref *The Era*, 30 January, 1897, p 18.
2 *Church Parade of Troops* (Month and year uncertain) [N-F]
   Ref *The Era*, 30 January, 1897, p 18.
3 *Practising for the Oxford and Cambridge University Boat Race* (March) [N]
   Ref *British Journal of Photography*, vol 44, no 1930 (30 April 1897) p 286.
   Photographic News, vol 41, no 96, N.S. (29 October 1897) p 710.
4 *Oxford and Cambridge University Boat Race* (3 April) [N]
   The film does not appear to have materialised, probably owing to bad weather.
   Ref British Journal of Photography, vol 44, no 1930 (30 April 1897) p 286.
5 *The Great Northern Mail Train Catching the Post Bags at Barnet* (April) [N-F]
   Ref *British Journal of Photography*, vol 44, no 1930 (30 April 1897) p 286.
6 *A visit to the Northern Photographic Works, Barnet* (April) [N]
   Reception of editors of the photographic press during a visit to the Works.
   Ref *Optical Magic Lantern Journal*, vol 8, no 96 (June 1897) p 81.
7 *Clouds* (April) [S]
   Study of clouds by time-lapse cinematography
   Ref *Journal of the Camera Club*. vol 11 (May 1897) p 66.
8 *Queen Victoria's Diamond Jubilee Procession* (22 June) [N]
   Supposedly taken from precincts of Buckingham Palace. The film does not seem to have materialised.
   Ref *Amateur Photographer*, vol 25, no 654 (16 April 1897) p 310.
9 *Coaching in North Devon* (Month uncertain) [N-F]
   Ref *The Era*, 2 April 1898, p 31d.
10 *Band marching down a street* (Year and month uncertain) [N-F]
   Ref R. Child Bayley, *Modern Magic Lanterns*, 2nd edn (London, n.d.) p 102 (Copy in David Henry Collection) This edition of Bayley's book, contains frame illustrations from the film.
   (Illustration 9).
11 *Promenade scene* (Year and month uncertain) [N-F]
   Ref As for no 10, above.
   (Illustration 9)

R. J. Appleton & Son

1 *Queen Victoria's Diamond Jubilee Procession* (22 June) [N]
The procession passing St George's Church in the Borough. Consisting of five sequences.
Ref *British Journal of Photography*, vol 44, no 1930 (2 July 1897) p 418.
Ibid, vol 44, no 1949 (10 September 1897) pp 590–91.
2 *High Tide on the Rocks at Flamborough Head* (August) [N-F]
Ref *British Journal of Photography*, vol 44, no 1949 (10 September 1897) pp 590–91.

Bender & Co.

1 *Demolition of Old Railway Station, Croydon* (January) [N] 70mm
Photographed by Adolphe Langfier
Ref *British Journal of Photography*, vol 44, no 1916 (22 January 1897) p 61.
2 *Yacht Landing Pleasure Party, Hastings* (January) [N-F] 70mm
Photographed by Adolphe Langfier
Ref *British Journal of Photography*, vol 44, no 1916 (22 January 1897) p 61.
3 *Skating on Moreland Pond* (27 February) [N-F] 70mm
Photographed by Adolphe Langfier
Ref *British Journal of Photography*, vol 44, no 1918 (5 February 1897) p 94.

British Cinematographe Co, Ltd (Prof. Jolly's Cinematographe)

1 *Queen Victoria's Diamond Jubilee Procession* (22 June) [N]
Taken at the corner of Piccadilly and St James's Street.
Ref *The Era*, 24 July 1897, p 16.
2 *Spithead Naval Review* (26 June) [N]
Ref Souvenir programme, Windsor Castle, 23/11/97
(*Barnes Museum of Cinematography*)
3 *Hussars Passing Through Dublin* (Month uncertain) [N]
Ref Souvenir programme, Windsor Castle, 23/11/97
4 *A Scene in Parliament Street* (October) [N-F]
Ref Souvenir programme, Windsor Castle, 23/11/97
5 *Scene Taken from a Moving Train Near Clapham Junction* (October) [N-F]
Ref Souvenir programme, Windsor Castle, 23/11/97

Chard & Co

1 *Spring Races, Epsom Downs* (27 April) [N]
Photographed by H. V. Tovey
Ref *British Journal of Photography*, vol 44, no 1939 (2 July 1897) p 428.
2 *Church Parade, Woolwich* (May) [N-F]
Ref *The Era*, 22 May 1897, p 28.
3 *Flying Dutchman at Full Speed* (May) [N-F]
Ref *The Era*, 22 May 1897, p 28.
4 *Grenadier Guards Entering the Tower of London* (May) [N-F]
Ref *The Era*, 22 May 1897, p 28.
5 *London: Hyde Park Corner* (May) [N-F]
Ref *The Era*, 22 May 1897, p 28.
6 *London: Marble Arch* (May) [N-F]
Ref *The Era*, 22 May 1897, p 28.

7 *London: Zoological Gardens* (May) [N-F]
   a. Feeding the Pelicans
   b. Polar Bears
   Ref *The Era*, 22 May 1897, p 28.
8 *Naval Brigade at Single Stick Exercises* (May) [N-F]
   Ref *The Era*, 22 May 1897, p 28.
9 *Portsmouth Fire Brigade* (May) [N-F]
   Ref *The Era*, 22 May 1897, p 28.
10 *The Royal Artillery Leaving for Africa* (May) [N]
   Ref *The Era*, 22 May 1897, p 28.
11 *Wiltshire Regiment Leaving Church* (May) [N-F]
   Ref *The Era*, 22 May 1897, p 28.
12 *Woodside Ferry, Liverpool* (May) [N-F]
   Showing the wreck of Nelson's old Flagship "The Foudroyant"
   Ref *The Era*, 19 June 1897, p 25.
13 *Maypole Dance* (May) [N]
   Ref *The Era*, 19 June 1897, p 25.
14 *The Derby* (2 June) [N]
   Ref *The Era*, 19 June 1897, p 25.
15 *Oaks Day - On The Coaches* (4 June) [N]
   Ref *The Era*, 19 June, 1897, p 25.
16 *The Oaks* (4 June) [N]
   Ref *The Era*, 19 June 1897, p 25.
17 *Queen Victoria's Diamond Jubilee Procession* (22 June) [N]
   a. The Queen at Temple Bar - Lord Mayor Handing the City Sword to the Queen.
   b. Procession entering the City.
   c. The Queen entering the Borough.
   d. Procession Crossing London Bridge.
   e. Procession in St James's Street.
   f. Colonial Premiers in St James's Street.
   Ref *The Era*, 26 June 1897, p 26.
   Ibid, 17 July 1897, p 26.
   Ibid, 24 July 1897, p 17.
18 *The Bolster Fight* (August) [F]
   Ref *The Era*, 14 August 1897, p 25.
19 *Firing Disappearing Gun* (August) [N]
   Ref *The Era*, 4 September 1897, p 29.
20 *Garrison Artillery in Action* (August) [N]
   Ref *The Era*, 4 September 1897, p 29.
21 *Royal Horse Artillery in Action* (August) [N]
   Ref *The Era*, 4 September 1897, p 29.
22 *Teddington Lock, River Thames* (August) [N-F]
   Ref *The Era*, 14 August 1897, p 25.
23 *Donkey Racing on Ramsgate Sands* (September) [N-F]
   Ref *The Era*, 2 October 1897, p 29.
24 *Passengers Landing from the Koh-i-nor at Ramsgate* (September) [N-F]
   Ref *The Era*, 2 October 1897, p 29.
25 *Roman Catholic St Augustine Centenary at Ebbsfleet* (14 September) [N]
   Ref *The Era*, 2 October 1897, p 29.
26 *Launch of HMS Canopus at Portsmouth* (13 October) [N]
   Ref *The Era*, 23 October 1897, p 30.
27 *The Lord Mayer's Show* (9 November) [N]
   Ref *The Era*, 13 November 1897, p 28.

28 *Marines at Vaulting Horse Excercise* (November) [N-F]
   Ref *The Era*, 13 November 1897, p 19.

Edisonia Ltd

1 *H.R.H. The Prince of Wales on Board his Yacht Britannia* (5 August) [N]
   Ref *The Era*, 28 August 1897, p 29.

F. Havard

1 *Queen Victoria's Diamond Jubilee Procession* (22 June) [N] 75ft
   The Queen's Carriage
   Ref *The Era*, 10 July, 1897, p 25.

Haydon & Urry Ltd

1 *The Derby* (2 June) [N] 75ft
   Ref *The Era*, 5 June 1897, p 29.
2 (?) *Alexander Park Racecourse and Paddock* (19 June) [N]
   Ref *The Era*, 21 August 1897, p 16.
3 *Queen Victoria's Diamond Jubilee Procession* (22 June) [N] 450ft
   Series of six films, each 75ft
   Ref *The Era*, 3 July 1897, p 7.
4 *Royal Henley Regatta* (14 July) [N] 756ft
   a. Grand Challenge Cup (Leander v Dutch)
   b. Ladies Challenge Plate (Emanuel v Christ Church)
   c. Review of Boats
   d. Small Boats passing under Henley Bridge
   e. New College, Oxford crew at Landing Stage
   f. Arrival of Eton Crew at the Landing Stage
      Each 75ft
      Ref *The Era*, 17 July 1897, pp 17 and 26
5 (?) *Cornish Coast and Sea* (August) [N-F]
   Ref *The Era*, 21 August 1897, p 16.
6 *Funeral Procession of the Actor William Terriss* (21 December) [N] 75ft
   Terris met his death by assasination on 16 December. He was buried at Brompton
   Cemetery.
   Ref *The Era*, 1 January 1898, p 36 (a)

W. C. Hughes

1 *Queen Victoria's Diamond Jubilee Procession* (22 June) [N] 2,000ft
   Ref *The Era*, 3 July 1897, p 7.
2 *Jubilee - The Queen's Carriage and Escort* (22 June) [N] 120ft. Shorter version 75ft
   Ref *The Era*, 3 July 1897, p 7.

London Stereoscopic Co

1 *Queen Victoria's Diamond Jubilee Procession* (22 June) [N]
   a. The Queen's Carriage
   b. Royal Princes
   c. Colonial Troops
   Ref *Optician*, vol 13 (19 August 1897) p 385.

Ludgate Kinematograph Film Co

1 *The Procession which Accompanied the Prince and Princess of Wales to the Opening of the Blackwall Tunnel* (22 May) [N]
Taken from the offices of the *Sydney Morning Herald*, 78 Queen Victoria Street, London E.C.
Ref *Photographic News*, vol 41, no 75, N.S. (4 June 1897) p 355.

2 *Queen Victoria's Diamond Jubilee Procession* (22 June) [N]
Taken from the offices of the *European Mail* in Ludgate Circus
Ref *Photograpic News*, vol 41, no 75, N.S. (4 June 1897) p 355.

Lumière

This list of the Lumière films made in England during 1897 is mainly compiled from the list published by Maguire & Baucus in the *Optician* (see Appendix 2), and one published in the Warwick Trading Company's general catalogue of 1898 (copy in the Science Museum, London). Each film is preceded by the official English catalogue number (where known) which differs from the original Lumière catalogue number in that the former starts from one thousand and the latter from zero.

The length of each film is about 55 feet (running time 50 to 60 seconds).

1 *1425- Hyde Park* (London). (Month uncertain) [N-F]
2 *1426- Carriages at Marble Arch (London).* (Month uncertain) [N-F]
3 *1488- Arrival of the Queen from Windsor.* (21 June) [N]
'Shows the arrival of the Queen and Royal Members at Paddington, on the eve of the Jubilee.' Photographed by Jules Fuerst.
Refs *British Journal of Photography*, vol 44, no 1940 (9 July 1897) p 445.
Amateur Photographer, vol 26, no 667 (16 July 1897) p 57.
4 *Queen Victoria's Diamond Jubilee Procession* (22 June) [N] Approx: 755ft.
Taken from Parliament Square. Photographed by Jules Fuerst.
  a. *1489- Crowd following Procession.*
  b. *1490- The Queen's Carriage and Escort.*
    'Showing Queen Victoria and the Princess of Wales seated in Her Majesty's Carriage, which is drawn by the eight famous cream-coloured ponies. Following the carriage is a squadron of Life Guards on their magnificent black horses, and numerous members of the Royal Family, etc., all mounted. This and the six following photos (sic) were taken from one point of view, namely, Parliament Square, and can therefore be joined so as to make one continuous exhibition of over six minutes duration.' (WTC catalogue 1898, p 18).
  c. *1491- Foreign Princes and Nobility.*
  d. *1492- Ambassadors.*
  e. *1493- Mounted Bands of the Life Guards and Dragoons.*
  f. *1494- Marine Artillery.*
  g. *1495- Colonial Cavalry and Premiers.*
  h. *1496- Royal Horse Artillery.*
See frame illustration in WTC catalogue 1898, p 18.
Copy in National Film Archive [N.23]
(Illustration 97)
5 *Aldershot Jubilee Review* (1 July) [N] 250ft
Comprising five sequences, including the Queen's arrival and departure.
Ref *Amateur Photographer*, vol 26, no 668 (23 July 1897) p 62.
6 *Henley Royal Regatta* (14 July) [N] 110ft
Photographed by Jules Fuerst
  a. *Race for the Diamond Sculls.*

b. *Grand Challenge Cup.*

Refs *Amateur Photographer*, vol 26, no 668 (23 July 1897) p 62.

British Journal of Photography, vol 44, no 1943 (30 July 1897) p 494.

7 *English Military Views* (July) [N-F] 330ft

  a. *1520- London: Guards Leaving St James's Palace* (Also known as *Musical Lunch*)
    'Another excellent view showing the famous Guards preceded by their band marching
    slowly by the camera. Effective perspective. Splendid subject.'

  b. *1521- London: Scots Guards in Hyde Park.*
    'In Highland costume, preceded by Scotch Pipers. Fine definition and interesting
    subject.'

  c. *1522- London: Guards on foot — Rifle Drill.*
    'Several detachements of the Foot Guards drilling in Hyde Park.'

  d. *1523- London: Guards on foot — Bayonet Exercise.*

  e. *1524- London: Guards on foot — Muscular Drill.*

  f. *1525- London: Guards on foot — March to the Front.*

All the above 55ft each

Ref *The Era*, 7 August 1897, p 27; ibid, 21 August 1897, p 16.

8 *1695- London: Pleasure Boats on Lake of St James's Park* (Month uncertain) [N-F]
'A beautiful scene on the picturesque lake, showing many pleasure boats skimming over
the surface of the water. The scene is further animated by the presence of scores of ducks
and other water fowl. Sharp and clear.'

9 *1696- Departure of River Steamer on the Thames, London.* (Month uncertain) [N-F]
'Showing the steamer "Cardinal Wolsey" crowded with passengers arriving and departing
from Victoria Embankment stations. Waterloo Bridge and Surrey shore of the Thames
form an appropriate background, while various river craft is seen sailing up and down.'
Ref: *The Era*, 11 December 1897, p 20.

10 *1698- Panorama of Westminster Palace, London.* (Month uncertain) [N-F]
Taken from the deck of the Thames steamer. 'An excellent view of the Parliament
Buildings from the embankment side is shown. Victoria Tower looms up conspicuously in
the background.'

11 *1700- Church Street, Liverpool.* (September/October) [N-F]

12 *1701- Lime Street, Liverpool.* (September/October) [N-F]

13 *The Mersey and Liverpool Docks.* (October) [N-F]
Panoramas taken from Liverpool Electric Railway.

  a. *1704- Sailing Vessels and Slips.*

  b. *1705- Locks, Slips, Docks and Station.*

  c. *1706- Lumber Docks and Vessels.*

'Hundreds of thousands of sightseers annually patronize the Liverpool Elevated Electric
Road which skirts the docks and vast shipping district of this famous sea port. An
ever-varying scene is presented which is full of interest.'
Ref *The Era*, 23 October 1897, p 19.

14 *Irish Views* (October) [N-F]
Probably photographed by A. Promio.

  a. *1708- The O'Connell Bridge, Dublin.*

  b. *Sackville Street, Dublin.*

  c. *Dublin Fire Brigade.*

  d. *Blackrock, Drogheda.*

  e. *Belfast Street Scene.*

Ref *The Era*, 23 October 1897, p 19.

15 *Cavalry Jumping Hurdles* (October) [N-F]
Probably taken in Ireland.
Ref *The Era*, 23 October 1897, p 19.

16 *1729- Panorama Taken from Train on Railway Line Between Belfast and Wigtown (Ireland)*

(September/October) [N-F]

'Showing fields, farms, villages, and a picturesque park with its lake, pavillion, and winding paths. Beautiful landscape throughout the entire length of the film.'

Dr. John Macintyre

1 *X-Ray Cinematography of Frog's Legs.* (April) [S] 35ft.
Ref *British Journal of Photography*, vol 44, no 1929 (23 April 1897) p 260.
Copy in National Film Archive [891]

Mutoscope & Biograph Syndicate Ltd (Biograph)

All films 70mm.

1 *Arrival of HRH The Prince of Wales at Ascot* (15 June) [N]
Ref Palace Theatre programme, 11 October 1897 (*Barnes Museum of Cinematography*)
2 *The Race for the Ascot Gold Cup* (15 June) [N]
Ref Palace Theatre programme, 13 December 1897 (*Barnes Museum of Cinematography*)
3 *Departure of HRH The Prince of Wales from Ascot* (15 June) [N]
Ref Palace Theatre programme, 11 October 1897 (*Barnes Museum of Cinematography*)
4 *Queen Victoria's Diamond Jubilee Procession* (22 June) [N]
Ref *The Era*, 24 July 1897, p 17.
5 *Aldershot Jubilee Review* (1 July) [N]
Ref *The Era*, 24 July 1897, p 17.
6 *Spithead Naval Review* (26 June) [N]
Ref *The Era*, 24 July 1897, p 17.
7 *The Royal Family at Afternoon Tea in the Garden of Clarence House* (July) [N]
Ref *The Era*, 24 July 1897, p 17.
(Illustration 79)
8 *Henley Regatta* (14 July) [N]
Ref Palace Theatre programme, 30 August 1897 (*Science Museum, London*)
9 *The Eclipse Stakes, Sandown Park* (July) [N] Horse race
Ref Palace Theatre programme, 30 August 1897 (*Science Museum, London*)
10 *H.R.H. The Prince of Wales Proceeding from Marlborough House to St James's Palace to Hold the Investiture on Behalf of the Queen* (August) [N]
Ref *The Era*, 4 September 1897, p 18.
11 *The Koh-i-noor with the Colonial Guests* (September) [N]
Ref Palace Theatre programme, 11 October 1897 (*Barnes Museum of Cinematography*)
12 *H.M. Battleship "Terrible"* (September) [N-F]
Ref Palace Theatre programme, 11 October 1897 (*Barnes Museum of Cinematography*)
13 *Aldershot Military Camp — Bayonet Assault* (November) [N-F]
Ref *The Era*, 20 November 1897, p 21.
14 *The Gordon Highlanders* (November) [N-F]
Returning to Camp
Leisure Hours in Camp
Alarm and Response
Ref *The Era*, 20 November 1897, p 21
Palace Theatre programme, 13 December 1897 (*Barnes Museum of Cinematography*)

R. W. Paul

This list of Paul's films for 1897, has been compiled from the following sources: 1. A list of films advertised by Paul in *Photography Annual for 1897*, published in August (referred to below as Phot. Anl 1897). The films listed in this advertisement are numbered from 1 to 60, and stated as being 'the best of hundreds of scenes taken and the most interesting and exciting for public display.' Only about half the films listed were made in 1897, the rest being 1896 productions. 2. A list of films advertised by Paul in *The Magic Lantern Journal Almanac & Annual for 1897–8*, published in October, 1897 (referred to below as MLjl.Al.Oct.1897). The films listed in this advertisement are numbered from 1 to 75, but it should be noted that many of the titles are of films previously issued by Paul in 1896. 3. A catalogue of films published by Paul in August, 1898, as 'List No 15' (referred to below as L.15 Aug 1898). In addition to the 1898 productions listed, Paul has included a number of his more successful films of previous years. A copy of List No 15 is preserved in the National Film Archive, London. 4. Paul films mentioned in advertisements and reviews published in *The Era* during 1897.

1 *The Geisha* (Month uncertain) [F] 80ft
    a. *Mountainous:* Scene from "The Geisha" specially played for the Animatographe (40ft)
    b. *Marquis:* do. (The Marquis and Wun Hi) (40ft)
    Ref: L.15 Aug 1898, p 28.

2 *24-Sisters Hengler, specialite dancers* (Year and month uncertain) [F] 40ft
    Refs *The Era*, 16 January 1897, p 18.
    Phot.Anl. 1897 — No 24 Henglers. The Sisters Hengler, specialite dancers; a pretty subject, suited for colouring.
    MLJl.Al. Oct. 1897, p xcv
    Subject of Filoscopes in the Barnes Collection and Kodak Museum, Harrow.
    (Illustration 4)

3 *72-Jealousy:* Dramatic scene in gardens; jealous husband shot (Month uncertain) [F] 40ft
    Ref *Mljl.Al.* Oct. 1897, p xcv

4 *69-Robbery:* A wayfarer compelled partially to disrobe (Month uncertain) [F] 40ft
    Ref *MLjl.Al* Oct. 1897
    Copy in National Film Archive (F.529)
    (Illustration 5)

5 *26-Dirty:* "You Dirty Boy" statue comes to life (Month uncertain) [F] 40ft
    Refs: *MLjl.Al.* Oct. 1897
    Phot.Anl. 1897—Dirty: A living representation of "the Dirty Boy" statue.

6 *25-Flag:* The Union Jack fluttering (Month uncertain) [N–F] 40ft
    Refs: *MLjl.Al* Oct. 1897
    Phot.Anl 1897—Flag: The Union Jack fluttering in the breeze; nearly covers the screen.
    Copy in Barnes Collection. Probably the flag flying above Alhambra Theatre.
    Paper print of six consecutive frames in Science Museum, London (Inv.no 1913–557)

7 *13-Chimney:* Underpinning a chimney-stack and the overthrow (Month uncertain) [N] 80ft
    'Overthrow of a chimney stack, by Mr. Jack Smith'.
    Refs: *MLjl.Al.* Oct. 1897
    Phot.Anl. 1897— 13-Chimney: Underpinning a chimney-stack, burning the struts, and the overthrow.
    Vitamotograph programme (David Francis Collection)
    Paper print of six consecutive frames in Science Museum, London (Inv. no 1913–557)

8 *61-Traffic on Tower Bridge* (Month uncertain) [N-F] 40ft
    Ref: *MLjl.Al.* Oct 1897.

9 *Fountains:* Fountains playing in Trafalgar Square (Month uncertain) [N-F] 40ft
    Ref L.15.Aug. 1898

10 *12-Carting Snow at Leicester* (February) [N] 40ft
    Refs *MLjl.Al.* Oct. 1897
    Phot.Anl. 1897—No 12—Shovelling: Carting snow in the Market Place, Leicester.

11 *Carting Snow* (February) [N] 40ft
    Roadmen at work shovelling snow into carts in a busy West End thoroughfare.
    Ref *The Era*, 13 February 1897, p 18

12 *Egypt* (March/April) [N-F] 520ft

Photographed by H. W. Short

  a 35-An Arab knife grinder at work (Knife Grinder)

  b. 36-An Arab exercising his monkey (Arab and Monkey)

  c. 37-Women fetching water from Nile (Water)

  d. 38-A Caravan arriving at Pyramids which are seen in the background (Pyramids)

  e. 39-A Cairo scene; selling water from a goat skin (Drinkman)

  f. 40-Loading camels in a Cairo street (Camels-Cairo)

  g. 41-Arabs at work breaking old iron with primitive machinery (Iron)

  h. 42-An Egyptian bullock-pump; drawing water (Bullock Pump)

  i. 43-Fishermen and boat at Port Said (Fishermen - Port Said - Fisher)

  j. 44-Egyptian scene, primitive saw mill (Sawyers)

  k. 75-Procession of the Holy Carpet from Cairo

  l.   -Dervishes - Dancing

  m.   -Cigarette maker

All the above 40ft each

Refs *The Era*, 24 April 1897, p 8

MLjl.Al. Oct. 1897

Phot.Anl. 1897

Frame illustrations of d and f published in Paul's catalogues for 1901 and 1903 (Barnes Collection)

Paper print of six consecutive frames of f in Science Museum, London (Inv. no 1913–557)

13 *60-City & Surburban Handicap, Newmarket* (21 April) [N] 40ft

The final of the race

Refs *MLjl.Al.* Oct. 1897

Phot.Anl. 1897: 60-Surburban: City and Surburban, Finish, 1897

14 *71-Prince of Wales reviewing Yeomanry, Cheltenham* (13 May) [N] 120ft

Ref *MLjl.Al.* Oct. 1897

15 *The Derby* (2 June) [N] 40ft

The victory of Galtee More

Ref *The Era*, 10 July 1897, p 16

MLjl.Al Oct. 1897

Phot,Anl. 1897 -Derby: The 1897 Derby; a fine picture.

16 *Queen Victoria's Diamond Jubilee Procession* (22 June) [N] 480ft

Photographed by R. W. Paul and others

  a.   Sailors — Head of Procession, including bluejackets

  b.   Colonial — Head of Colonial procession, Canadians, etc.

  c.   Cavalcade — Royal Carriages passing Westminster

  d.   Troops — Colonial Troops passing Westminster

  e.   Troopers — Continuation of, and can be joined to preceding one

  f.   Rifles — Cape Mounted Riflemen passing St Paul's

  g.   Dragoons — Dragoons passing St Paul's

  h.   Royal — Royal Carriages arriving at St Paul's

  i.   Royalties — Guards and escort arriving at St Paul's

  j.   Carriage — Queen's carriage and Indian escort arriving

  k.   Princes — Guards and Princes north of St Paul's

  l.   Queen and escort in Churchyard, showing Queen's face

All the above 40ft each

Ref *MLjl.Al.* Oct. 1897

L.15.Aug. 1898, p 28

17 *56 — Fire Brigade Review at Windsor* (28 June) [N] 40ft

Gallop past

Refs *MLjl.Al.* Oct. 1897

Phot.Anl. 1897 — 56-Review: Fire Brigade Review at Windsor, June, 1897.

Vitamotograph programme (David Francis Collection): No 7 'Review of Fire Brigades in the Home Park, Windsor.'

18 *Sweden* (July) [N-F] 460ft

Photographed by R. W. Paul

The title of each film is followed by the code word in brackets

a. 28-Passengers arriving at Stockholm and leaving the boat (Disembarking)

b. 45-A Laplander feeding his Reindeer (Reindeer)

c. 46-Laplanders arriving at their village; a welcome home (Laplanders)

d. 47-Children at play in the King's garden, Stockholm (Garden)

e. 48-Derricks at work discharging coal from a steamer (Derricks)

f. 49-Electric Trolley Car coming through pine forest, Sweden (Trolley) 60ft

g. 50-The King's Guard marching at Stockholm (Guard)

h. 51-The Steamboat "Aeolus" leaving Stockholm (Aeolus)

i. 52-A Swedish National Dance at Skansen (Swede)

j. 53- Do. Do. Eight performers (Sweden)

k. 54- Do. Do. Four performers (Swedish)

All the above 40ft each, unless otherwise stated.

Refs *MLjl.Al.* Oct. 1897

L.15.Aug. 1898, pp 28 and 30

Phot.Anl. 1897

19 *73 — Bank Holiday Picture at Hampstead* (Roundabout) (1 August) [N] 40ft

Ref *MLjl.Al.* Oct. 1897

20 *66 — Ferries arriving at landing stage* (Liverpool Landing Stage) (August) [N-F] 60ft

Ref *MLjl.Al.* Oct. 1897

21 *Douglas, Isle of Man* (August) [N-F] 360ft

a. 62 — A lively picture at Douglas Diving at Port Skillion, I.O.M. (Diving) 80ft

b. 63 — Landing visitors from small boats (Douglas) 40ft

c. Laxey Electric Railway. 40ft

d. Scene on Douglas Beach. 40ft

e. SS Empress Queen. 40ft

f. The Clock Tower. 40ft

g. The Parade. 40ft

h. Douglas Ferry. 40ft

Ref *MLjl.Al.* Oct. 1897

L.15.Aug. 1898, pp 28 and 30

Vitamotograph programme (David Francis Collection)

22 *30 — Diving and Bathing in the Sea* (August) [N-F] 40ft

Probably the same film as 21a, above.

Ref *MLjl.Al.* Oct. 1897

23 *74 — Donkey Riding on the Beach* (August) [N-F] 40ft

Ref *MLjl.Al.* Oct. 1897

Copy in the Barnes Collection

24 *65 — Rottingdean Electric Railway (Electric)* (August) [N-F] 80ft

The Brighton-Rottingdean Electric Marine Car coming through the sea to the pier, and passengers disembarking

Ref *MlJl.Al.* Oct. 1897

L.15.Aug. 1898, p 27

25 *14 — Meet of Staghounds at Aylesbury* (Month uncertain) [N]

Ref *MLjl.Al.* Oct. 1897

Phot.Anl. 1897: No 14-Hounds: Meet of Lord Rothschild's staghounds at Aylesbury.

26 *A Phantom Ride* (Month uncertain) [N-F]
    'Taken from a train entering a tunnel'
    Ref: Vitamotograph programme (David Francis Collection): Film no 4.
    Attribution uncertain.

Prestwich Manufacturing Co

1 *Queen Victoria's Diamond Jubilee Procession* (22 June) [N]
    Ref *Amateur Photographer*, vol 26, no 677 (24 September 1897) p 267
2 *Photographic Convention, Great Yarmouth: Members Leaving the Town Hall* (14 July) [N]
    Photographed by W. H. Prestwich
    Ref *Amateur Photographer*, vol 26, no 680 (15 October 1897) p 34
    Photograms, of the Year 1897, p 34
    Frame illustrations published in *The Practical Photographer*, vol 8, no 93 (September 1898)
    pp 280-81; and Alfred T. Story, *The Story of Photography* (London, 1898) p 139, fig 38
    (Illustration 27)

J. H. Rigg

1 *Switchback in operation at Shipley Glen* (September) [N-F]
    Ref *British Journal of Photography*, vol 44, no 1956 (29 October 1897) p 699

J. W. Rowe & Co

1 *Boy washing a dog* (June) [F]
    Ref *Photogram*, vol 4, no 41 (July 1897) p 214
2 *London* (June) [N-F]
    a   The Mansion House
    b.   Cheapside
    c.   Ludgate Circus
    d.   Oxford Circus
    e.   Rotten Row
    Ref *Photogram*, vol 4, no 41 (July 1897) p 214
3 *Queen Victoria's Diamond Jubilee Procession* (22 June) [N]
    Ref *Photogram*, vol 4, no 41 (July 1897) p 214

G. A. Smith

1 *Football* (April) [F] 75ft
    With Tubby Edlin as one of the players
    Ref Smith's cash book
    Hove Echo, 8 May 1897, p 3
    Prestwich Catalogue 1898, p 6: 33 — Football. Game and Scrimmage
    Warwick Trading Co catalogue 1898, p 60: 3017 — Football. Game Scrimmage. Code
    word: Skater
2 *Westminster* (18 May) [N-F] 75ft
    Ref Smith's Cash book
    Prestwich Catalogue 1897, p 7: 53 — Street traffic by Clock Tower.
    Warwick Catalogue 1898, p 30: 3031 — Westminster: Street Traffic by Clock Tower.
    Code Skim.
3 *(Midget film)* (20–21 May) [F] 75ft
    Apparently a failure
    Ref Smith's cash book

4 *Sailing Boat* (June) [N-F]
   Ref Smith's cash book
   Prestwich catalogue 1898, p 6: 34 — Sailing Boat. Sails ashore in rough sea
5 *Queen Victoria's Diamond Jubilee Procession* (22 June) [N]
   a   Colonials
   b.   Queen's Carriage
   Ref Smith's cast book
   Hove Echo, 27 November 1897, p 5
6 *The Miller and the Sweep* (First version) (24 June) [F] 75ft
   Apparently a failure
   Ref Smith's cash book
7 *Mohawk Minstrels* (1 July) [N] 75ft
   Audience leaving Hastings Pier Pavilion, headed by Messrs. Danvers & Schofield, of the
   Mohawk Minstrels, in costume.
   Ref: Smith's cash book (?)
   Prestwich Catalogue, October 1898, p 6, no 41
   N.B. The entry in Smith's cash book shows that on 1st July he made an excursion to
   Hastings, where he exposed two negatives. The fare cost him three shillings, and tips, one
   shilling. Smith does not refer to the subject taken, but the above is the only film
   commensurate with the place and date. We know the Mohawk Minstrels were appearing
   at the Hastings Pier Pavilion on that date, from a report published in *The Hastings & St
   Leonards Advertiser*, 1 July, 1897, p 6, column four.
8 *Yachting* (Month uncertain) [N-F] 75ft
   Ref *Hove Echo*, 27 November 1897, p 5
   Prestwich catalogue 1898, p 7: 58 — Yachting. Rounding the buoy; sailing boats racing
9 *Miss Ellen Terry* (9 August) [N] 225ft
   Taken at her cottage in Winchelsea
   Ref Smith's cash book
   Prestwich catalogue 1898, p 6:
   49- Miss Ellen Terry appears at her country cottage window, kisses hand, throws flower,
   etc. Characteristic portrait.
   50- Miss Ellen Terry gathering flowers in her garden, with pet dog.
   51- Miss Ellen Terry. Afternoon tea with a lady friend in the garden.
   Also listed in the Warwick catalogue 1898, pp 59-60 - Nos 3014, 3015 and 3016. Each
   75ft
10 *Pierrot Troupe* (28 August) [N-F] 75ft
   Ref Smith's cash book
   Prestwich catalogue 1898, p 6: 39 — Pierrot Troupe. Performing at sea-side. Showing crowd.
11 *Brighton Sea-Going Electric Car* (3–4 September) [N-F]
   Magnus Volk's Brighton-Rottingdean Seashore Electric Railway.
   Ref Smith's cash book
   Hove Echo, 27 November 1897, p 5
12 *Brighton Sea-Going Electric Car* (3–4 September) [N-F] 75ft Taken in rougher sea
   Ref Smith's cash book
   Warwick catalogue 1898, p 60: 3025 — Brighton Sea-going Electric Car in rough sea.
   Novel and interesting. Code word: Skeiy
13 *Sailing & Car* (September) [N-F] 75ft
   Two subjects on one film. Comprising numbers 4 & 10
   Ref Smith's cash book
   Prestwich catalogue 1898, p 6: 34 & 35 — (The above Two Subjects, which are both
   printed on one 75ft film, with blank space between, afford a pleasing contrast in methods
   of marine travelling)

14 *Walking Greasy Pole* (11 September) [N] 75ft
Filmed at Southwick, Sussex.
Ref Smith's cash book
Prestwich catalogue 1898, p 6: 31 — Walking Greasy Pole; winning the pig. Very pretty
and amusing scene at regatta.
Also listed in Warwick catalogue 1898, p 6 as number 3022, code word: Skew

15 *Paddling* (18 September) [F] 75ft
Filmed at Southwick, Sussex after two previous attempts.
Ref Smith's cash book
Prestwich catalogue 1898, p 6: 37 — Children Paddling at Sea-side. With comic fat old
lady and lovers. An amusing scene on the beach.
Also listed in Warwick catalogue 1898, p 60, as number 3026, code word: Skiff.

16 *Hanging Out the Clothes* (20 September) [F] 75ft
Featuring Mr & Mrs Tom Green
Ref Smith's cash book
Hove Echo, 27 November 1897, p 5
Prestwich catalogue 1898, p 6: 40 — Hanging out the Clothes, or Master, Mistress, and
Maid. Very comic and popular.
Also listed in Warwick catalogue 1898, p 60 as number 3028, code word: Skill
Copies in the National Film Archive (F.535) and the New Zealand National Film Unit
Archive.
(Illustration 44)

17 *The Lady Barber*, or *Comic Shaving* (23 September) [F] 75ft
Featuring Tom Green and W. Carlile
Ref Smith's cash book
Prestwich catalogue 1898, p 6: 29 — The Lady Barber. What we shall come to, and how
to make the best of a "bad job".
Also listed in Warwick catalogue 1898, p 60, as number 3023, code word: Skewer

18 *The Miller and the Sweep* (Second version) (24 September) [F] 52ft
Ref Smith's cash book
Hove Echo, 27 November 1897, p 5
Prestwich catalogue 1898, p 5: 27 — The Miller and Sweep. A dusty fight between soot
and flour; windmill at work in background. Very funny and popular. 52ft
Also listed in Warwick catalogue 1898, p 60; as number 3021
Copy in the National Film Archive (F. 536)
Illustration 43)

19 *Comic Face* (28 September) [F] 75ft
Featuring Tom Green
Ref Smith's cash book
Prestwich catalogue 1898, p 6: 42 — Comic Face. Old man drinking glass of beer, old women
taking snuff. Two subjects on one film.

20 *Wearie Willie* (30 September) [F] 75ft
Featuring Mr & Mrs Tom Green
Ref Smith's cash book
Prestwich catalogue 1898, p 6: 43 — Wearie Willie. Tramp engaged to beat carpets, beats
employer by mistake — rewarded by pail of water.

21 *Waves and Spray* (September) [N-F] 75ft
Ref Smith's cash book
Prestwich catalogue 1898, p 6: 38 — Waves and Spray. Fine effect. Rough sea dashing
against stone groyne.
Also listed in Warwick catalogue 1898, p 60, as number 3027, code word: Skilful

22 *Indian Clubs* (September) [N-F] 75ft
Ref Smith's cash book

Prestwich catalogue 1898, p 7: 62 — Indian Clubs. Performance by Instructor
Also listed in Warwick catalogue 1898, p 61, as number 3035 — Gymnastics — Indian Club Performer. Code word: Skinless

23 *Football and Cricket* (September) [N-F] 75ft
Ref Smith's cash book
Prestwich catalogue 1898, p 6: 33a — Football and Cricket. Batsman stumped. Two different subjects on one film.
Also listed in Warwick catalogue 1898, p 61, as number 3038, code word: Skipper

24 *Passenger Train* (September) [N-F] 75ft
Ref Smith's cash book
Hove Echo, 27 November 1897, p 5
Prestwich catalogue 1898, p 6: 47 — Passenger Train. Arrival at station — passengers change — train moves off. Good example of this subject.
Also listed in Warwick catalogue 1898, p 60: as number 3030, code word: Skillett

25 *Love on the Pier* (2 October) [F] 75ft
Filmed at Hastings
Ref Smith's cash book

26 *The X Rays* (6 October) [F] 54ft
With Tom Green
Ref Smith's cash book
Hove Echo, 27 November 1897, p 5
Prestwich catalogue 1898, p 6: 32 — The X Rays. The Professor turns his apparatus upon the lovers and makes a startling revelation. Very surprising and amusing. 54 feet.
Also listed in Warwick catalogue 1898, p 60, as number 3032, code word: Skin.

27 *Portsmouth Express* (20 October) [N-F] 75ft
Filmed at Southwick, Sussex
Ref Smith's cash book
Prestwich catalogue 1898, p 6: 48 — Portsmouth Express and another train passing signal box.
Also listed in Warwick catalogue 1898, p 61, as number 3039, code word: Skittish

28 *Trafalgar Day* (21 October) [N] 75ft
Ref Smith's cash book
Prestwich catalogue 1898, p 7: 54 — Nelson's Monument (decorated) Trafalgar Square, London. Traffic on Trafalgar Day.
Also listed in Warwick catalogue 1898, p 61, as number 3040, code word: Skittles.

29 *Making Sausages* (October) [F] 75ft
Ref Smith's cash book
Hove Echo, 27 November 1897, p 5
Prestwich catalogue 1898, p 6: 30 — Making Sausages. Live cats and dogs put into a machine, sausages come out. Four cooks. Always goes well.
Also listed in Warwick catalogue 1898, p 60, as number 3024, code word: Skid

30 *Tipsy, Topsy, Turvey* (Reversal) (19 November) [F] 75ft
With Tom Green
Ref Smith's cash book
Hove Echo, 27 November 1897, p 5
Prestwich catalogue 1898, p 7: 56 — Tipsy, Topsy, Turvey. The reveller's return from his club

31 *Yachting* (Month and year uncertain) [N-F] 150ft
Perhaps filmed at Hastings on 1st July, 1897. Cf entry for that date in Smith's cash book.
See also no 7, which may have been filmed on the same occasion.
Ref Warwick catalogue 1898, p 61:
3037 — Yachting (150ft) Price £6
Code word: Skirt.

3036 — Yachting (Shortened version of the above)
Code word: Skip.
A continuous procession of yachts passing and repassing quite close to camera.

Velograph Syndicate Ltd

1 *The Derby* (2 June) [N] 120ft
Ref *Photogram*, vol 4, no 43 (July 1897) p 214
Printed programme, Palace Theatre, Croydon, 9/8/97 (*Science Museum, London*)
2 *The Ascot Gold Cup* (15 June) [N]
Ref Printed programme, Palace Theatre, Croydon, 9/8/97 (*Science Museum*)
3 *Queen Victoria's Diamond Jubilee Procession* (22 June) [N] 180ft
Ref *British Journal of Photography*, vol 44, no 1939 (2 July 1897) p 427
Ibid, *Monthly Supplement*, 2 July 1897, p 49
Frame illustrations published in the *Magic Lantern Journal Annual 1897-8*.
(Illustration 98)
4 *Queen Victoria and Royal Family at the State Garden Party, Buckingham Palace* (28 June) [N]
Ref Printed programme, Palace Theatre, Croydon, 9/8/97 (*Science Museum*)
5 *Royal Henley Regatta* (14 July) [N]
Ref Printed programme, Palace Theatre, Croydon, 9/8/97 (*Science Museum*)
6 *The Flying Scotsman* (July) [N-F]
Ref Printed programme, Palace Theatre, Croydon, 9/8/97 (*Science Museum*)
7 *London Life* (July) [N-F]
Ref Printed programme, Palace Theatre, Croydon, 9/8/97 (*Science Museum*)
8 *Military Drill* (July) [N-F]
Ref Printed programme, Palace Theatre, Croydon, 9/8/97 (*Science Museum*)
9 *The Seaside* (July) [N-F]
Ref Printed programme, Palace Theatre, Croydon, 9/8/97 (*Science Museum*)

Walker & Co

1 *Queen Victoria's Arrival at Ballater* (May) [N]
The Royal Guard of Honour, the Royal Scots and Deeside Highlanders
Ref *British Journal of Photography*, vol 44, no 1958 (12 November 1897) p 732
2 *Queen Victoria's Departure from Ballater for Balmoral* (22 May) [N] 75ft
Ref *British Journal of Photography*, vol 44, no 1935 (4 June 1897) p 354
3 *Queen Victoria's Diamond Jubilee Celebrations, Aberdeen* (22 June) [N]
Ref *British Journal of Photography*, vol 44, no 1958 (12 November 1897) p 732
4 *Children's Fresh Air Fund* (July) [N]
2,000 Aberdeen children marching to station
Ref *British Journal of Photography*, vol 44, no 1958 (12 November 1897) p 732
5 *Gordon Highlanders, Castlehill Barracks, Aberdeen* (Month uncertain) [N-F]
a Bayonet Exercise
b. Volley Firing
Ref *British Journal of Photography*, vol 44, no 1958 (12 November 1897)
6 *Braemar Gathering* (September) [N]
a March past of the Clans
b. A Highland Reel
Ref *British Journal of Photography*, vol 44, no 1958 (12 November 1897) p 732
7 *Aberdeen, Near Union Bridge* (Month uncertain) [N-F]
Ref *British Journal of Photography*, vol 44, no 1958 (12 November 1897) p 732
8 *Aberdeen, Union Street* (Month uncertain) [N-F]
Ref *British Journal of Photography*, vol 44, no 1958 (12 November 1897) p 732

W. Watson & Sons

1 *Queen Victoria's Diamond Jubilee Procession* (22 June) [N] 1,000ft
Photographed by H. A. Saunders. Issued in lengths of 75 ft
Ref *The Optician*, vol 13 (15 July 1897) p 295
Optical Magic Lantern Journal, vol 8, no 99 (August 1897) p 126
2 *Trafalgar Day* (21 October) [N]
'The Nelson Monument during the recent decorations, and the people passing at the time.'
Ref: *The Practical Photographer*, vol 8, no 96 (December 1898) p 380

James A. Williamson

1 *Ring-a-Ring-of-Roses* (Month uncertain) [F] 75ft
The Williamson children playing the traditional game of that name
Ref *Hove Echo*, 9 October, 1897, p 3
2 *Fox-and-Geese* (Month uncertain) [F] 75ft
The Williamson children playing the traditional game of that name
Ref *Hove Echo*, 9 October 1897, p 3
3 *Hove Coastguards at Cutlass Drill* (Month uncertain) [N-F]
Ref *Hove Echo*, 9 October 1897, p 3; ibid, 27 November 1897, p 5
4 *Hove Coastguards at Flag Drill* (Month uncertain) [N-F]
Ref *Hove Echo*, 27 November 1897, p 5

J. Wrench & Son

1 *Queen Victoria's Diamond Jubilee Procession* (22 June) [N] 800ft
Photographed by Alfred Wrench from a position at the corner of King William Street, E.C.
Issued as 7 films, six 75ft long and one 100ft.
Ref *The Optician*, vol 13 (8 July, 1897) p 278
Optical Magic Lantern Journal, vol 8, no 99 (August 1897) p 126
2 *Spithead Naval Review* (26 June) [N]
Ref *The Optician*, vol 13 (8 July 1897) p 278

Appendix 4

AMENDMENTS AND ADDITIONS TO THE PREVIOUS VOLUME.

ERRATA

Page 5, line 7. *For* Theatograph *read* Theatrograph.

Page 12, illustration 3. *For* 1898 *read* 1897.

Page 12, line 25. *For* Copyright *read* Copyrighted.

Page 13, illustration 4. The bottom edge has been cropped losing the portion printed with the address of the Continental Commerce Co. This should read: 70 Oxford Street, W., London.

Page 19, line 7. *For* New Orange *read* West Orange.

Page 29, line 42. *For* March *read* May.

Page 31, line 4. *For* tree *read* three.

Page 60, illustration 27. Add: The original drawing is in the British Film Institute, and was donated by Sydney Birt Acres.

Page 65, Line 12. *For* Birt Acres *read* Mr. Acres.

Page 89, line 43. *For* July *read* May.

Page 90, line 3. *Delete* into.

Page 108, illustration 40. *For* Storey *read* Story.

Page 108. The missing word on the last line is Chorus.

Page 109, illustration 40. This is incorrectly printed and shows the image reversed.

Page 113, line 40. *For* correctly *read* precisely.

Page 144, line 3. *For* 9 March *read* 19 March.

Page 148, line 3. *For* making *read* selling.

Page 149, line 41. *For* 70 *read* (70).

Page 150, line 38. *For* [57] *read* (57).

Page 155, bottom line. *Delete* or no.

Page 173, line 25. The address should read: 368 rue St Honoré.

Page 184, illustration 70. *For* 60mm *read* 70mm.

Page 188, line 3. *For* November *read* October.

Page 205, line 21, film number 9. *For* [N–F] *read* [F].

Page 210, film 18 (*Children at Play (2)*) *Add:* Copy in Barnes Collection.

Pages 211–12. The two illustrations on page 211 should appear on page 212, and those on page 212 should appear on page 211.

Page 225, note 30. *Amend note to read*: The first prototype is conserved at the Musée du Cinéma de Lyon. The second prototype is at the Conservatoire des Arts et Métiers, Paris (Inv. no. 16966-E. 1942). Examples of the definitive model are to be found in several collections, including the Science Museum, London, and the Kodak Museum, Harrow.

Page 230, note 27. *For* pl. xix *read* p lxix.

Page 232, note 115. *For* Great Glasgow Fair *read* Blockley Wakes (North Manchester).

Page 234, note 1. *For* November *read* October.

ADDENDA

Since the publication of the first volume of this history some additional information has come to my attention, which although necessitating certain amendments to my text, does not effect in any way the general conclusions reached by me concerning those first formative years of the cinema's history in England. Among the contributors to this additional data I particularly wish to acknowledge Messrs R. Brown, David Francis, David Henry and Roy H. Thornton.

From material submitted, I have been able to date more accurately a few of the films listed in Appendix I. Of particular help in this respect is an advertisement of R. W. Paul's which appeared in the *English Mechanic* for 14 June 1895, brought to my notice by Mr Brown. Here five

Kinetoscope films are mentioned which can only have been photographed with the Paul-Acres Camera. This advertisement is the earliest reference to these films found so far, and necessitates certain amendments to my list on pages 203–5, viz:

Page 203. After the film listed as number 4, add the following:

4a *Comic Shoeblack* (May) [F]
Ref. *English Mechanic*, vol 61, no 1577 (14 June 1895) p vi advertisement.
4b *Performing Bears* (May [F]
Ref. Same as for 4a.
4c *Arrest of a Pickpocket* (May) [F]
Ref. Same as for 4a.

Page 203. The dates of numbers 5 and 7 should be amended in each case to read: (May).
Page 204, lines 13–15. Delete all reference to *Arrest of a Pickpocket*, since this has now been established as a Paul-Acres film.
Page 205. Delete film number 3.

Another valuable source of information on the films of the period, is an Alhambra Theatre programme for 31 August 1896, a Xerox copy of which has also been kindly supplied by Mr Brown. It lists twenty films by R. W. Paul, some of which are dated. We are thus enabled to make the following amendments:

Pages 214–15, films numbered 32–34. *For* (August) [N–F], *read* (14 August) [N].
Page 215, film number 35. *For* (August) [N–F], *read* (15 August) [N].
Page 215, film number 36. *For* (August) [N–F], *read* (15 August) [N].
Page 216, films numbered 38–40. *For* (August/September) *read* (August).
Page 216, film number 41. *For* (September) *read* (August).

The references for entries 32–41 should read: Alhambra Theatre programme, 31 August 1896 (*R. Brown Collection*).

A hitherto unrecorded film by R. W. Paul, *Gardener Watering Plants*, is listed on a Paragon Theatre programme for 21 September 1896, a Xerox copy of which has been kindly sent to me by Mr David Henry. The following entry should therefore be made on page 218: After film number 55, add:

55a *Gardener Watering Plants* (September) [N–F]
Ref. Paragon Theatre programme, 21 September 1896 (*David Henry Collection*).

A film in the National Film Archive catalogued as *A Rush-hour Record on London Bridge* (N.7), has since been identified by Mr R. H. Thornton as Paul's film *Blackfriar's Bridge*. Mr Thornton went to the exact spot where Paul must have set up his camera and took photographs to prove his point. The following amendments are therefore called for:

Page 207. Delete film number 3.
Page 209, illustration 78. This should read: *Blackfriar's Bridge*, by R. W. Paul, July 1896 (*National Film Archive*).
Page 214, film number 29. After the reference, add: Copy in National Film Archive. Formerly catalogued incorrectly as *A Rush-Hour Record on London Bridge* (N.7) (Illustration 78).

The London street scene shown in illustration 77 on page 208 is also the subject of a Filoscope in the Barnes Collection and so we know the film to be one of Paul's. The caption to this illustration therefore, should be amended to read:

London Street Scene, R. W. Paul, 1896 (*Kodak Museum, Harrow*).

Likewise, the reference to the film on page 207 (film number 1) should read:

1 *London Street Scene* (April) [N–F] Ref *The Era*, 25 April, 1896, p 17. Subject of a Filoscope in the Barnes Museum (Illustration 77).

My attention has since been directed to a list of films advertised by R. W. Paul in *Photography Annual for 1897*; among the sixty films listed are two 1896 productions omitted from my list. One is another event taken at the Music Hall Sports, and the other is an additional film of Morris Cronin. On page 210, film number 15 should be amended to read:

15 *Music Hall Sports* (14 July) [N]

Held at Herne Hill, London.

   a) Cat No 22: *Sports* — A Comic Costume Race at the Music Hall Sports, July 14th, 1896.
   Refs: *The Era*, 8 August 1896, p 25. *Photographic Annual for 1897* (August 1897) p 1,
   advertisement: 57 — Sports — Comic Costume Race at the Music Hall Sports.

A similar film was taken at the Music Hall Sports held on 5 July 1898 (Paul List No 15, August
1898, p 20).

   A copy of one or other of these films is in the National Film Archive. The indications are that it
is the earlier event which is recorded on the Archive print (186).
(Illustration 79)

   b) 59 — *Race*: The Juvenile Plate Race, 1896 Ref: *Photography Annual for 1897* (August 1897)
   p 1, advertisement.

On page 216, film number 41 should be amended to read:

   41 *Morris Cronin, American Club Manipulator* (August) [F]

   a) 22: *Club*. Morris Cronin, the marvellous American club manipulator.

   Ref: *Photography Annual for 1897* (August 1897) p 1, advertisement.

   b) 23: *Clubs*. Cronin with three clubs; a wonderful feat.

   Ref: *The Era*, 25 September 1896, p 18, *Photography Annual for 1897* (August 1897) p 1,
   advertisement.

From the list of films by Birt Acres on pages 204–6, I inadvertently omitted *Tower Bridge*,
which is one of the films mentioned on the handbill advertising the Kineoptikon at Piccadilly
Circus (p 70, illustration 30). Unfortunately, the poor quality of the reproduction renders the
text partially illegible so that not all the titles are discernible. We now know from information
published by Mr. Brown (see below) that the performances of the Kineoptikon ceased on 10 June
1896, so the handbill is not likely to be later than that date. Most probably it was printed for the
opening of the exhibition which took place on 21 March. 'May' is written in ink on the original
but I am inclined to believe that this refers to the month when visited by the handbill's recipient.
Accordingly, we must make the following amendments to my list:

   Page 205. After film number 5, add:

   5a *Tower Bridge, Working* (March) [N–F]

   Ref. Handbill of the Kineoptikon Exhibition, Piccadilly (*Mrs. Audrey Wadowska Collection*).
   Page 205, film number 11. *For* (June/July) *read* (March).
   Page 206, film number 24. *For* (June/July) *read* (March).
   Page 206, film number 31. *For* (October) *read* (March).

The reference to entries 11, 24 and 31 should read:

   Handbill of the Kineoptikon Exhibition, Piccadilly (Mrs. Audrey Wadowska Collection).

   I have since come across two further films of Birt Acres which must be added to his 1896 list;
these are:

   Brighton on a Bank Holiday (1 August) [N]

   a. *The King's Road and West Pier*

   b. *Landing at Low Tide*

   Ref *The Era*, 30 January 1897, p 18.

and

   Gatwick Races (October/November) [N]

   a. *Arrival of a Race Train at Gatwick Station*

   b. *The Paddock*

   Ref *The Era*, 30 January 1897, p 18.

12 films which can be attributed to Birt Acres, are listed on a poster reproduced in Stephen
Peart, *The Picture House in East Anglia* (Lavenham, 1980) p xii. The poster advertises the 'Royal
Cinematographe', one of the items in a programme presented by Gilbert's Modern Circus at the
Agricultural Hall, Norwich, for the week commencing 11 January, 1897. The films listed are:

   The Derby (Probably the Paul-Acres film no 4 of 1895).

   Boxing Kangaroo (Paul-Acres film no 5).

   The South Western Railway at Dover

A Prize Fight by Jem Mace and Burke
Tom Merry, Lightning Cartoonist (No 25 or 26).
Highgate Tunnel: The Goods Train (No 11).
Yarmouth Beach (No 14).
The Dancing Dogs
The Royal Films:-

    1. Arrival of the Royal Party at Marlborough House (No 27).
    2. Departure of the Royal Party from Marlborough House (No 27).
    3. Garden Party on the Lawn at Marlborough House.
    4. Arrival of the Prince and Suite (Possibly no 36).

Attention must be drawn to Mr. R. Brown's article 'England's First Cinema' in *The British Journal of Photography* (24 June, 1979, pp 520–21; 530–31). Here he has delved more deeply than I into the Olympia Theatrograph exhibitions and presents evidence to show that two special buildings were designed and erected to house Paul's Theatrograph there. To the first of these, Mr. Brown is happy to designate the term 'England's First Cinema', defining his term cinema as 'a building designed and exclusively used for exhibiting projected films'. I will not quarrel with him on this point, but I would prefer to regard these temporary structures at Olympia as sideshow booths. Besides, his definition, if strictly adhered to, would eliminate more than half the cinemas (so-called) that were to come into being during the first half of the 20th century. In the same article, mention is made of the performances given by Birt Acres at 2 Piccadilly Mansions, and Mr Brown is able to present evidence to show that the fire which put an end to the performances there occurred at 9.44 pm on Wednesday 10 June 1896, indicating that the show had lasted over two and a half months, whereas in my book (p 70) I was able to give only an approximate period of 'a few weeks'.

On page 197, I raised the question of Paul's suggestion for a repository of films at the British Museum. He did in fact send a copy of his film of the 1896 Derby, but this, Dr Thomas informs me, was later transferred to the Science Museum. Frame illustrations from this film are reproduced on page 111 (41a), but the accompanying illustration (41b) does not depict the finish of the race, as stated, but shows the Derby of 1900, and is therefore out of context in the present work. The unidentified film reproduced on page 203 (75), formerly thought likely to be the Derby of 1895, filmed by Birt Acres, is now believed to be the Derby of 1898. Since the publication of my book, the Derby material in the National Film Archive has come under more careful scrutiny and I am grateful to Mr Roger Holman for giving me the opportunity of benefitting from this research to make these corrections. It is therefore necessary to make the following amendments to my text:

    Page 111. Expunge illustration 41b and delete reference to same in the caption.
    Page 202, film number 4. Delete reference to illustration 75.
    Page 203. Expunge illustration 75 and delete caption.

My piece on Randall Williams, 'King of Showmen' also needs some slight revision in the light of fresh information supplied by his grandson, Mr Paul Williams, of Leeds. On page 167 I stated that Randall Williams had two sons who carried on the show after their father's death. In fact, he had no sons. His family history is recorded in an interesting letter sent me by his grandson, which I quote:

    ' . . . For your information, my grandfather Randall Williams had no sons. My grandfather died at Grimsby after he left Hull Fair about 1898. There were only two daughters, Carrie Williams and Annie Williams. Annie Williams was my mother. She was the oldest daughter. I am the oldest grandson. My father Ruben Williams was my mother's cousin. Her mother was Randall Williams' sister.

    My mother married after my grandfather died. Her mother died when she was a child. They have told me that they came from Warrington, Lancs.

    Mrs George Proctor was another of Randall Williams' sisters. They travelled with a circus. My father showed the pictures in the Hall in London [ie the Royal Agricultural Hall, Islington] with my grandfather, but what I have been told they had to be wound on a spool after they left the projector. For your information, Carrie Williams married a man called Richard Monte. He was a Jew. He had two brothers when he married my Aunt Carrie. He used her Randalls name on his show fronts. He traded in the name of Randall Williams.

Neither my mother or my Aunt Carrie could read or write. I used to write the letters for my mother and father.

I was born on November 19th 1899 so you see I had not the pleasure of meeting my grandfather. So you see your facts are slightly out.

Yours faithfully

Paul Williams

I am again indebted to Mr Brown for additional information on the first film performances in Bradford. It turns out that the date given by me on page 144 in respect to Wray's first performance in that town, is far too late. In fact, an exhibition of Wray's Kineoptoscope, under the name Cinetograph, was given in Bradford on 11 June, 1896, a review of which appeared the next day in the *Bradford Observer* (p 7, col 1). The actual exhibitors were the Scientific Entertainment Company, of Matlock, Bath, whose advertisements appeared in the same paper from 11 to 29 June. Later in the year, on the 21st of November, Wray's Kineoptoscope is advertised in the *Bradford Observer* (p 1, col 1) by Riley Brothers, who by then had acquired the patent rights. A week previously R. J. Appleton & Co advertised their Cieroscope in the *Observer* (14 November, p 1, col 2) and so that apparatus should also have found a place in my first volume. However, as the reader is aware, I have carried over its 1896 history into this volume.

The list of Lumière films on page 219, also calls for revision. It transpires that the Lumière films are remarkably well documented. Maurice Bessy and Lo Duca, in their book *Louis Lumière: Inventeur* (Paris, 1948) pp 54–59, reproduce the first Lumière catalogue of 1897. A catalogue in English also appears in *The Optician*, vol 14 (23 September 1897) pp 122–27. The Warwick Trading Company (WTC) too, publish a list of Lumière films in their general catalogue of 1898 (copy in Science Museum, London). In each case the original Lumière catalogue numbers are given, except that in the English lists, the numbers start from one thousand instead of from number one. For example, *A Fire Call, London* is numbered 1246, whereas in the original Lumière catalogue it appears as number 246–*Alerte de pompiers*.

It should be noted that certain films depicting French scenes, are sometimes passed off in England as English subjects. We can cite three such examples:

> *1016–A Boxing Match (16-Boxeurs)* is described as a contest between English boxers; *1039–Departure of a Trans-Atlantic Liner (39-Départ d'un transatlantique)* is described as a departure from Liverpool; and *1052–Gale at Sea (52-Gros temps en mer)* is described as a Cornish coast scene.

The Lumière films made in England during 1896 include the following:

1 *1246–Answering a Fire Call (London)* / *246–Alerte de pompiers (Londres)* (Month uncertain) [N–F]
This depicts the Metropolitan Fire Brigade Southwark Bridge, London.
Refs: Empire Theatre programme, 5 October 1896 (*Barnes Museum*)
Optician, vol 14 (23 September 1897) p 124 WTC catalogue 1898, p 43.

2 *1247–Arrival of Cyclists and Cavaliers* / *247–Cyclistes et cavaliers arrivant au cottage (Londres)* (Month uncertain) [N]
'Another interesting scene in Hampstead, London. A number of people before a cottage, evidently awaiting the arrival of several persons seen approaching from the distance, who, as they come closer, dismount from their cycles and horses, and are heartily greeted by the first group mentioned. A pretty picture.'
Refs: WTC, p 32.

3 *1248–Procession at the Wedding of Princess Maud* / *248–Cortège au mariage du la princesse Maud (Londres)* (22 July) [N]
Refs: Empire Theatre programme, 5 October 1896 (*Barnes Museum*).

4 *1249–London Street Dancers* / *249–Danseuses des rues (Londres)* (Month uncertain) [N–F]
'Two little urchins are dancing to the airs of a grind organ, under the masterly manipulation of a dusky Italian, surrounded by an admiring crowd.'
Ref: WTC, p 30.

5 *1250–Entrance to the Cinematograph Exhibition / 250–Entrée du Cinématographe (Londres)* (July) [N]
Showing cabs arriving and departing, with Dundas Slater, the acting-manager of the [Empire] theatre, and other members of the staff.
Probably taken by Felicien Trewey with the Empire's Cinématographe.
Ref: *The Era*, 1 August 1896, p 16.

6 *1251–Rotten Row, Hyde Park Corner (London) / 251–Hyde Park (Londres)* (Month uncertain) [N–F]
'Showing the parade of fashionable London on this famous Drive on a bright morning.'
Ref: WTC, p 15.

7 *1252–The Wandering Negro Minstrels / 252–Negres dansant dans la rue (Londres)* (Month uncertain) [N–F]
'Shows five lively negroes dancing and playing Banjos, Tamborines, and "Bones", to the delight of a typical London curb-stone audience.'
Ref: WTC, p 31.

8 *1253–The Tower Bridge / 253–Pont de la Tour (Londres)*. (Month uncertain) [N–F]
Ref: *Optician*, p 124.

9 *1254–Westminster Bridge (London) / 254–Pont de Westminster (Londres)*. (Month uncertain) [N–F]
'Showing Houses of Parliament.'
RefL WTC, p 14.

10 *1255–Piccadilly Cirus / 255–Piccadilly Circus (Londres)*. (Month uncertain) [N–F]
Ref: Empire Theatre programme, 21 December 1896 (*Barnes Museum*).

11 *1256–Regent Street, London / 256–Regent Street (Londres)*. (Month uncertain) [N–F]
'One of the busiest sections of the world's largest city.'
Ref: WTC, p 13.

12 *1257–Change of Guards at St James's Palace / 258–Gardes montante au palais de Buckingham* (sic) (*Vues militaires*). (Month uncertain) [N–F]
'One of the most popular of English Military subjects. The Band of the Horse Guards is seen approaching, followed by Scotch Pipers and Guards as they march close to the camera. Crowds of spectators line one side of the walls. Palace in background. Sharp and clear.'
Refs: *The Era*, 1 August 1896, p 16 WTC, p 20.

13 *1258–Horse Guards / 258–Gardes a cheval (Vues militaires)*. (Month uncertain) [N–F]
Ref: *Optician*, p 124.

14 *A String of Winners belonging to the Popular Owner of the Two Thousand Guineas*. (Month uncertain) [N–F]
Ref: Empire Theatre programme, 5 October 1896 (*Barnes Museum*)
Not in Lumière catalogue.

15 *Trafalgar Square on Lord Mayor's Day*. (9 November) [N]
Police arresting Scottish piper and dancer for obstruction.
Ref: Empire Theatre programme, 21 December 1896 (*Barnes Museum*)
Not in Lumière catalogue.

Regarding the exhibition of Lumière films, I stated on page 92 that in no instance was the Lumière machine ever exhibited except at the Empire Theatre in Leicester Square. This statement I now find to be incorrect. Mr D. J. Scott has kindly sent me information proving that the Cinématographe-Lumière was exhibited in Cardiff. An advertisement published in the *South Wales Echo*, dated Monday, 11 May, 1896, states that 'The Lumière Machine — The Original, not a Copy under Mons. Trewey' would be at the Empire Theatre, Cardiff for that week. This apparatus was also exhibited at the same theatre for the weeks commencing 6 July, 17 August, 5 October, and 14 December, 1896. It is probable that the Cinématographe-Lumière was exhibited in other towns in the United Kingdom during 1896 under Trewey's direction, but during the whole of this period, the apparatus was never for sale on the open market.

Mention must be made of a French 35mm projector called the Lapiposcope, which may have been available for sale in England as the example in the Barnes Collection bears the mark: 'Patent applied for. Made in France,' suggesting an English market for the apparatus. It was patented in England, as well as in France (British patent no 26,765. 25 November 1896. French patent no 259549) and was the invention of A. Lapipe, who gave his name to the instrument. The

102 Paul's Theatrograph Projector, 1896. Specially adapted for touring (*British Film Institute*)

roll of film is suspended above the machine on a hanger and driven by a single sprocket wheel moved intermittently by a ratchet and pawl device somewhat similar to Watson's Motorgraph, which it also resembles in outward appearances. There is no take-up provided, and the film is allowed to issue freely from the lower front panel of the machine, to be caught in some convenient receptacle provided by the operator. The shutter is situated in front of the picture aperture and is of the segmental cylinder type, with two opaque celluloid blades. The mechanism is contained in a mahogany case (16 × 16 × 14.5cm) with front and rear sliding panels. Racking adjustment is provided by a milled-headed screw at the top of the case. (See also Trutat, *La Photographie Animée* (Paris, 1899) pp 87–90, figs 72 & 73).

On pages 142–3, I refer to 'Living Pictures' being exhibited at the Palace Theatre, Cambridge Circus. For some time I have had my doubts about the true nature of these 'living pictures', realising that they may well refer to posed tableaux of live models (Tableaux Vivants) and not to a cinematograph performance as at first thought. My doubts have since been confirmed by Mr. Barry Anthony, an expert on the history of the music hall, who informs me that the reference is indeed to living tableaux. The following amendment therefore should be made to my text:

p 142, line 30: After the word, previously, delete the remainder of the paragraph which ends on page 143, line 3. Delete also note 44 on page 231.

In my chapter on R. W. Paul, I made only passing reference (p 50) to a projector specially adapted for travelling showmen. Since then, more specific details of this machine have come to hand. It consisted of the ordinary Theatrograph No 2 mechanism, but arranged so that it could be bolted to the top of a sturdy travelling case instead of to the iron pillar-stand normally used. The mechanism was belt driven by a 'mangle-wheel' crank fitted to the side of the case. There was no take-up spool, the film being allowed to spill into a bag suspended from the front (102). The apparatus is described and illustrated in an article on Paul written by Will Day entitled 'An Early Chapter on Kinematograph History' which was published in the *Kinematograph Year Book*, 1915, pp 43–48. I have to thank David Henry for kindly drawing my attention to this article which previously was unknown to me.

The same article also refers (p 47) to Paul's first coloured film, which we learn was hand-painted by Doubell, a painter of magic lantern slides for the Royal Polytechnic Institution, Regent Street. Although the film was only about 40ft long, it took the artist over one month to execute. The film was also referred to in the *Evening News* of 10 April, 1896 (p 1f), so this reference too should be added to my note 44 on page 228.

For the sake of completeness, attention must be drawn to a description and illustration of Paul's first Theatrograph projector in the *Photography Annual For 1896*, p 528, although no fresh facts are to be gathered from this source. Of more importance is a first hand account of Paul's public début at the City and Guild Technical College on the 20th February, published in *Lightning*, vol 9, no 228 (27 February 1896), and brought to my notice by Mr R. Brown. Had space permitted I would have wished to have quoted this account in full, as the writer had, on the same day, also witnessed the first performance of the Lumière Cinématographe at the Polytechnic, Regent Street. As neither machine worked well on the day, a satisfactory comparison was impossible and he found there was nothing to choose between the two machines.

Lastly, a few words need to be said about the Will Day catalogue of historic cinematograph equipment. This exists in two editions. The first published from Day's private address in Highgate, which is not dated; and the second, the auctioneer's edition published in 1930. It is the first which has been used in the volume under discussion. Unfortunately, the item numbers in each edition do not tally and many of the entries also differ. Both are lamentably inaccurate. However, I should have taken note of item 323 (or 306) when compiling my list of films by Esmé Collings, for this item records an original positive print reputably to have been taken by Collings in 1896 of some bathers on the beach at Brighton. It is necessary therefore to add the following to the list on page 219:

Bathers on the Beach at Brighton (Month uncertain) [N–F]
Ref Will Day catalogue, item 323.
Copy in Cinématheque Française, Paris.

Notes

1 Robert W. Paul and Birt Acres

1 *British Journal of Photography*, vol 44, no 1930 (30 April 1897) p 273.
2 Ibid, loc cit.
3 Ibid, loc cit.
4 Ibid, loc cit. See also *The Era*, 24 April 1897, p 8, where Paul's prospectus is printed in full.
5 *British Journal of Photography*, vol 14, no 1930 (30 April 1897) p 277.
6 *The Optician*, vol 13 (29 April 1897) p 110.
7 *Proceedings* of the British Kinematograph Society, no 38 (3 February 1937) p 4.
8 Paul's catalogue in the Barnes Museum of Cinematography. The film's original length was 80ft but by 1903 it had evidently been edited and reduced to 60ft.
9 *Amateur Photographer*, vol 25, no 658 (14 May 1897) p 394.
10 National Film Archive F.529.
11 *The Era*, 16 January 1897, p 18.
12 Ibid, 23 January 1897, p 18.
13 Ibid, 10 April 1897, p 18.
14 Ibid, 14 August 1897, p 16.
15 Ibid, 17 April 1897, p 16.
16 Ibid, 10 July 1897, p 16.
17 Ibid, 6 February 1897, p 30.
18 Ibid, 10 April 1897, p 18.
19 Ibid, 16 January 1897, p 18.
20 *Optical Magic Lantern Journal*, vol 8, no 99 (August 1897) p 126.
21 *The Wrench Illustrated Catalogue 1908–9*, p 301, fig 561. Copy in the Barnes Museum of Cinematography.
22 See for example: *The Optician*, 1897, vol 13, p 140; Ibid, vol 14, pp 150, 240 and 313. Also *The Era*, 19 June 1897, p 16.
23 *Amateur Photographer*, vol 25, no 662 (11 June 1897) p 474; Ibid, no 663 (18 June 1897) p 491; Ibid, no 664 (25 June 1897) p 514; Ibid, vol 26, no 665 (2 July 1897) pp 4–5.
24 *Proc* BKS, no 38 (3 February 1936) p 5.
25 Paul's previous projector, the Theatrograph, was being advertised in July 1897 @ £25, complete (see *The Era*, 3 and 10 July 1897, pp 7 and 25 respectively).
26 *Magic Lantern Journal Annual 1897–8* (October 1897) p xciv advertisement.
27 *Amateur Photographer*, vol 26, no 682 (29 October 1897) p 369.
28 Ibid, loc cit.
29 See for example Paul's advertisement in the *Magic Lantern Journal Annual 1897–8* (October 1897) p xciv.
30 *Amateur Photographer*, vol 26, no 674 (3 September 1897) p 183.
31 Ibid, loc cit.
32 *The Era*, 24 April 1897, p 8.
33 *Amateur Photographer*, vol 25, no 643 (29 January 1897) p 83: 'We notice from the provincial papers that Mr. Birt Acres is showing his kineopticon before many of the societies in the country.'
34 Ibid, no 642 (22 January 1897) p 76.
35 Ibid, no 640 (8 January 1897) p 38; ibid, no 642 (22 January 1897) p 76.
36 Ibid, no 643 (29 January 1897) p 83.
37 Ibid, loc cit.
38 Ibid, no 643 (29 January 1897) p 83.
39 *Journal of the Camera Club*, vol 11 (May 1897) pp 65–7.
40 Ibid, p 66.
41 Ibid, loc cit.
42 Ibid, loc cit.
43 *British Journal of Photography*, vol 44, no 1930 (30 April 1897) p 286.
44 *Amateur Photographer*, vol 25, no 649 (12 March 1897) p 202.
45 Ibid, no 654 (16 April 1897) p 310.
46 Ibid, loc cit.
47 *British Journal of Photography*, vol 44, no 1927 (9 April 1897) p 227.
48 *Photogram*, vol 4, no 42 (June 1897) p 178.
49 *Optical Magic Lantern Journal*, vol 8, no 96 (June 1897) p 81.
50 Ibid, loc cit.
51 *Photogram*, vol 4, no 42 (June 1897) p 178.
52 *British Journal Photographic Almanac for 1898*, (1 December 1897) p 659.

53 *Optical Magic Lantern Journal*, vol 8, no 96 (June 1897) p 81.
54 *Amateur Photographer*, vol 25, no 659 (21 May 1897) p 426.
55 See Barnes, *The Beginnings of the Cinema in England* [vol 1] (Newton Abbot, 1976) pp 158–60. A two-lens system of cinematography for alternate exposure or projection, was also the subject of a patent issued to Charles Rubie Neve, a photographer of 2 Wordsworth Road, Wealdstone (No 19,805. 28 August, 1897). Two rolls of film running side by side were alternately moved by means of tappet-levers; one shutter serving both lenses.
56 Henry V. Hopwood, *Living Pictures* (London, 1899) p 159.
57 *Amateur Photographer*, vol 26, no 677 (24 September 1897) p 242.
58 Ibid, no 678 (1 October 1897) p 277.
59 Ibid, loc cit.
60 Ibid, loc cit.
61 For a discussion of the Birt Acres experimental camera and Birtac see the previous volume of this history pages 59–62.
62 *Photogram*, vol 4, no 42 (June 1897) p 178.
63 *Amateur Photographer*, vol 25, no 662 (11 June 1897) p 474.
64 *British Journal Photographic Almanac for 1898* (1 December 1897) p 344.
65 Ibid, p 1091.
66 Ibid, p 17.
67 Ibid, p 540.
68 Ibid, p 1362.
69 *Photogram*, vol 4, no 48 (December 1897) p 382.
70 *Amateur Photographer*, vol 26, no 677 (24 September 1897) p 242. See also *The Optician*, vol 14, (23 September 1897) p 74.
71 *Photogram*, vol 4, no 48 (December 1897) p 382.
72 *The Era*, 2 January 1897, p 34; 9 January, p 29; 16 January, p 29; 13 February, p 30; 20 February, p 35; 27 February, p 30.

2 Manufacturers and Dealers in London 1896–7

1 *Optical Magic Lantern Journal*, vol 8, no 100 (September 1897) p 142; Ibid, vol 8, no 101 (October 1897) p 173.
2 Ibid, vol 8, no 86 (July 1897) p 113.
3 *The Optician*, vol 13 (25 March 1897) p 43. See also same issue, p 50.
4 *Magic Lantern Journal Annual 1897–8* (October 1897) p 125.
5 *Optical Magic Lantern Journal*, vol 8, no 103 (December 1897) p 213.
6 *The Era*, 11 December 1897, p 32.
7 *Optical Magic Lantern Journal*, vol 8, no 103 (December 1897) p 199.
8 *The Era*, 11 December 1897, p 32 advertisement.
9 British Patent no 17,881, 12 August 1896.
10 *Optical Magic Lantern Journal*, vol 8, no 93 (February 1897) p 23. See also *The Journal of the Camera Club*, vol 11 (March 1897) pp 36–41.
11 *Amateur Photographer*, vol 25, no 641 (15 January 1897) p 55.
12 The jet was made by C. W. Locke, 244 Tottenham Court Road, London.
13 *British Journal of Photography*, vol 44, Suppl. (2 April 1897) pp 28–31.
14 *Optical Magic Lantern Journal*, vol 8, no 93 (February 1897) p 23.
15 *Amateur Photographer*, vol 25, no 641 (15 January 1897) p 55.
16 *Ibid*, vol 25, no 648 (5 March 1897) p 186.
17 *The Optician*, vol 13 (3 June 1897) p 196.
18 *Optical Magic Lantern Journal*, vol 8, no 99 (August 1897) p 126. See also *The Optician*, vol 13 (8 July 1897) p 278.
19 *Amateur Photographer*, vol 26, no 668 (23 July 1897) p 63.
20 *Magic Lantern Journal Annual 1897–8* (October 1897) p xxv advertisement.
21 *Amateur Photographer*, vol 26, no 677 (24 September 1897) p 266.
22 From information printed on the patent specification (no 17,248).
23 *Amateur Photographer*, vol 26, no 677 (24 September 1897) p 265.
24 *Optical Magic Lantern Journal*, vol 8, no 103 (December 1897) p 213.
25 *Ibid, loc cit.*
26 *Amateur Photographer*, vol 26, no 677 (24 September 1897) p 265.
27 Example in the Barnes Museum of Cinematography. The only other known example of this cinematograph was auctioned at Sotheby's on 24 May 1973. An illustration of the Wrench Cinematograph appears in the next volume of this history.
28 *The Optician*, vol 13 (3 June 1897) p 196.

29 See the previous volume of this history, pp 141–3.
30 *The Era*, 2 January 1897, p 33 advertisement; and *British Journal Photographic Almanac 1898* (1 December 1897) p 1121 advertisement.
31 *British Journal of Photography*, vol 44, Suppl. (1 January 1897) p 6.
32 *Amateur Photographer*, vol 25, no 660 (28 May 1897) p 444.
33 *Ibid, loc cit.*
34 *British Journal of Photography*, vol 44, Suppl. (1 January 1897) p 6.
35 *Amateur Photographer*, vol 26, no 677 (24 September 1897) p 265. Xylonite — a light vulcanite material similar to celluloid.
36 *Magic Lantern Journal Annual 1897–8* (October 1897) p 120.
37 *Amateur Photographer*, vol 25, no 660 (28 May 1897) p 444. See also *The Optician*, vol 13 (3 June 1897) p 194.
38 *Magic Lantern Journal Annual 1897–8* (October 1897) Advertisement on end paper.
39 *The Optician*, vol 13 (3 June 1897) p 194.
40 *British Journal of Photography*, vol 44, no 1955 (22 October 1897) p 683.
41 *Optical Magic Lantern Journal*, vol 8, no 87 (August 1897) p 126.
42 See previous volume of this history, pp 146–7.
43 *Magic Lantern Journal Annual 1897–8* (October 1897) pp 123–4. See also *The Photographic News*, vol 41, no 53, N.S. (1 January 1897) p 9.
44 *Amateur Photographer* vol 26, no 677 (24 September 1897) p 267.
45 *The Optician*, vol 12 (19 November 1896) p 128.
46 *Magic Lantern Journal Annual 1897–8* (October 1897) p 124.
47 *Photogram*, vol 4, no 43 (July 1897) p 219.
48 *Amateur Photographer*, vol 25, no 661 (4 June 1897) p 464.
49 Ibid, vol 26, no 677 (24 September 1897) p 267.
50 *British Journal of Photography*, vol 44, no 1961 (3 December 1897) p 770.
51 *Ibid, loc cit.*
52 *The Era*, 12 September 1896, p 28.
53 Ibid, 3 July 1897, p 7.
54 Ibid, 4 September 1897, p 29.
55 Ibid, 17 July 1897, p 26.
56 Ibid, 13 November 1897, p 19.
57 Ibid, 14 August 1897, p 25.
58 Ibid, 3 July 1897, p 7.
59 Ibid, 14 August 1897, p 25.
60 Ibid, 23 October 1897, p 30.
61 Ibid, 3 July 1897, p 7.
62 *British Journal of Photography*, vol 44, no 1939 (2 July 1897) p 428.
63 Ibid, vol 44, no 1942 (23 July 1897) p 478.
64 *The Era*, 1 May 1897, p 29.
65 *British Journal Photographic Almanac for 1897* (November 1896) p 278.
66 *Magic Lantern Journal Annual 1897–8* (October 1897) p xxxiii advertisement.
67 *British Journal Photographic Almanac for 1898* (1 December 1897) p 292.
68 *The Era*, 10 July 1897, p 25 advertisement. See also *Magic Lantern Journal Annual 1897–8* (October 1897) p ci advertisement. One of the English films advertised by Wolff was *Garden Party at Buckingham Palace*, see *The Optician*, vol 14 (23 September 1897) p 41.
69 *Photogram*, vol 4, no 42 (June 1897) p 179.
70 *Optical Magic Lantern Journal*, vol 8, no 102 (November 1897) p 177. *The Death of Nelson* was advertised by Wolff in *The Era*, 23 October 1897, p 30.
71 *Optical Magic Lantern Journal*, vol 8, no 102 (November 1897) p 177.
72 Ibid, vol 8, no 103 (December 1897) p 212. *The Indian Mutiny* was advertised by Wolff in *The Era*, 4 December 1897, p 32.
73 *Optical Magic Lantern Journal*, vol 8, no 103 (December 1897) p 212.
74 *The Era*, 2 January 1897, p 33 advertisement. See also the issue for 16 January, p 28 advertisement.
75 *Photogram*, vol 4, no 42 (June 1897) p 179.
76 *Magic Lantern Journal Annual 1897–8* (October 1897) p 144.
77 *Photographic News*, vol 41, no 75, N.S. (4 June 1897) p 366. A description of the Vitaphotoscope also appears in *The Optician*, vol 14 (23 September 1897) p 100.
78 *Photograms of '97*, p xxi advertisement.
79 *Photogram*, vol 4, no 42 (June 1897) p 179.
80 *Amateur Photographer*, vol 26, no 677 (24 September 1897) pp 266–7.
81 Ibid, loc cit.
82 Henry V. Hopwood, *Living Pictures* (London, 1899) p 185.
83 See the previous volume of this history, pp 74, 162–4.

84 *The Era*, 9 January 1897, p 29 advertisement.
85 Ibid, loc cit.
86 Ibid, loc cit.
87 *Amateur Photographer*, vol 26, no 677 (24 September 1897) pp 267–8.
88 Complete Specification left 4 May 1897; accepted 7 August 1897. The patent is in the name of Thomas Henry Blair, manufacturer, Naylor House, Chiswick, Surrey.
89 Hopwood, *Living Pictures*, p 244.
90 Complete Specification left 20 March 1896; accepted 27 June 1896. The patent is in the names of The European Blair Camera Co. Ltd., and Thomas Henry Blair.
91 Complete Specification left 15 March 1897; accepted 17 April 1897. This specification was communicated from abroad and is in the name of Thomas Henry Blair, The Chestnuts, Northborough, Massachusetts, USA.
92 *British Journal Photographic Almanac for 1898* (1 December 1897) p 344.
93 *British Journal of Photography*, vol 43, no 1905 (6 November 1896) pp 715–16.
94 British Patent No 17,049, 1 August 1896.
95 *British Journal of Photography*, vol 44, no 1916 (22 January 1897) p 61.
96 Ibid, vol 44, no 1918 (5 February 1897) p 94.
97 *Photogram*, vol 4, no 42 (June 1897) p 178.
98 *The Optician*, vol 13 (10 June 1897) p 216. See also *Photogram*, vol 4, no 43 (July 1897) p 214.
99 *Photogram*, vol 4, no 43 (July 1897) p 214.
100 *Magic Lantern Journal Annual 1897–8* (October 1897) illustration facing p xlix.
101 *Photogram*, vol 4, no 42 (June 1897) p 178.
102 *The Era*, 21 November 1896, p 30 advertisement.
103 Ibid, 27 March 1897, p 29 advertisement.
104 Ibid, 4 December 1897, p 32 advertisement.
105 Ibid, loc cit.
106 Ibid, 24 July 1897, p 26 advertisement.
107 Ibid, 4 December 1897, p 32 advertisement.
108 See the first volume of this history, p 157.
109 *The Era*, 23 January 1897, p 28 advertisement. In quoting this advertisement, the layout and frequent use of capital letters in the original has been ignored.
110 *The Era*, 23 January 1897, p 28 advertisement.
111 See the first volume of this history, p 157.
112 Cecil M. Hepworth, *Came the Dawn* (London, 1951) p 30.
113 *Proc*. BKS (3 February 1936) pp 7–8.
114 *The Era*, 20 March 1897, p 29 advertisement.
115 Ibid, 2 January 1897, p 33 advertisement.
116 Ibid, 29 May 1897, p 29 advertisement.
117 Ibid, 2 January 1897, p 33 advertisement.
118 Ibid, loc cit.
119 Ibid, 29 May 1897, p 29 advertisement.
120 Ibid, loc cit.
121 Ibid, 10 July 1897, p 16.
122 Ibid, 7 August 1897, p 23 advertisement.
123 Ibid, 29 May 1897, p 29 advertisement.

3 London Manufacturers and Dealers 1897

1 *Photographic News*, vol 41, no 53, N.S. (1 January 1897) Suppl. p 4. See also *The Era*, 16 January 1897, pp 19 and 28; *Optical Magic Lantern Journal*, vol 8, no 93 (February 1897) p 22; and *Photogram*, vol 4, no 38 (February 1897) p 63.
2 *British Journal of Photography*, vol 44, no 1924 (19 March 1897) p 186. See also *British Journal Photographic Almanac for 1898* (1 December 1897) p 926.
3 *Magic Lantern Journal Annual 1897–8* (October 1897) p 124.
4 *Amateur Photographer*, vol 26, no 677 (24 September 1897) p 266.
5 *Optical Magic Lantern Journal*, vol 8, no 94 (March 1897) p 58.
6 Ibid, loc cit.
7 Ibid, loc cit.
8 *Photograms of '97*, p xxi advertisement. See also *The Era*, 26 June 1897, p 26 advertisement; and *British Journal Phorographic Almanac for 1898* (1 December 1897) p 369.
9 *Optical Magic Lantern Journal*, vol 8, no 94 (March 1897) p 58.
10 *The Era*, 26 June 1897, p 26 advertisement.
11 Ibid, 9 October 1897, p 29 advertisement.

12 Ibid, 23 October 1897, p 30 advertisement.

13 *Magic Lantern Journal Annual 1897–8* (October 1897) p Lvi advertisement.

14 Ibid, loc cit.

15 Ibid, loc cit.

16 Ibid, loc cit.

17 One of Hughes' most interesting patents was for a mechanically operated lantern slide called the Choreutoscope. By means of an intermittent movement, the illusion of motion was imparted to a series of figures representing for example, a dancing skeleton (British Patent No 13,372. 9 October 1884).

18 *Optical Magic Lantern Journal*, vol 8, no 93 (February 1897) p 24.

19 *Magic Lantern Journal Annual 1897–8* (October 1897) p Lvi advertisement. See also *The Era*, 3 July 1897, p 7 advertisement.

20 See obituary in *The Kinematograph & Lantern Weekly* (13 August 1908) p 301.

21 Both studios are advertised on the backs of *cartes-de-visite* in the Barnes Collection. Other *cartes* in the collection, have the name W. H. Prestwich and addresses at 98 Cheapside, and 87 Broad St, Reading.

22 See the first volume of this history, pp 158–60.

23 See D. J. Buchanan, *The J.A.P. Story 1895–1951* (London, 1951).

24 *Photograms of '97*, p lxxi advertisement.

25 *British Journal of Photography*, vol 44, Suppl. (16 April 1897) p 252.

26 *Photogram*, vol 4, no 42 (June 1897) p 186.

27 *British Journal of Photography*, vol 44, Suppl. (16 April 1897) p 252.

28 *Magic Lantern Journal Annual 1897–8* (October 1897) p lvi advertisement.

29 *The Era*, 1 May 1897, p 29 advertisement. A previous advertisement published in the same paper on 24 April 1897, p 29, states: 'Now in construction, the Moto-Photoscope Camera, for taking Living Pictures, will be the best and simplest made, so that amateurs can take their own subjects.'

30 *British Journal of Photography*, vol 44, no 1933 (21 May 1897) p 335. See also *Amateur Photographer*, vol 25, no 659 (21 May 1897) p 424.

31 *Photogram*, vol 4, no 42 (June 1897) p 178.

32 *British Journal Photographic Almanac for 1898* (1 December 1897) p 17 advertisement.

33 Ibid, loc cit.

34 Ibid, loc cit.

35 *Photograms of '97*, p 34.

36 *Photogram*, vol 4, no 44 (August 1897) p 248.

37 *Photograms of '97*, pp 36–7. See also frame illustrations published in *The Practical Photographer*, vol 8, no 93 (September 1897) pp 280–81, and Alfred T. Story, *The Story of Photography* (London, 1898) p 139, fig 38.

38 *Amateur Photographer*, vol 26, no 668 (23 July 1897) p 72.

39 Ibid, vol 26, no 677 (24 September 1897) p 267.

40 *Photograms of '97*, p lxxi advertisement.

41 *Illustrated Catalogue of the International Photographic Exhibition, Glasgow, September 1897*. A copy of this catalogue is in the Glasgow University Library (Ref. 3/256).

42 *Amateur Photographer*, vol 26, no 680 (15 October 1897) p 316.

43 *British Journal of Photography*, vol 44, no 1952 (1 October 1897) p 636.

44 Data on Models 1, 2 and 3, obtained from illustrated advertisement in *Photograms of '97*, p lxxi.

45 *British Journal Photographic Almanac for 1898* (1 December 1897) p 937.

46 Buchanan, *The J.A.P. Story* (London, 1951).

47 *Amateur Photographer*, vol 25, no 645 (12 February 1897) p 137.

48 *Optical Magic Lantern Journal*, vol 8, no 92 (January 1897) pp 3–4.

49 Ibid, loc cit.

50 *The Optician*, vol 12 (11 February 1897) p 274.

51 *The Era*, 24 April 1897, p 29 advertisement. See also *Amateur Photographer*, vol 25, no 654 (16 April 1897) p xiv advertisement facing page 323.

52 *Amateur Photographer*, vol 25, no 663 (18 June 1897) p 506.

53 *Magic Lantern Journal Annual 1897–8* (October 1897) p xlvii advertisement. See also *The Era*, 24 April 1897, p 29 advertisement.

54 *Magic Lantern Journal Annual 1897–8* (October 1897) p xlvii advertisement.

55 *Amateur Photographer*, vol 25, no 654 (16 April 1897) p xiv advertisement. See also *The Era*, 6 and 20 March 1897, pp 17 and 29 respectively; and 1 and 8 May, pp 29 and 28 respectively.

56 *The Era*, 20 June 1896, p 25 advertisement.

57 Science Museum Inv. no 9482–79.

58 *The Era*, 20 February 1897, p 38 advertisement.

59 Ibid, 6 March 1897, p 29 advertisement.

60 Ibid, 24 April 1897, p 29 advertisement.

61 Ibid, loc cit.

62 Ibid, 3 April 1897, p 30 advertisement.

63 Ibid, loc cit.

64 Ibid, 14 August 1897, p 25 advertisement.
65 Ibid, 4 December 1897, p 32 advertisement.
66 *Magic Lantern Journal Annual 1897–8* (October 1897) p 254 advertisement. For the Wigan award, see also *The Era*, 11 December 1897, p 32 advertisement.
67 *The Era*, 3 April 1897, p 30 advertisement.
68 Ibid, 1 May 1897, p 29 advertisement.
69 Ibid, 5 June 1897, p 29 advertisement.
70 Ibid, 3 July 1897, p 7 advertisement.
71 Ibid, 17 July 1897, p 17.
72 Ibid, loc cit.
73 *Magic Lantern Journal Annual 1897–8* (October 1897) p 254 advertisement.
74 *The Era*, 17 July 1897, p 26 advertisement.
75 Ibid, 6 March 1897, p 28 advertisement.
76 Ibid, loc cit.
77 *Photogram*, vol 4, no 41 (July 1897) p 214.
78 *Amateur Photographer*, vol 25, no 660 (28 May 1897) p 444.
79 *Photogram*, vol 4, no 41 (July 1897) p 214.
80 *Amateur Photographer*, vol 25, no 651 (26 March 1897) p 247; Ibid, vol 25, no 660 (28 May 1897) p 444; Ibid, vol 26, no 677 (24 September 1897) p 267.
81 *The Era*, 6 March 1897, p 28 advertisement.
82 *Photogram*, vol 4, no 41 (July 1897) p 214.
83 *Amateur Photographer*, vol 26, no 668 (23 July 1897) p 62.
84 *British Journal of Photography*, vol 44, no 1939 (2 July 1897) p 427.
85 *Amateur Photographer*, vol 26, no 668 (23 July 1897) p 62.
86 Ibid, loc cit.
87 Obituary in *The Optical Magic Lantern Journal*, vol 11, no 137 (October 1900) p 119.
88 *Magic Lantern Journal Annual 1897–8* (October 1897) p xviii advertisement. See also Cecil M. Hepworth, *Animated Photography* (London, 1897) p xx advertisement.
89 *Amateur Photographer*, vol 26, no 677 (24 September 1897) p 267.
90 *British Journal of Photography*, vol 44, no 1932 (14 May 1897) p 306. See also *The Optician*, vol 13 (13 May 1897) p 142.
91 *British Journal of Photography*, vol 44, no 1955 (22 October 1897) pp 682–3.
92 *Photograms of '97*, p lxxvi advertisement.
93 *Optical Magic Lantern Journal*, vol 8, no 98 (July 1897) p 111. See also obituary notices in *To-day's Cinema*, 5, 8, 11 February 1932; *Southend Standard*, 11.2.32; *British Journal of Photography*, 12.2.32; *Amateur Photographer*, 17.2.32.
94 *Magic Lantern Journal Annual 1897–8* (October 1897) p xcvi advertisement.
95 R. Child Bayley, *Modern Magic Lanterns*, 2nd edn. (London, N.D.) advertisement.
96 Will Day, *Illustrated Catalogue of the Will Day Historical Collection of Cinematograph and Moving Picture Equipment* (London: undated), p 22, item 145 (Pl 20a), copy in the Barnes Museum. Another edition of this catalogue was published in 1930, a copy of which is in the Science Museum, London.
97 *Magic Lantern Journal Annual 1897–8* (October 1897) p xxxii advertisement.
98 Ibid, p 129.
99 *Magic Lantern Journal Annual 1898–9* (October 1898) p 168.
100 Ibid, loc cit.
101 *The Era*, 13 February 1897, p 26 advertisement.
102 Ibid, 3 July 1897, p 7 advertisement.
103 Ibid, loc cit.
104 Ibid, loc cit.
105 Ibid, loc cit.
106 Ibid, 14 August 1897, p 25 advertisement.
107 *Magic Lantern Journal Annual 1897–8* (October 1897) p xxiv advertisement.
108 *Photographic News*, vol 41, no 75, N.S. (4 June 1897) p 355.
109 Ibid, loc cit.
110 Ibid, loc cit.
111 This apparatus was discovered in a cellar in Soho Square, London, in 1939 by John and William Barnes, and led directly to the formation of the Barnes Collection, subsequently to become the Barnes Museum of Cinematography.
112 British patent no 15,195. 11 July, 1898.
113 Hopwood, *Living Pictures*, pp 173 and 253.
114 Ibid, p 155.
115 Accepted 3 April, 1897.
116 Accepted 2 October 1897.
117 Patent no 12,128, 3 June 1896; see the previous volume of this history, p 157.

118 Complete specification left 24 January 1898 — Accepted 5 March 1898.
119 Complete specification left 20 August 1898 — Accepted 20 October 1898.
120 Hopwood, *Living Pictures*, p 251.
121 Complete specification left 23 May 1898 — Accepted 9 July 1898.
122 Moy was an electrical engineer of 3 Greenland Place, Camden Town. He subsequently formed his own company as Ernest F. Moy Ltd.
123 *Amateur Photographer*, vol 23, no 590 (24 January 1896) p 75.
124 Robert Bartlett Haas, *Muybridge – Man in Motion* (Los Angeles, 1976) p 110.
125 *Photogram*, vol 4, no 42 (June 1897) p 178.
126 *Magic Lantern Journal Annual 1897-8* (October 1897) p 134. See also *The British Journal Photographic Almanac for 1898* (Published 1 December 1897) p 75.
127 *British Journal of Photography*, vol 44, no 1917 (29 January 1897) p 75.
128 Ibid, vol 44, no 1923 (12 March 1897) p 171.
129 *Photograms of the Year 1897*, p lxxxv advertisement.
130 *British Journal Photographic Almanac for 1898* (1 December 1897) p 38 advertisement.
131 Ibid, p 225 advertisement.
132 Ibid, p 1352 advertisement.
133 Ibid, p 17 advertisement.
134 See example in the Barnes Museum of Cinematography.

4 Brighton

1 The Brighton and Bath studios are listed on the reverse of the cabinet photograph reproduced as illustration 39; the London studios appear on the obverse.
2 Alfred Darling's work-book consists of an ordinary quarto hard-backed exercise book with faintly ruled pages, with about half the leaves missing from the front of the book. The existing entries cover the period from 31 August 1896 to 5 March 1897. The work-book is at present in the possession of Messrs Alfred Darling & Sons, Adas Works, South Road, Preston Park, Brighton.
3 The information on St Ann's Well and Gardens is taken from an advertisement published in *The Hove Echo*, 4 September, 1897, p 1, column 4.
4 After falling in disrepair, the Old Pump House was finally demolished in 1935. The site is now marked by a pseudo well-head erected by the local council.
5 *Hove Echo*, 8 May 1897, pp 3-4.
6 The film showed a 'corner' incident of a football match staged in St Ann's Well Gardens. Smith enlisted as players a few of the gardeners, including a young man named Tubby Edlin, who later made a name for himself as a comedian (Interview with G. A. Smith published in the *Brighton & Hove Herald*, 7 May, 1955.
7 *Optical Magic Lantern Journal*, vol 8, no 98 (July 1897) p 110.
8 Ibid, vol 8, no 100 (September 1897) p 142.
9 *Hove Echo*, 28 August 1897, p 7.
10 A copy of this catalogue is preserved in the National Film Archive.
11 Roger Manvell, *Ellen Terry* (London, 1968) pp 226-7.
12 *Hove Echo*, 3 July 1897, p 7.
13 200 copies of this list were printed (cf. Smith's cash book, entry for 4 December 1897).
14 *British Journal of Photography*, vol 44, Supplement (5 November 1897) p 88.
15 *Optical Magic Lantern Journal*, vol 8, no 96 (May 1897) p 91.
16 Maguire & Baucus Ltd advertised 'The Bioscope Reverser' @ £2.10s. [£2.50]. This could be fitted to any machine, which could then be operated in the regular way (Advertisement in Cecil M. Hepworth, *Animated Photography* (London, 1897) p iv.
17 This was probably the Lumière film: 277 *Bains de Diane (Swimming Baths, Milan)*.
18 *The Era*, 11 December, 1897, p 20.
19 *Optical Magic Lantern Journal*, vol 8, no 103 (December 1897) p 216.
20 Smith's cash book measures approximately 4½ × 7 inches, with the pages ruled for cash. It has typical marbled end-papers, the first of which carries the trade label of Carter Bros., manufacturing stationers of 173 Western Road, Brighton. Smith's entries date from 1 January, 1897 and terminate on 8 October, 1907. Expenses are recorded on the right-hand pages and the receipts on the left. Four pages of the book are devoted to 'colour work' carried out during the period 1907–1912.
21 See Smith's cash book, which is headed: 'Film Factory'.
22 There is the possibility that the 'whiskers and spirit gum' were purchased for the photograph shown in our illustration 41(c), where a man, obviously wearing false whiskers, is seen posing outside the Old Cave at St Ann's Well Gardens.
23 National Film Archive No F.536.
24 Frederick Harrison, editor, *Brighton & Hove Archaeologist* (Brighton, 1924) p 92 and Pl XX. I am indebted to the late Mr Graham Head for kindly bringing this reference to my attention.

25 According to my informant, Graham Head, Tom Green was resident comedian at the Brighton Hippodrome.
26 National Film Archive No F.535.
27 *Photograms of the Year 1896* (London, 1896) p 46.
28 The identical subject is shown in a frame illustration reproduced in Albert A. Hopkins, *Magic* (New York, 1897) p 504. It is taken from a film called *The Sausage Factory*, made by the American Mutoscope & Biograph Co. A review of this film appeared in the English periodical *The Optical Magic Lantern Journal*, vol 8, no 96 (May 1897) p 78, so it would seem that Smith was guilty of outright plagiarism. In turn, the American film may have been copied from a similar subject issued by Lumière: *107 Chareuterie Mecanique* (*Mechanical Butcher*).
29 The original building still stands, but the shop-front has been greatly altered. The present occupiers are Messrs Charles Television Ltd.
30 *Hove Echo*, 24 April, 1897, p 2 advertisement.
31 Ibid, 28 August, 1897, p 3.
32 Ibid, 9 October, 1897, p 3: 'Animated Photographs and the Magic Lantern. A Chat with Mr Williamson'.
33 Ibid, 27 November, 1897, p 4. See also: *Brighton & Hove Guardian*, 24 November, 1897, p 8, column 2: 'An interesting feature of the exhibition was a display of Cinematographs and the "X" Ray photographic apparatus, shown by Mr J. Williamson, any visitor being able to see the bones of his own hands by means of the "X" Rays'.
34 *Hove Echo*, 27 November, 1897, p 5.
35 A copy of the Warwick Trading Company's catalogue for 1898 is in the Science Museum, London.
36 See entry in Smith's cash book for 18 September 1897.
37 Reminiscences from unpublished notebooks of James Williamson, 1926, quoted by Rachael Low, *The History of the British Film* (London, 1949) vol 1, p 115.
38 My visit to 47 Chester Terrace, Brighton, took place on 3 June, 1978.
39 The premises were demolished in about 1970 and a small factory now occupies the site, in which display signs are manufactured under the management of Bernard Bush.
40 Inv. no 1978–287.
41 Inv. no 1978–286.
42 I am indebted to Mr A. S. Clover for information on Alfred West.

5 Bradford and Leeds

1 *Photogram*, vol 4, no 37 (January 1897) p 27. See also *The Era*, 16 January 1897, p 28 advertisement.
2 *Photogram*, vol 4, no 39 (March 1897) pp 80–81.
3 *The Optician*, vol 14 (23 September 1897) p 99.
4 *Photograms of '97*, p lxi advertisement. See also *The Optician*, vol 14 (23 September 1897) p 73.
5 *Magic Lantern Journal Annual 1897–8* (October 1897) p xlv advertisement. See also *The Optician*, vol 14 (23 September 1897) p 33.
6 *Photogram*, vol 4, no 43 (July 1897) p 214.
7 Ibid, loc cit.
8 *Amateur Photographer*, vol 26, no 677 (24 September 1897) p 267.
9 *Photogram*, vol 4, no 39 (March 1897) p 81.
10 *The Optician*, vol 14 (21 October 1897) p 192.
11 Ibid, vol 14 (23 September 1897) p 98.
12 Ibid, loc cit.
13 *Photograms of '97*, p lxvii advertisement.
14 Hopwood, *Living Pictures* (London, 1899) p xv advertisement.
15 *Amateur Photographer*, vol 26, no 677 (24 September 1897) p 267.
16 Ibid, loc cit.
17 *Journal of the Motion Picture and Television Engineering Society of Japan* (Tokyo, 1970) pp 3; 70–72.
18 *Photogram*, vol 4, no 43 (July 1897) p 214.
19 *Photograms of '97*, p lxvii advertisement.
20 Ibid, loc cit.
21 *British Journal of Photography*, vol 44, no 1939 (2 July 1897) p 427.
22 *Photograms of '97*, p lxxxv advertisement.
23 Several *cartes-de-visite* by Appleton & Co are in the Barnes Museum of Cinematography.
24 *Photogram*, vol 4, no 39 (March 1897) p 81. Prior to its appearance on the open market, the Cieroscope was being exhibited by its makers as early as November 1896 (Cf. *Bradford Observer*, 14 November 1896, p 1, column 2) I am indebted to Mr R. Brown for kindly bringing this reference to my attention.
25 *Photograms of the Year 1897*, p Lxxxv advertisement.
26 *The Optician*, vol 14 (23 September 1897) p 69.

27 *Amateur Photographer*, vol 26, no 677 (24 September 1897) p 141.
28 *British Journal of Photography*, vol 44, no 1949 (10 September 1897) pp 590–91.
29 From a communication received from Mr R. Brown, dated 6 December 1978.
30 *Bradford Observer*, 14 November 1896, p 1, column 2.
31 Ibid, 14 December 1896.
32 Ibid, 15 December 1896, p 7, column 1.
33 *English Mechanic & World of Science*, vol 66, no 1707 (10 December 1897) p 396.
34 *British Journal Photographic Almanac for 1898* (1 December 1897) p 341 advertisement.
35 Hopwood, *Living Pictures* (London, 1899) p 185. Here the apparatus is incorrectly listed as Vever's Viviograph.
36 Accepted, 9 October, 1897.
37 Hopwood, *Living Pictures*, p 250.

6   The Foreign Influx

1 *Amateur Photographer*, vol 25, no 639 (1 January 1897) p 15.
2 Wolff had offices at 32 rue Le Peletier, Paris, and 5 Jerusalemer-str., Berlin; see *The Era*, 16 January 1897, p 28 advertisement.
3 *Amateur Photographer*, vol 26, no 677 (24 September 1897) p 266.
4 *Photogram*, vol 4, no 38 (February 1897) p 64.
5 *Optical Magic Lantern Journal*, vol 8, no 95 (April 1897) p 63.
6 *Photogram*, vol 4, no 44 (August 1897) p 241.
7 Ibid, loc cit.
8 *Magic Lantern Journal Annual 1897–8* (October 1897) pp xcvii — ci.
9 Ibid, loc cit.
10 *Photograms of '97*, p 38.
11 Ibid, pp 34 and 37.
12 *Photogram*, vol 4, no 39 (March 1897) pp 78–9.
13 The latest and most thorough of the Méliès filmographies is that published in Paul Hammond, *Marvellous Méliès* (London, 1974).
14 See *Photograms of '97*, p 37, where frame-illustrations from the film are reproduced.
15 See Georges Sadoul, *L'Invention du Cinéma 1832–1897* (Paris, 1946) pp 304–7.
16 *Photogram*, vol 4, no 42 (June 1897) p 179.
17 *Amateur Photographer*, vol 25, no 648 (5 March 1897) p 186.
18 Wolff's advertisements, where particular films are mentioned, appear in *The Era*, 15 May 1897, p 28; Ibid, 5 June 1897, p 29; Ibid, 3 July 1897, p 7; Ibid, 23 October 1897, p 30; Ibid, 4 December 1897, p 32; *The Optician*, vol 14 (23 September 1897) p 41. See also *Optical Magic Lantern Journal*, vol 8, no 95 (April 1897) p 63; Ibid, vol 8, no 101 (October 1897) p 173; Ibid, vol 8, no 102 (November 1897) p 177; Ibid, vol 8, no 103 (December 1897) p 212.
19 See *Photogram*, vol 4, no 39 (March 1897) pp 78–9, and *Photograms of '97*, pp 34 and 37.
20 *Amateur Photographer*, vol 24, no 633 (20 November 1896) p 409.
21 *The Era*, 24 July 1897, p 16.
22 *Photogram*, vol 4, no 40 (April 1897) p 124.
23 *Amateur Photographer*, vol 26, no 665 (2 July 1897) p 17. See also *The Optician*, vol 13 (1 July 1897) p 260; Ibid, vol 13 (15 July 1897) p 297; *Optical Magic Lantern Journal*, vol 8, no 99 (August 1897) p 138.
24 Robert Hooke, *Micrographia* (London, 1665) See Barnes Museum of Cinematography, *Catalogue of the Collection Part 2: Optical Projection* (St Ives, 1970).
25 *Amateur Photographer*, vol 26, no 667 (16 July 1897) p 55. Film archivists should note that Lumière films cannot always be identified by perforations alone.
26 Ibid, loc cit.
27 *Photogram*, vol 4, no 47 (November 1897) p 347.
28 *British Journal Photographic Almanac for 1898* (1 December 1897) p 409.
29 *Amateur Photographer*, vol 25, no 662 (11 June 1897) p 483.
30 Ibid, loc cit.
31 Ibid, vol 26, no 675 (10 September 1897) p 205.
32 Ibid, vol 26, no 691 (31 December 1897) p 550.
33 The Model B was subsequently transformed by Pathé Frères Cf. Jean Vivié, *Histoire du Cinema* (Paris, 1946) p 54.
34 *The Era*, 31 July 1897, p 16.
35 Ibid, 21 August 1897, p 16.
36 Ibid, 18 September 1897, p 18.
37 Ibid, 23 October 1897, p 18 and 11 December, p 20.
38 Advertisements for the Cinématographe at the Empire no longer appear in *The Era* after the issue of 24 April 1897.

39 *The Era*, 9 January 1897, p 18.
40 Ibid, 30 January 1897, p 18.
41 Ibid, 24 April 1897, p 18.
42 *British Journal of Photography*, vol 44, no 1955 (25 October 1897) p 684.
43 Ibid, vol 44, no 1958 (12 November 1897) pp 721–2.
44 Ibid, vol 44, no 1963 (17 December 1897) p 810.
45 *The Era*, 31 July 1897, p 14.
46 *The People*, Sunday, 1 August 1897; quoted in *The Era*, 7 August 1897, p 27.
47 *Entr'acte*, 31 July 1897; quoted in *The Era*, 7 August 1897, p 27.
48 *The Era*, 7 August 1897, p 27 advertisement.
49 Ibid, 18 December 1897, p 17.
50 Ibid, 7 August 1897, p 27 advertisement.
51 Ibid, 28 August 1897, p 18.
52 Ibid, 18 December 1897, p 17.
53 Ibid, 21 August 1897, p 16.
54 Ibid, 18 December 1897, p 16.
55 Ibid, 18 September 1897, p 18.
56 See Promio's memoires quoted in G.-Michel Coissac, *Histoire du Cinématographe* (Paris, 1925) pp 195–99.
57 *The Era*, 23 October 1897, p 18.
58 Ibid, loc cit.
59 Ibid, 23 October 1897, p 19.
60 Ibid, 18 December 1897, p 17.
61 Ibid, 11 December 1897, p 20.
62 British Patent No 21,382. 26 September 1896.
63 *The Daily Telegraph*, Friday 7 May 1897.
64 Hopwood, *Living Pictures* (London, 1899) p 145.
65 *The Era*, 24 July 1897, p 16.
66 Ibid, 27 November 1897, p 19.
67 Example in the Barnes Museum of Cinematography.
68 *The Era*, 27 November 1897, p 19.
69 Ibid, 4 December 1897, p 21.
70 Ibid, 11 December 1897, p 32 advertisement.
71 Eug. Trutat, *La Photographie Animée* (Paris, 1899) pp 96–8.
72 *Amateur Photographer*, vol 26, no 677 (24 September 1897) p 267.
73 *Photograms of '97*, p xli advertisement.
74 Ibid, loc cit.
75 *Amateur Photographer*, vol 26, no 677 (24 September 1897) p 268.
76 *Photogram*, vol 4, no 42 (June 1897) p 178.
77 *Magic Lantern Journal Annual 1897–8* (October 1897) p 126.
78 Trutat, *La Photographie Animée*, pp 95–6.
79 *Photogram*, vol 4, no 39 (March 1897) p 79.
80 *Amateur Photographer*, vol 26, no 677 (24 September 1897) p 268.
81 Ibid, vol 26, no 690 (24 December 1897) p 529.
82 *Photogram*, vol 4, no 38 (February 1897) p 64.
83 *Photogram*, vol 4, no 42 (June 1897) p 179. See also *Bulletin* de la Societé Française de Photographie (2) xiii 1897, p 295.
84 *Optical Magic Lantern Journal*, vol 8, no 97 (June 1897) pp 101–2.
85 *Amateur Photographer*, vol 26, no 681 (22 October 1897) 334–5.
86 Ibid, vol 26, no 677 (24 September 1897) p 268.
87 *Photograms of '97*, p lxii advertisement.
88 *Photogram*, vol 4, no 43 (July 1897) p 214.
89 *Amateur Photographer*, vol 26, no 677 (24 September 1897) p 268.
90 *Photogram*, vol 4, no 46 (October 1897) p 314.
91 Cf. Hopwood, *Living Pictures* (London, 1899) p 246.
92 The earliest reference to the Mutoscope which I have been able to find in an English publication appears in *The Amateur Photographer*, vol 25, no 648 (5 March 1897) p 182.
93 Gordon Hendricks, *Beginnings of the Biograph* (New York, 1964).
94 *The Era*, 20 March 1897, p 18.
95 *Amateur Photographer*, vol 25, no 651 (26 March 1897) p 247.
96 *Photogram*, vol 4, no 41 (May 1897) p 151.
97 Ibid, loc cit.
98 Ibid, loc cit.
99 *Amateur Photographer*, vol 25, no 651 (26 March 1897) p 247.
100 *The Era*, 9 September 1899, p 19.

101 Ibid, 20 March 1897, p 18.
102 *Amateur Photographer*, vol 25, no 651 (26 March 1897) p 247.
103 *The Era*, 15 May 1897, p 18.
104 For an illustration of this, see Jacques Deslandes, *Histoire Comparée du Cinéma* (Tournai, 1968) p 354.
105 *Amateur Photographer*, vol 26, no 682 (29 October 1897) p 354.
106 *The Era*, 30 October 1897, p 19.
107 Ibid, 9 April 1898, pp 19 and 27.
108 *Photographic News*, vol 41, no 96, new series (29 October 1897) p 710.
109 *British Journal of Photography*, vol 44, no 1930 (30 April 1897) p 286.
110 Ibid, loc cit.
111 Ibid, loc cit.
112 *The Era*, 30 January 1897, p 18.
113 Hendricks, *Beginnings of the Biograph*, p 70.
114 Printed programme in the Barnes Museum of Cinematography. The Science Museum, London, has a similar programme for the week commencing 9 August 1897, which gives the same list of films (See Charles Urban Collection).
115 *The Era*, 4 September 1897, p 18.
116 R. H. Mere, The Wonders of the Biograph: *Pearson's Magazine*, vol 7 (London, 1899) pp 194–9.
117 *The Era*, 20 November 1897, p 21.
118 *Optical Magic Lantern Journal*, vol 8, no 97 (June 1897) p 101.
119 *Hove Echo*, 13 November 1897, p 7.
120 *British Journal of Photography*, vol 44, no 1936 (11 June 1897) p 380.
121 *The Era*, 24 July 1897, p 17.
122 *Survey of London*, vol 31 (London, 1963) p 50.
123 Terry Ramsaye, *A Million and One Nights* (New York, 1926) p 286.
124 Diana Howard, *London Theatres and Music Halls 1850–1950* (London, 1970) p 120.
125 See the previous volume of this history, p 130.
126 *British Journal of Photography*, vol 44, Supplement (1 October 1897) p 73.
127 *The Era*, 2 October 1897, p 18.
128 *Photographic News*, vol 40, no 47, new series (20 November 1896) p 753.
129 An example of the Edison Projecting Kinetoscope is in the Barnes Museum of Cinematography; see illustration 81.
130 *The Optician*, vol 13 (6 May 1897) p 128.
131 Ibid, vol 13 (27 May 1897) p 176. The agent for the north of England was A. Lomax, who operated the Edison Phonograph Office, 28 Caunce Street, Liverpool; see *English Mechanic*, vol 66 (September 1897) pp 76 and 122.
132 Ibid, loc cit.
133 Ibid, loc cit.
134 Ibid, vol 14 (11 November 1897) p 253.
135 Ibid, vol 13 (27 May 1897) p 177.
136 *The Era*, 29 May 1897, p 29 advertisement.
137 Ibid, 28 August 1897, p 29 advertisement; see also the issue for 4 September 1897, p 29 advertisement.
138 Ibid, 28 August 1897, p 29 advertisement.
139 Ibid, 2 January 1897, p 19; see also the issue for 9 January 1897, p 16 advertisement.
140 Ibid, 6 March 1897, p 30 advertisement.
141 Ibid, 6 November 1897, p 18.
142 *Amateur Photographer*, vol 26, no 677 (24 September 1897) p 266.
143 Ibid, vol 26, no 691 (31 December 1897) p 550.
144 *The Optician*, vol 13 (22 July 1897) p 313.
145 Ibid, vol 13 (2 September 1897) p 422.
146 *Amateur Photographer*, vol 26, no 691 (31 December 1897) p 550.
147 Ibid, loc cit.
148 *The Optician*, vol 13 (2 September 1897) p 422; see also the issue for 18 November, p 262.
149 *Amateur Photographer*, vol 26, no 691 (31 December 1897) p 550.
150 *The Optician*, vol 13 (2 September 1897) p 422; see also the issue for 18 November, p 262.
151 *British Journal Photographic Almanac for 1898* (1 December 1897) p 1294.
152 *The Optician*, vol 14 (18 November 1897) p 260.
153 Ibid, vol 13 (22 July 1897) p 313.
154 Ibid, vol 14 (23 September 1897) pp 122–27.
155 Ibid, vol 14 (23 December 1897) p 349.
156 Ibid, vol 14 (23 September 1897) p 74.
157 Ibid, vol 13 (9 September 1897) p 438.
158 It is as Manager that Charles Urban signs a letter which is reproduced in *The Optician*, vol 14, (11 November 1897) p 253.

159 The photographs were first published in *The Optician*, vol 14 (20 January 1898) pp 426–27.
160 See obituary in *Brighton & Hove Herald*, 5 September 1942, p 1, columns 1 and 2.
161 *The English Mechanic & World of Science*, vol 65, no 1678 (21 May 1897) p 326 advertisement. Eclipse were also dealers in Edison phonographs, projectors and films (Ibid, vol 65, no 1666 (26 February 1897) p vi.)
162 British patent no 925, 18 March, 1868. A Kineograph in the Barnes Museum of Cinematography depicts the famous violinist Paganini.
163 Hopwood, *Living Pictures*, p 35.
164 *British Journal of Photography*, vol 44, no 1937 (18 June 1897) p 386.
165 Ibid, vol 44, no 1934 (28 May 1897) p 342.
166 British patent no 17,930. 25 September, 1895.
167 British patent no 23,183. 19 October, 1896.
168 *British Journal of Photography*, vol 44, no 1950 (17 September 1897) p 604.
169 *English Mechanic*, vol 65, no 1667 (5 March 1897) p v.

7 The Showmen

1 *The Era*, 7 August 1897, p 27 advertisement.
2 Ibid, 13 February 1897, p 26. Another example of an adopted name for a cinematograph projector is the 'Eventographe' advertised by Herbert Wyndham, see *Hove Echo*, 16 October 1897, p 5, column 3.
3 Edmund A. Robins, Hints on Exhibiting Cinematographs, in *The Optical Magic Lantern Journal*, vol 8, no 99 (August 1897) p 129.
4 Ibid, pp 129–31.
5 *The Photogram*, vol 4, no 41 (May 1897) p 149.
6 Robins, The Development of Kinetograph Films, in *The Optical Magic Lantern Journal*, vol 8, no 97 (June 1897) pp 102–3; see also *The Photogram*, vol 4, no 41 (May 1897) p 149.
7 *The Era*, 26 June 1897, p 16.
8 Ibid, 2 January 1897, p 33 advertisement; see also the issues for 9 January, p 27; 23 January, p 28; 6 February, p 24; 13 February, p 27; 20 February, p 38; and 27 February, p 28.
9 Ibid, loc cit.
10 Ibid, 12 June 1897, p 14 advertisement.
11 Ibid, 2 January 1897, p 16.
12 Ibid, 28 August 1897, p 19.
13 Printed programme in the Barnes Collection.
14 From information kindly sent to the author by Mr Clive Sowry of Wellington, New Zealand.
15 *The Era*, 19 June 1897, p 16.
16 For example, compare the report in *The Optician* (7 October 1897) p 150 with that in *The Optical Magic Lantern Journal*, vol 8, no 102 (November 1897) p 181.
17 J. H. Rigg was the inventor and patentee of a machine known as Rigg's Kinematograph (see previous volume of this history, pp 130–33).
18 *British Journal of Photography*, vol 44, no 1956 (29 October 1897) p 699.
19 viz: The Temperance Hall, Guisborough, 5 November 1897; and the Rochdale Circus of Varieties, 3 December 1897 (See *The Optician*, vol 14, pp 240 and 313.
20 *The Era*, 30 January 1897, p 18.
21 Ibid, 3 April 1897, p 18.
22 Ibid, 8 May 1897, p 18.
23 *Hove Echo*, 7 August 1897, p 12, column 4, advertisement.
24 *The Era*, 2 January 1897, p 34, advertisement; see also issues for 9 January, p 29; 16 January, p 29; 30 January, p 29; 6 February, p 30; 13 February, p 30; 20 February, p 35; and 27 February, p 30.
25 Ibid, 30 January 1897, p 18.
26 Ibid, 3 April 1897, p 18.
27 Compare the list of Birt Acres' films published in the previous volume of this history.
28 *Hove Echo*, 7 August 1897, p 12; see also issues for 14 August, p 12; 21 August, p 1; 28 August, p 12; 4 September, p 12; 11 September, p 1; and 18 September, p 1.
29 *The Era*, 11 September 1897, p 18.
30 Ibid, 9 January 1897, p 29; 16 January, p 29; 20 February, p 20; 6 March, p 30; 10 April, p 29.
31 Ibid, 9 January 1897, p 29; 16 January, p 29; 6 March, p 30.
32 Ibid, loc cit.
33 Ibid, 20 February 1897, p 20; 21 August, p 16.
34 Ibid, 6 March 1897, p 16.
35 Ibid, 11 September 1897, p 18.
36 Ibid, 20 February 1897, p 20.
37 Ibid, 6 March 1897, p 16.

38 Ibid, 6 March 1897, p 30.
39 Ibid, 10 April 1897, p 29.
40 Ibid, 21 August 1897, p 16.
41 Ibid, 11 September 1897, p 18.
42 Ibid, loc cit.
43 Ibid, 21 August 1897, p 16.
44 Ibid, 18 September 1897, p 18.
45 Ibid, 9 January 1897, p 19.
46 Ibid, 26 June 1897, p 16.
47 Ibid, loc cit.
48 Ibid, 3 July 1897, p 17.
49 Ibid, 16 January 1897, p 29.
50 Ibid, 23 January 1897, p 28.
51 *Chat*, 6 November 1896.
52 Norton's press cutting book reveals several shows of this kind, but unfortunately, most of the clippings are undated and from unidentified sources. The press book is now in the possession of Mr David Henry, whom I wish to thank for his kindness in allowing me to consult this and other clippings in his own collection.
53 Quoted in *The Era*, 2 January 1897, p 33, advertisement.
54 *The Era*, 2 January 1897, p 33; 9 January, p 27; 23 January, p 28; and 6 February, p 24.
55 Ibid, 21 August 1897, p 16.
56 Ibid, loc cit.
57 Ibid, 13 February 1897, p 26.
58 Printed programme in the Barnes Museum of Cinematography.
59 *The Era*, 7 August 1897, p 27 advertisement.
60 Ibid, 6 February 1897, p 30 advertisement; see also the issue for 30 January, p 29 advertisement.
61 Ibid, 6 February 1897, p 30.
62 Ibid, 7 August 1897, p 27 advertisement.
63 Ibid, 17 July 1897, p 16.
64 *Magic Lantern Journal Annual 1897–8* (October 1897) p xcviii advertisement.
65 *The Era*, 24 July 1897, p 17.
66 Ibid, 17 July 1897, p 16.
67 *Magic Lantern Journal Annual 1897–8* (October 1897) p 254 advertisement.
68 *The Era*, 21 August 1897, p 16.
69 Ibid, 17 July 1897, p 16.
70 Ibid, 25 December 1897, p 25 advertisement.
71 Ibid, loc cit.
72 Ibid, loc cit.
73 Ibid, 13 February 1897, p 26 advertisement.
74 Ibid, loc cit.
75 Ibid, 7 August 1897, p 17.
76 Ibid, 28 August 1897, p 29 advertisement.
77 Ibid, 6 November 1897, p 19.
78 *British Journal of Photography*, vol 44, no 1963 (17 December 1897) p 811.
79 Ibid, loc cit.
80 Ibid, loc cit.
81 *The Era*, 2 January 1897, p 19; see also issue for 9 January, p 16.
82 Ibid, 2 January 1897, p 19.
83 Ibid, 6 February 1897, p 30.
84 Ibid, loc cit.
85 Ibid, 9 January 1897, p 19.
86 Ibid, 6 March 1897, p 30 advertisement.
87 Ibid, loc cit.
88 Ibid, loc cit.
89 Ibid, loc cit.
90 Ibid, 21 November 1896, p 30.
91 Ibid, 27 March 1897, p 29 advertisement.
92 Ibid, 13 February 1897, p 26 advertisement.
93 *The Optician*, 10 September 1896, p 350. See Barnes, *The Beginnings of the Cinema in England* (Newton Abbot, 1976) p 133.
94 Science Museum Inv. no 1930–486.
95 *The Era*, 13 February 1897, p 26 advertisement.
96 Ibid, loc cit.
97 Ibid, loc cit.

98 *Optical Magic Lantern Journal*, vol 8, no 94 (March 1897) p 62.

99 Cecil M. Hepworth, *Came the Dawn: Memories of a Film Pioneer* (London, 1951) p 30.

100 Low Warren, *The Film Game* (London, 1937) p 16.

101 British patent no 11,923. Date of application, 13 May 1897. Complete specification left, 14 February 1898. Accepted, 13 May 1898.

102 The Ross-Hepworth Arc Lamp is described and illustrated in the previous volume of this history.

103 British patent no 13,315.

104 Editions appeared in 1888, 1889, 1890, 1891, 1894 and 1899. Copies of each of these editions are in the Barnes Collection.

105 *Amateur Photographer*, vol 26, no 689 (17 December 1897) p 509.

106 *British Journal of Photography*, vol 44, no 1935 (4 June 1897) p 354.

107 Ibid, loc cit.

108 *The Era*, 30 October 1897, p 19.

109 *British Journal of Photography*, vol 44, no 1958 (12 November 1897) p 732.

110 *The Era*, 11 December 1897, p 32 advertisement; see also *Optical Magic Lantern Journal*, vol 8, no 103 (December 1897) p 199.

111 *The Optician*, vol 14 (28 October 1897) p 204.

112 *Optical Magic Lantern Journal*, vol 9, no 115 (December 1898) p 180.

113 *British Journal of Photography*, vol 44, no 1957 (5 November 1897) p 719.

114 *Optical Magic Lantern Journal*, vol 8, no 101 (October 1897) p 158.

115 *The Era*, 26 December 1896, p 18.

116 The Randall Williams handbill is illustrated in the previous volume of this history, p 166.

117 *The Era*, 7 August 1897, p 18.

118 Ibid, 14 August 1897, p 17.

119 Ibid, loc cit.

120 Ibid, 28 August 1897, p 19.

121 Ibid, loc cit.

122 Ibid, loc cit.

123 Ibid, 4 September 1897, p 18.

124 Ibid, loc cit.

125 Ibid, 11 September 1897, p 20.

126 Ibid, loc cit.

127 Ibid, loc cit.

128 Ibid, loc cit.

129 Ibid, 18 September 1897, p 18.

130 Ibid, loc cit.

131 Ibid, loc cit.

132 Ibid, loc cit.

133 Ibid, 25 September 1897, p 19.

134 Ibid, loc cit.

135 Ibid, loc cit.

136 Ibid, loc cit.

137 Ibid, 9 October 1897, p 19.

138 Ibid, 16 October 1897, p 22.

139 Ibid, loc cit.

140 Ibid, loc cit.

8 The Jubilee

1 *Amateur Photographer*, vol 25, no 648 (5 April 1897) p 186.

2 *The Photogram*, vol 4, no 39 (March 1897) p 78.

3 *British Journal of Photography*, vol 44, no 1930 (30 April 1897) p 286.

4 *Ibid*, vol 44, no 1931 (7 May 1897) p 292.

5 *Amateur Photographer*, vol 25, no 662 (11 June 1897) p 469.

6 Ibid, p 470.

7 Ibid, p 474.

8 *The Photogram*, vol 4, no 43 (July 1897) p 214.

9 *Photographic News*, vol 41, no 75, n.s. (Friday 4 June 1897) p 355.

10 Ibid, loc cit.

11 John Munro, 'Living Photographs of the Queen', in *Cassell's Family Magazine* (July 1897) p 328; see also *The Era*, 3 July 1897, p 17.

12 *Cassell's Family Magazine* (July 1897) p 328.

13 Ibid, loc cit.

14 Ibid, loc cit.

15 *The Era*, 3 July 1897, p 17.

16 Inv. No 1913–552.

17 *Cassell's Family Magazine* (July 1897) p 329.

18 I am indebted to Mr David Francis for kindly calling my attention to this important article.

19 *Cassell's Family Magazine* (July 1897) p 329.

20 Ibid, loc cit.

21 *Proceedings of the British Kinematograph Society*, No 38 (3 February 1936) pp 4–5.

22 *Amateur Photographer*, vol 26, no 665 (2 July 1897) p 2.

23 *The Era*, 12 June 1897, p 14 advertisement.

24 *British Journal of Photography*, vol 44, no 1960 (26 November 1897) p 763; see also *The Optician*, vol 14 (25 November 1897) p 275.

25 *British Journal of Photography*, vol 44, no 1939 (2 July 1897) p 418.

26 *Optical Magic Lantern Journal*, vol 8, no 99 (August 1897) p 126.

27 Ibid; loc cit. See also *The Optician*, vol 13 (15 July 1897) p 295.

28 *Hove Echo*, 3 July 1897, p 7, column two.

29 *Optical Magic Lantern Journal*, vol 8, no 99 (August 1897) p 126.

30 *The Era*, 3 July 1897, p 7 advertisement.

31 Printed programme, Palace Theatre of Varieties, for the week commencing 13 September 1897 (in the collection of the Barnes Museum of Cinematography).

32 *British Journal of Photography*, vol 44, Supplement (3 September 1897), p 65.

33 Sir Herbert Maxwell, *Sixty Years a Queen* (London, 1897) pp 204, 212 and 214. Other illustrations in this work are useful for identifying locations on the Jubilee route.

34 *British Journal of Photography*, vol 44, Supplement (2 July 1897) p 49.

35 *The Era*, 24 July 1897, p 16.

36 *Amateur Photographer*, vol 25, no 654 (16 April 1897) p 310.

37 Ibid, vol 26, no 665 (2 July 1897) p 2.

38 *The Era*, 3 July 1897, p 7 advertisement.

39 *Optical Magic Lantern Journal*, vol 8, no 99 (August 1897) p 126.

40 *Amateur Photographer*, vol 26, no 667 (16 July 1897) p 57.

41 *British Journal of Photography*, vol 44, no 1939 (2 July 1897) p 427.

42 *The Era*, 3 July 1897, p 7 advertisement.

43 *Optical Magic Lantern Journal*, vol 8, no 99 (August 1897) p 126.

44 *The Optician*, vol 13 (8 July 1897) p 278.

45 Ibid, loc cit.

46 *Optical Magic Lantern Journal*, vol 8, no 99 (August 1897) p 126; see also *The Optician*, vol 13 (15 July 1897) p 295.

47 *British Journal of Photography*, vol 44, Supplement (2 July 1897) p 49.

48 *Photographic News*, vol 41, no 79, n.s. (2 July 1897) p 418.

49 *Photogram*, vol 4, no 44 (August 1897) p 241; see also *Photograms of '97*, p 34; and *The Photographic News*, vol 41, no 79, n.s. (2 July 1897) p 426.

50 *Photogram*, vol 4, no 44 (August 1897) p 241.

51 *British Journal of Photography*, vol 44, no 1949 (10 September 1897) pp 590–91.

52 *The Era*, 26 February 1898, p 19.

53 *Photographic News*, vol 41, no 79, n.s. (2 July 1897) p 418.

54 *The Era*, 3 July 1897, p 7.

55 Ibid, p 17.

56 Ibid, 10 July 1897, p 17.

57 *The Optician*, vol 13 (15 July 1897) p 294.

58 *Optical Magic Lantern Journal*, vol 8, no 99 (August 1897) p 126.

59 *Amateur Photographer*, vol 26, no 668 (23 July 1897) p 63.

60 *Optical Magic Lantern Journal*, vol 8, no 99 (August 1897) p 126.

61 Ibid, vol 8, no 100 (September 1897) p 143.

62 *The Era*, 10 July 1897, p 16.

63 Ibid, p 25 advertisement.

64 Ibid, 14 August 1897, p 16.

65 Ibid, 10 July 1897, p 25 advertisement.

66 Ibid, 26 February 1898, p 19.

67 Ibid, 24 July 1897, p 16.

68 Ibid, 7 August 1897, p 16.

69 Ibid, 27 November 1897, p 19.

70 Ibid, 24 July 1897, p 17.

71 Ibid, 7 August 1897, p 16.

72 Ibid, 30 October 1897, p 19.

73 Ibid, 11 December 1897, p 32 advertisement.
74 *The Optician*, vol 14 (28 October 1897) p 204.
75 *The Era*, 7 August 1897, p 27 advertisement.
76 Ibid, 11 September 1897, p 18.
77 Ibid, 21 August 1897, p 16.
78 Ibid, 24 July 1897, p 17; see also issue for 21 August, p 16.
79 Ibid, 1 May 1897, p 29 advertisement.
80 Ibid, 3 July 1897, p 7 advertisement.
81 From information given on a poster advertising a performance at the Corn Exchange, Chelmsford, Essex, dated 1st & 2nd of October [1897]. Original in the Kodak Museum, Harrow. See illustration 100.
82 Quoted in the *Optical Magic Lantern Journal*, vol 8, no 101 (October 1897) p 158.
83 *Optical Magic Lantern Journal*, vol 8, no 102 (November 1897) p 178.
84 *English Mechanic*, vol 66, no 1694 (10 September 1897) p 89. See also *The British Journal of Photography*, vol 44, no 1955 (22 October 1897) p 677.
85 *Photograms of the Year 1897* (November 1897) p 34.
86 *Photographic News*, vol 41, no 96, N.S. (29 October 1897) p 710.
87 *British Journal of Photography*, vol 44, no 1944 (6 August 1897) p 508.
88 *Photographic News*, vol 41, no 54, N.S. (8 January 1897) p 26.
89 *Journal of the Camera Club*, vol 11 (May 1897) p 65.
90 *British Journal of Photography*, vol 44, no 1929 (23 April 1897) p 260. See also *Photograms of the Year 1897*, p 34.
91 *Archives of Skiagraphy*, vol 1, 1897, p 37. See also *Photogram*, vol 4, no 44 (August 1897) p 246.
92 *Photogram*, vol 4, no 46 (October 1897) p 311.
93 Ibid, vol 4, no 48 (December 1897) p 381.
94 *The Optician*, vol 14 (23 December 1897) p 346.
95 *Photographic News*, vol 41, no 69, N.S. (23 April 1897) p 257.
96 *The Optician*, vol 12 (11 February 1897) p 273; Ibid, vol 14 (30 September 1897) p 130.

Acknowledgements

First and foremost I wish to thank my wife, Carmen, and my brother William Barnes, for their continued help and encouragement. Without my brother's constant quest for original source material, this book would have been much the poorer. Also, I particularly wish to thank Alfred Darling's two grandsons, Philip and Kenneth Darling, for giving me access to their grandfather's effects and for supplying much valuable information on his life and career. At the National Film Archive I have received valuable assistance from David Francis / Curator; Roger Holman / Chief Cataloguer; Harold Brown / Preservation Officer; and Michelle Snapes / Chief Stills Officer. Likewise I wish to thank Dr. D. B. Thomas; John Ward; C. P. Harris and Kate Lloyd at the Science Museum, South Kensington. Equally I wish to thank Judith Dale / Local History Librarian, Hove Area Library; and Brian Coe / Curator, Kodak Museum. In my quest for information on C. Goodwin Norton, I have been helped by Mrs Sylvia Bexley and Brian Cummings. For information on R. R. Beard I was fortunate to contact three of his descendants, namely, Professor R. E. Beard (son), Mrs Dorothy G. Fowler (daughter) and F. Royou Cox (grandson). Information on the showman Randall Williams was very kindly volunteered by his grandson Paul Williams.

Others who have assisted me in my work, and to whom I give thanks, are: Mrs Sydney Birt Acres, Uwe H. Breker, R. Brown, Albert Couch, David J. Dednum, Graham Head, Gordon Hendricks, David Henry, Susan Julian-Huxley, Stanley Jones-Frank, Feroze Sarosh, Clive Sowry, and Roy H. Thornton. Finally, I wish to acknowledge the following corporate bodies for services rendered: Science Museum, and Science Library, London; National Film Archive; British Film Institute, Kodak Museum; The Patent Office; Alfred Darling & Sons; Westminster Central Reference Library; Westminster Public Library; British Library — Newspaper Library (Colindale) and Science Reference Library (Holborn); Royal Photographic Society; East Sussex County Libraries, Hove Area Library and Brighton Reference Library; Guildhall Library; GLC Record Office & Library; and the Public Library, St Ives, Cornwall.

Items from the Barnes Collection were photographed by Ray Holland Photographics and St Ives Printing & Publishing Company.

Film Index

General Index

268

269

271